James Herman De Ricci

Fiji

Our New Province in the South Seas

James Herman De Ricci

Fiji

Our New Province in the South Seas

ISBN/EAN: 9783337471965

Printed in Europe, USA, Canada, Australia, Japan

Cover: Foto ©Andreas Hilbeck / pixelio.de

More available books at **www.hansebooks.com**

FIJI:

OUR NEW PROVINCE IN THE SOUTH SEAS.

BY

J. H. DE RICCI, F.R.G.S.,

BARRISTER-AT-LAW, AUTHOR OF 'HOW ABOUT FIJI.'

WITH TWO MAPS.

LONDON:
EDWARD STANFORD, 55 CHARING CROSS.
1875.

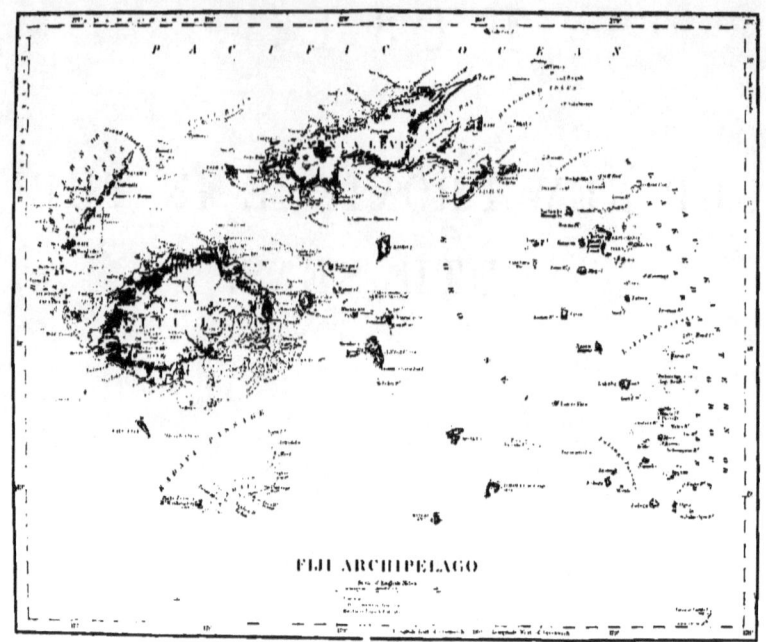

PREFACE.

In the following pages I have essayed to put together in a succinct and practicable form all such information concerning our new Colony as I have thought likely to prove of interest or importance.

Much of this information has hitherto existed under conditions rendering it difficult of access, not only from the fact of its being scattered piecemeal throughout various Parliamentary Returns, Official Reports, and other publications, but also owing to the comparative difficulty of sometimes identifying the subject by the title of that publication in which it is contained.

Commodore Wilkes' exhaustive description of the natives, and their manners and customs, contained in the narrative of the United States Exploring Expedition, would be difficult to improve upon, and to that author and Dr. Berthold Seemann I am especially indebted.

In writing Fijian words I have endeavoured as far as possible to spell them as they are pronounced, the consonants being sounded as in English, and the vowels as in Italian.

If in this undertaking, embarked upon with considerable diffidence, and which, owing to the course of rapid events, has been less perfectly executed than I could wish, I have in any degree satisfied an immediate want or particular necessity, I shall feel amply rewarded.

The Temple. London,
  20th February, 1875.

CONTENTS.

CHAP.		PAGE
	MAPS.	
	PREFACE.	
I.	PHYSICAL ASPECT OF THE ISLANDS	1
II.	CLIMATE	17
III.	THE NATIVES	23
IV.	THE LANGUAGE	37
V.	MANNERS AND CUSTOMS	39
VI.	INDUSTRIES	62
VII.	POLITY	67
VIII.	AN ACCOUNT OF THE VARIOUS PROPOSALS FOR THE CESSION OF FIJI	79
IX.	THE ANNEXATION	121
X.	PRODUCTIONS	129
XI.	TRADE	143
XII.	LABOUR	170
XIII.	THE WHITE POPULATION	183
XIV.	EMIGRATION	191
XV.	ETHNOLOGY	204
XVI.	FAUNA	213
XVII.	HISTORICAL NOTICE	219

APPENDIX.

	PAGE
TONGA ISLANDS.	279
AN ACT FOR THE REGULATION OF POLYNESIAN LABOURERS	283
A STATEMENT BY DR. MACDONALD CONTAINING:—	
(1) A TOPOGRAPHICAL RÉSUMÉ OF THE PLACES VISITED BY THE EXPEDITION FOR THE EXPLORATION OF THE RIVER REWA	298
(2) A GENERAL SUMMARY OF TREES AVAILABLE AS TIMBER	300
(3) A ZOOLOGICAL LIST	303
A SYSTEMATIC LIST OF ALL THE FIJIAN PLANTS AT PRESENT KNOWN	305
INDEX	325

FIJI.

CHAPTER I.

PHYSICAL ASPECT OF THE ISLANDS.

THE Fijian Archipelago is situated in the South Pacific, within the tropics, between the meridians of 176° E. and 178° W. longitude, and the parallels of 15° and 20° S. latitude. The islands composing the group have been variously estimated as numbering from 200 to 255, and they are roughly computed to have a superficial area of 7403 square miles, which is about equal to that of Wales. Viti Levu and Vanua Levu are the two largest islands, the former having an area of 4112 square miles, and the latter an area of 2432½ miles. The areas here given can only be considered as approximately correct, as up to the present date no systematic trigonometrical survey of the lands has been made. The remaining islands are of lesser magnitude, the more important being included in the following statement :—

Approximate Area, in English Statute Miles, of the Fiji Group.

	Sq. Miles.		Sq. Miles.
Viti Levu	4112	Brought forward . .	6886¾
Vanua Levu	2432½	Windward Isles	59
Taviuni	217¾	Angau	46
Kandavu	124½	Ovalau	42½
Carried forward . .	6886¾	Carried forward . .	7034½

Approximate Area, in English Statute Miles, &c.—continued.

	Sq. Miles.		Sq. Miles.
Brought forward	7034¾	Brought forward	7232¼
Rabi	28	Mango	10
Moala	28	Cicia	10
Gamia	26	Nairai	10
Lomo Lomo	24	Goro	5¾
Vatu Lele	18½	Laucala	9
Ono	13	Kea	9
Mbega	13	Maitamba	9
Yedua	13½	Kanacia	8
Lakemba	12	Mokani	4¾
Matuku	11	Mbatiki	4
Totoga	11	Other isles, probably	40
Carried forward	7232¼	Total	7403¼

7403 square miles equal 4,738,350 acres.

Owing to a more constant rainfall and plentiful moisture, the aspect of the weather side of these islands forms a remarkable contrast to the lee side. While the former in its innumerable creepers, thick jungles, forests, and luxuriant foliage exhibits all the characteristics of a tropical vegetation, the latter is, on the contrary, remarkable for its fertile undulating plains and valleys of the richest alluvial soil.

Viewed from the sea, with their bold, broken, picturesque outlines profusely adorned with the rich dark green foliage of teeming exotic growth, these islands present a very lovely scene. They are all more or less mountainous, rising abruptly from the sea, and otherwise indicating by their geological formation their volcanic origin. Many of the mountains attain a considerable height, several of them exceeding 3000 feet, and the highest, Voma, in Viti Levu, having an altitude of nearly 5000 feet.

The glorious panoramic views displayed from the summits of many of these mountains may be more easily imagined than described, and rich is the reward of the climber of their tortuous heights.

Picture to yourself a mass of luxuriant tropical foliage, extending for miles over hill and dale, interspersed here and there with patches of cultivation and majestic groves of cocoa-nut trees. Towns and villages perched upon apparently inaccessible cliffs overhanging picturesque and secluded valleys; the broken and fantastic peaks of the various mountains towering against an azure sky, and the surrounding calm, blue, boundless sea dotted with innumerable islands, each more interesting than another for its own peculiar beauty; and then the foamy reefs stretching far beyond, fading imperceptibly away, until lost in the hazy distance.

Though there are at present no active craters, earthquakes are occasionally experienced, and in some of the islands hot springs are found, thus indicating that Fiji is not secure from volcanic disturbance.

At the bay of Savu-savu, on the island of Vanua Levu, five of these hot springs, 'Waicama,' are clustered in a basin about fifty feet in diameter at some little distance from the beach. The water marks a heat of from 200° to 210°, and is frequently used by the natives for cooking their taros and yams. The water has a strong saline taste, and a faint smell of sulphur is perceptible. The mouths of the springs, which have been apparently enlarged by the natives, are from twelve to twenty-four inches in diameter. A small brook of fresh water flowing immediately in the vicinity unites with the waters of the springs at a little distance below the basin, and in the lower part of the bed of the united stream thus formed excavations have been made, where the natives bathe their persons, no doubt with much benefit and satisfaction.

The coasts of the larger islands are indented by numerous beautiful bays, having often good anchorage, and forming outlets for numerous rivers and streams. Some of the available harbours are enumerated in the following extract from the official report of Admiral Washington, Hydrographer to the Admiralty, dated March, 1859:—

Q. 2. Do the natural harbours now existing require much, if any, artificial development for naval purposes? Whether such harbours are few or many?

A. 2. There are several roadsteads and harbours in the Fiji group, the principal of which is the extensive harbour of Levuka, on the eastern side of Ovalau; this harbour has good holding ground, is easy of access, and has every facility for the supply of fruit, vegetables, wood, and water.

Angan, on its western side, has a sheltered roadstead of large extent.

Totoga is surrounded by a coral reef, within which is a spacious sheltered anchorage, with good holding ground and an entrance for ships.

All the above harbours have been thoroughly surveyed by order of the Admiralty, and plans of them on a large scale are available when required. These natural harbours will not require any artificial development for naval purposes.

3. There is nothing unusual in the tides and currents around the Fiji group; they depend chiefly on the prevailing winds; nor are they of sufficient strength to render the entrance into or egress from the harbours dangerous. There is no present necessity for buoys, beacons, or lights; but should trade greatly increase, or should mail-steamers call by night, a light would become necessary.

The harbour of Goloa, in the island of Kandavu, has been selected as the port of arrival and departure of the steamers carrying the mails *viâ* San Francisco for the colonies of New South Wales and New Zealand. It is pleasantly situated, and the south-east trade-winds, to which it is exposed, causes this island to be one of the healthiest in the group. The soil is very fertile, being capable of producing everything that requires a tropical climate, and accordingly, notwithstanding that it is hilly, is highly cultivated.

Mbua Bay, the place from whence sandal-wood was formerly obtained, though interspersed with large reefs, offers ample space for safe anchorage. The form of the bay, into which several streams flow, is not unlike the figure of the larger segment of a circle, formed by Lecumba Point on the east, and on the west by the point of Naithombothombo, which is also supposed to be the starting-point for the future abode of departed spirits. In the immediate vicinity the land is low-lying, but as you go inland, gradually it becomes more undulating, until within a few miles of the bay it rises in lofty picturesque peaks, culminating in that of Corobato, which is distinguishable from the Viti Levu shore, and has an altitude of over 2000 feet.

At the north-east extremity of the island Vanua Levu, Natewa Bay forms a fine harbour.

The bay of Savu-savu is a fine sheet of water, and also affords good anchorage. It is about ten miles in length by five in breadth, and is well protected by an extensive reef, which (excepting one large opening) reaches from Savu-savu Point on the east to Kombelau on the west.

The rivers, which afford a constant and unfailing water supply, are unusually large for the size of the islands, some of them varying from 50 feet to 120 feet in width, and navigable by small craft. The most important of the rivers yet explored is the Rewa, in Viti Levu, which was ascended by an expedition from H. M. S. *Herald* in 1856 for a distance of ninety-one miles. It is navigable for this distance; sixty miles by vessels drawing from four to five feet of water, and the remainder by boats of lighter draught.

The Rewa, otherwise termed Wai Levu, or great water, empties itself into the sea by four mouths, and its deltas are fertile and cultivated. One of these is traversed by a canal, the Kele Musu, cut by the natives to join the channels, Wai-ni-Ki and Wai-ni-Mbokasi, which saves a distance of nearly twenty miles between Rewa and Mbau, and also a considerable distance between the latter place and the main channel of the river. It is about two miles long and sixty feet wide, and admits of the passage of the largest canoes. It is said to have been constructed for military purposes, but further, its origin or *raison d'être* does not appear capable of elucidation. In any case it must be looked upon as a marvel in engineering, when we come to consider the means available for such an undertaking, namely: "staves to dig the ground, hands to shovel it up, and baskets to carry it away."

At about twelve miles from its mouth the Rewa receives the Wai Manu at Navuso. This tributary takes its source in the neighbourhood of Namosi, and courses in an easterly direction through a thickly-populated district. It is navigable by boats for about ten miles.

Here is a description of the scenery on the Wai Manu by Mr. Macdonald:—*

"It is very beautiful on account of the great diversity of the surface and the richness of the forests. The distant mountains now and again peeped between the slopes of the hills, or, when we gained an elevation, stood up boldly against the horizon.

"From the bank on which our canoe was hauled up, when the river

* Extract from the proceedings of an Expedition for the Exploration of the River Rewa, communicated to the Royal Geographical Society, June 22nd, 1857. *Vide* 'Journal R.G.S.' vol. xxvii.

was no longer navigable, we followed a well-beaten path over a ridge or spur, leading to the high land on which the town of Koroi stood. From this elevated spot the surrounding country presented the most charming aspect, enlivened by a narrow strip of the sea (our first glimpse of it for the space of six weeks), with the islands of Ovalau, Wakaya, Mbatiki, Nairai, and Nyau spread upon its bosom. The forests in this district are exceedingly dense and stored with valuable timber.

"The sedimentary rocks composing the height of Koroi abound in foraminifera. Fossil impressions, or rather casts of animal and vegetable structures, were everywhere to be seen, so case-hardened, apparently by a superficial layer of the oxide of iron, that their forms stand out in bold relief on the large slabs of rock over which the natives continually walk, the surrounding material being worn away by their feet. The original organised structures have been completely substituted by the common materials of which the rocks are composed. We noticed in many places large masses of breccia, like that of Namosi or Ovalau, scattered about amongst the stratified rocks in the most unaccountable manner. The whole region is full of interest to the geologist, who may examine the layers of an ancient marine bed now elevated about four hundred feet above the level of the sea; and abutting against mountain masses of breccia and conglomerate, consisting of fragments of close-grained primary lavas, cemented together by minute detritus of the same materials."

Retracing our steps to Navuso, on the Wai Levu, we find that—

"The banks of the Rewa here exhibit a richly ferruginous sandy basis, with a fine alluvial surface four to five feet in depth. The river runs at first nearly due north from Navuso to Kasavu, a distance of about three miles, and then winds suddenly to the westward, Mbau lying to the N.E. The banks on the right hand then passed rather abruptly into rude hilly country. Continuing our course from Navuso, we noticed a few beautiful Ninsawa trees (a species of areca) growing on the point opposite. Nakandi and every reach onward from this exhibited more loveliness and picturesque effect. * * * Naitasiri opened when we rounded a richly-wooded point of the river, called 'Wai-ni-Kumi,' literally water of the beard. A superstition connected with it exists among the people, that beardless boys may expedite the growth of their beard by bathing the chin in the water dripping from the rocks. The latter were of a sedimentary formation, presenting a nearly vertical face, over which a small stream of water was rushing down. This stream might possibly be much augmented after heavy rains, but it is the only approach to a waterfall occurring in the district.

* * * * * * * *

"Rich foliage embowered with creeping plants, beauteous trees, ferns, and Niu Sawa trees everywhere met the eye. All the intervening spaces, but more especially the immediate banks of the river, are covered with tall grass and humbler herbage. The river gradually closes from Wai-ni-Kumi towards Naitasiri, but widens out again at the latter place, the left bank in particular rising to a considerable height."

After leaving Naitasiri, the country is described as becoming gradually more elevated, and at the branching of the Rewa river into the smaller streams, Muna Ndonu, and Wai Ndina, the left bank is very precipitous, with a stratified rock peering here and there through rich vegetation.

Mr. Macdonald's party now ascended the Wai Ndina, taking its source in the mountains beyond the Namosi valley, and passing through the heart of Soloira, formerly a thickly-populated district, but then sadly decimated by the fierce intertribal wars. The waters of this stream have been so polluted with human gore that the natives call it 'the river of blood.'

"The force of the rapids frequently checked our speed, and the river bed being continually subject to change by the action of the floods, the position of the channel was rendered exceedingly uncertain. The river also was very tortuous, though trending mainly to the westward, and shallows often extended quite across its course, so as to prevent the possibility of navigation when the waters are low. After a more or less serpentine course for some distance the river suddenly turned to the southward, and when we got into position, with a bamboo forest on rising land bearing east, the Mbuggi Levu range became visible, bearing west.

"After this as we proceeded the mountains bore W. by S.W., and W.

PHYSICAL ASPECT OF THE ISLANDS.

by N. successively * * * When we had proceeded about ten miles in a westerly direction, the river took a southerly sweep. The flood was coming down with great force, widening its way by undermining the sides of the banks. A great mass of the right bank fell in just as we passed the spot, and we now and then observed trees rolling over and over, borne down with the body of water. In other places massive trees were torn up by the roots, and lying prostrate in the stream. The banks of the river here are composed of a basis of small rounded stones and pebbles, filled in with grit and sand, and overlaid with comparatively recent alluvial deposits, resembling those already alluded to. * * * Mr. Waterhouse and I went up a rather slippery path to the top of the nearest highland, from which we saw Mbuggi Levu about three miles distant, bearing W. N. W., and a range of mountains called Lutu was pointed out to us, bearing N. N. E., and appearing to be about thirty miles off, as the source of the river called Wai-ni-Mbuka, which opens into the Uluna Ndonu. The latter river flows through the heart of the country, arising in a N. N. W. direction * * * Here the vegetation was more beautiful than anything I could have conceived. We noticed a particularly remarkable species of Flagelaria, with a stem of about four inches in circumference, scaling the tallest trees by means of its prehensile leaves. Having left this place, we proceeded up the river to Vakandua, a rather small but well-inhabited town, most beautifully situated on elevated land, and surrounded with the river and forest scenery, * * * On the following morning after breakfast we resumed our journey, occasionally encountering a heavy shower of rain; and after having passed several difficult parts, and through numerous windings of the river, we arrived at the mouth of a tributary stream on the right hand, said to wind in a northerly direction to the base of Mbuggi Levu, and round along the eastern side of the range. We continued our course, however, up the main river, and ultimately reached the province of the Soloira tribe, ruled by Roko Tui Wai Maro, whose friendship was of the greatest importance to us. * * * Taking advantage of a dry interval to see the country, we ascended a hill near the town,* which is about two miles from Mbuggi Levu. This mountain bore N.W. by W., and the island of Ovalau was visible in the distance, the N.W. conical peak bearing N.E. The position of Namosi was pointed out to us behind some remarkable looking peaks in a W. by S. direction. From this point of view

---

* Vuni Mbua, the capital of the Soloira district.

Mendrau-Suthu-na-Mbasanga, a part of the serrated Mbuggi Levu range, bearing resemblance to the female breasts, and supposed to have yielded nourishment to a twin deity, connected after the manner of the Siamese Twins, were concealed by Mbuggi Levu. This elevation commands a very charming prospect of the surrounding country, more especially the mountain scenery. Mbuggi Levu rears its lofty head to the left, with many peaked and ragged mountain masses in the immediate vicinity. The winding bed of the river diversifies the hilly region through which it passes in the centre, and very distant mountains peer up, one behind the other, passing off by aërial perspective into the tints of sky on the right. On looking upon the scope through which the floods roll at certain periods of the year, and the comparatively small portion of it now traversed by the river, it may be easily conceived how the course of the latter, within certain boundaries, may vary with the casualties resulting from the action of the floods, breaking down existing banks, and filling up the previously open channels.   *   *   *   *   *   *   *

"After leaving the town of Nondo-Yavu-na-ta-Thaki we followed the winding of the river through the most charming mountain country, with occasional rapids and shallows, until we arrived at the town Na Seivau, famous for its hot springs. One of these was bubbling from the summit of an irregular mass of rock, apparently a portion of an ancient dyke, near the landing-place. The temperature of the water in this case was about 100°, and collecting in a wide recess in the rock below it, formed a very delightful natural bath. Some little distance farther on we visited another spring, with a temperature of 140°. Here also the water was gushing out from the summit of a very remarkable mass of rock; but the latter was very distinctly composed of a metamorphic breccia presenting a beautifully variegated surface. The natives state that the water occasionally emits a disagreeable odour, but this was not very apparent to us at the time of our visit.   *   *   *   From Na Seivau we continued our course as far as it was possible to perform it by water.

"We found the river filled with large boulders, over and between which the water was rushing with incredible force, so that all our little canoes were necessarily hauled up on land, and the traps and movables distributed amongst our party; and having got into marching order, we wended our way first through a deep mountain gorge of the most picturesque character, but afterwards through more open country, repeatedly crossing the stream, descending and climbing occasionally very precipitate banks."

The party reached Namosi toward evening.

"It lies on the right bank of the Wai Ndina in the luxuriant valley of Ono Mbalcanga, which trends nearly east and west between rugged and lofty mountains. The sublimity of the scenery cannot be faithfully described."

While in this lovely valley various expeditions were made, one of which was to the Wai-ni-Ura, where an individual named Harry—of whom more anon—imagined he had discovered the philosopher's stone.

"We ascended a mountain-ridge with precipitous sides, *titoko* * in hand, and having reached the top, commenced our descent into the next valley, through which the Wai-ni-Ura flows. The scenery was indeed very grand, but the footing was exceedingly difficult. Having selected some specimens of the rocks, and refreshed ourselves with a draught from the cool stream, two alternatives presented themselves to us, namely, to descend the valley with the course of the river, stepping from one huge boulder to another, and scrambling along vertical cliffs over which the water now and then came tumbling down, or to re-ascend the ridge and retrace our steps. The former was chosen, and from the difficulty experienced we have no particular desire to visit Wai-ni-Ura again. The *titoko* was of the greatest service to us in descending slippery rocks and jumping from one to another. The rocks are spangled with iron pyrites, which makes its appearance whenever the surface is broken, but we were not fortunate enough to discover gold.

* * * * * * * *

"Another interesting expedition was made to visit the celebrated Moti-vei-Tala, at the division of the two streamlets which respectively open into the Namosi and Navua rivers. Na Ulu Matua † and Harry accompanied us, and our walk through the vale of Ona Mbalcanga was very pleasing. We ascended a rich mountain valley to the left of Na-Ndela-ni-Solia, and soon reached a clear bubbling stream, dividing into two smaller streamlets at a very acute angle, the left branch trending to the Namosi river (Wai Ndina), the right one wending its way to the river flowing to Navua on the south coast of Viti Levu.

* A kind of native alpenstock, or stick.
† The Chief of Namosi.

"The natives say that a Moli (shaddock) tree formerly grew at this spot, and when the fruit of it fell into the last-mentioned stream, it might soon after be picked up at Navua in perfect condition; but falling into the Namosi streamlet, it became rotten before reaching the sea at Rewa. This is in short language the story of the Moli-vei-Tala, so called, and it is often adduced by the natives to afford an idea of the relative length of the two rivers. The distance of Nevua from this place by the river which leaves the valley of Nuku Tambua is computed to be about twenty miles, and it cannot be less than ninety-one from Rewa; so the tale of Moli-vei-Tala is very likely to have been founded on fact."

The party now returned to Naitasiri, where they formed another expedition to explore the Muna Ndonu; but unfortunately the hostility of the natives (who were then at war) on both banks of the river prevented them from carrying out their object. Otherwise the complete success of the expedition is well evidenced in the copious appendix herewith annexed.

The scenery on the Navua river is also very bold and fine, one of the most remarkable sights being the hundred waterfalls 'Na Savu Drau.' In the rainy season it is navigable by large boats, and during the remainder of the year by canoes.

Levuka, which is situated in a quiet pleasant valley, surrounded by a dense grove of cocoa-nut and bread-fruit-trees, on the north-east side of the island of Ovalau, is the most important town of the group, and the advantages of its central position and convenient anchorage, entirely sheltered by a reef, which runs nearly parallel with the shore, recommend it as the future capital of the colony. Built at the water's edge, it consists of one long narrow street of weather-boarded houses and stores, extending for upwards of half a mile, closely skirting the sea-beach, and contains about 550 European inhabitants.

Hotels there are many, both dubious and nondescript,

PHYSICAL ASPECT OF THE ISLANDS. 13

the charges of which vary from 5s. to 7s. per diem, *tout inclus*.

Mountains, thickly wooded to their summits, rise abruptly at the back of the town to a height of over 2,000 feet, while on the lower spurs and terraces villa residences are fast springing up. There is perhaps a no more conclusive or characteristic testimony of the barbarism and misgovernment of a country than the total absence of a system of conservancy or sanitary regulations, and Fiji in this respect forms no exception to the general rule.

Notwithstanding the considerable facilities which at least two streams, taking their source in the neighbouring mountain gorges, afford for the conservancy of the town, and which will assuredly be taken advantage of under the new *régime*, yet its present condition is somewhat akin to a bad kind of Turkish village, and bears forcible evidence of the sad neglect and misrule which have been rampant.

The Island of Ovalau, like most of the other islands, is of volcanic formation, and is about eight miles in length, by six in breadth. It is mountainous and rugged throughout, interspersed here and there with fertile and well-cultivated valleys. It possesses numerous safe and accessible harbours, which, like that of Levuka, are formed by coral reefs.

The site next best adapted for a white settlement (it has been described as the best adapted) is at the harbour of Suva, which possesses the recommendation of being situated on the largest of the islands, Viti Levu. The harbour is also good, and easy of access, but it is not so central as Levuka.

Mbau, the native capital, a straggling mass of reed huts, inverted canoes, and many other indescribable habitations, presents a strangely singular appearance. Conspicuous amongst the native houses, arranged in curious narrow little streets, is the principal *mbure* or temple, which is overshadowed by a few surrounding trees, and the Mbure-ni-Sa or stranger's house, thus described by Captain Erskine:—

"We came at last upon an irregular square, on which stood a building, probably 100 feet long, and about 100 feet in height, 'the stranger's house,' still occupied by the Mbutoni people,* and we entered by a door in the centre. The interior struck me at first as resembling the lower deck of a ship of war, there being a passage down the centre, and the families living in separate messes on either side, divided however from each other, in some cases, by partitions of coloured native cloth. We met the usual welcome from the people who happened to be there, and several of them followed our party out, through an opposite door to that by which we had entered, to a small level space between the back of the house and the hill, which rises somewhat abruptly behind."

The king resides in a large native house, in front of which there is a fairly presentable grass lawn, planted with native shrubs and trees.

The town is situated on and nearly covers a small island, which in one part attains an elevation of nearly 100 feet above the level of the sea, and is connected with Viti Levu, or the mainland, by a causeway of coral formation of nearly a mile in length, which during low water affords a ready means of communication, and is easily fordable at high tide.

Rewa, which is the town of next importance in the group, is situated to the south of the bay formed by the embouchure of the river of that name, along the banks of which it extends for nearly a mile. It contains a large

* This is a roving tribe, who spend much of their time at sea, and owe allegiance to Mbau, where at this time they had repaired for the purpose of paying tribute.

number of habitations of various sizes and dimensions, from the barn-like residences of the chiefs and the lofty *mbures* to the most rickety shanty and yam-house. The latter is a diminutive structure used for storing yams, and raised from the ground by four posts to protect them from the depredations of the rats. The town is everywhere intersected by narrow lanes bounded by high reed fences, and though its site is rather low, it has a characteristic and picturesque appearance.

The town of Nduri, the capital of the province of Mucuata, in Vanua Levu, though not so large as Rewa, resembles it much in style, and formerly was considered to be one of the best constructed towns of the group. Like Mbau and Rewa, it is unfortified, and very much exposed. Usually however the towns are fortified with a strong palisade, surrounded by a ditch, filled partly with water.

Many of the tribes possess mountain fastnesses, into which they retreat when hard pressed, and which bear a striking resemblance to those of the Maoris in New Zealand. They are constructed with considerable skill and ingenuity, and not only afford a good defence against an attack practised according to the more primitive modes of aboriginal warfare, but likewise against musketry.

Imagine a hill or rock as inaccessible as possible, with a small level space on the summit, surrounded by a stockade constructed of upright posts, at least six inches in diameter, and about eighteen inches apart, strongly bound together by wicker-work, either interwoven or lashed on the outside; a ditch, where practicable, surrounding the whole, with a couple of narrow logs for a bridge; as many entrances as may be necessary, over which are projecting platforms, from which the defenders guard the approaches by hurling spears, etc.; various gates, which are made fast by sliding bars, and defended on either side by structures resembling bastions, made of tough wicker-work, placed at intervals of about four yards—and you have a fair idea of a Fijian stronghold.

CHAPTER II.

CLIMATE.

THE climate is delightful, and notably salubrious. For three parts of the year the varied seasons mingle into one, and the bud, flower, and fruit may be truly said to

" Drop, as breezes blow, a shower of bread
And blossoms on the ground."

The thermometer marks a mean temperature throughout the year, sixty feet above the level of the sea, ranging from 78·9° to 80°, and there is a perfect immunity from the fevers which generally prevail in other islands of the South Pacific. A much lower temperature of course prevails in the highlands, and the numerous mountains afford considerable facilities for Hill Stations and Sanitaria.

The cold season obtains from May to October, during which period the rainfall is not so considerable as during the summer months, which as nearly as possible correspond to our winter months, from October to April.

In 1865 the rainfall was 83·62; for the year 1872, 127·03; and in 1873 the total fall was 104·19. Otherwise the dry and rainy seasons are not so marked as in most tropical climates. During the hot season the temperature is moderated by the north-east, and during the cold-weather season by the south-east trade-winds, which prevail.

The following meteorological tables give the results of observations taken up to March, 1874, but from the fact of their not affording any data from which the difference, which is considerable, between the climate on the windward and leeward sides of the islands can be accurately ascertained, and also owing to the fact of readings not having been taken at a greater altitude than sixty feet above the level of the sea, they cannot be considered satisfactory or complete.

Table No. 1.—Copy of Meteorological Table from Calvert's 'Fiji and Fijians,' taken daily at Levuka in 1865, at 9 A.M.

1865.	Thermometers.					Winds.		Rainfall.		
	Maximum.	Minimum.	Mean.	Maximum Wet and Dry.	Minimum Wet and Dry.	General, Direct.	Greatest Fall.	Total Fall.	No. Days Rain fell.
January	93·6	79·0	85·0	9·0	3·04	S.E., S.W.	2·00	6·11	15
February	97·6	73·5	83·3	9·2	1·07	S.E., N.W.	3·90	13·45	18
March .	95·0	70·0	82·5	8·5	1·08	E.N.	3·80	17·14	21
April .	87·7	72·0	81·5	9·2	1·10	S.E., E.	5·20	19·57	23
May .	89·3	70·5	80·7	9·0	2·00	S.E., N.	1·12	2·22	7
June .	87·0	67·0	79·0	8·0	1·09	S.E., N.E.	1·25	3·69	9
July .	85·0	68·0	77·9	7·6	1·07	S.E., N.E.	2·00	2·68	6
August	84·0	68·5	..	..	1·08	S.E., E.	0·55	1·15	3
September	84·0	65·0	78·7	8·3	2·05	S.E., N.E.	1·02	2·78	7
October	87·0	67·5	78·7	9·1	2·06	S.E.	9·92	4·38	8
November	84·3	68·0	79·5	10·0	2·05	S.E., N.E.	0·67	1·25	6
December	86·5	70·0	81·6	7·3	2·05	N.E., S.,	1·75	9·23	13
								83·62	136

CLIMATE.

Table No. 2.—*Abstract of Meteorological Observations taken at Bua, in Vanua Levu, 60 feet above sea, 1 mile from sea, in 1873, at 8 A.M.*

1873.	Thermometers.				Rainfall.			
	Mean.	Maximum.	Minimum.	Mean Daily Range.	Total Fall.	Greatest Daily Fall.	No. Days Rain fell.	Hours of Rain.
January	79·5	91·5	70·3	12·8	20·15	2·82	23	89
February	79·9	91·8	71·7	13·9	17·31	2·30	21	80
March	79·8	94·2	69·3	14·6	16·52	2·52	22	88
April	80·0	92·2	69·3	15·4	11·38	1·83	20	30
May	79·0	91·8	68·6	16·3	4·53	1·10	13	26
June	76·2	90·0	60·3	16·3	2·51	0·75	6	10
July	77·6	90·0	62·8	17·7	4·71	1·35	14	23
August	75·9	89·5	60·8	15·9	8·10	2·03	11	41
September	78·0	92·8	66·6	15·7	1·47	0·36	12	7
October	79·8	94·5	68·0	15·5	7·07	2·10	16	33
November	80·2	93·4	64·0	19·1	2·88	1·32	6	8
December	81·4	93·8	71·2	16·1	7·51	1·40	17	35
Year {1873	78·9	94·5	60·3	15·8	104·10	2·82	181	470
Year {1872	78·9	97·5	59·3	15·7	127·03	5·05	180	502

Table No. 3.—*Constructed by Surgeon O. T. Corrie, of Her Majesty's Ship 'Pearl,' from Observations taken on board that ship by Navigating-Lieutenant Henry Hoskins, R.N., during the visit of the 'Pearl' to different parts of the Group in 1873-74.*

Months.	Thermometers.							Rainfall.	
	Maximum.	Minimum.	Mean.	Maximum of Wet and Dry.	Minimum of Wet and Dry.	Mean of Wet and Dry.	Maximum Daily Fall.	Total.	Number of Days Rain fell.
1873.									
November	88·5	66·0	79·1	9·8	1·0	5·1	1·18	2·847	6
December	85·7	75·0	81·4	8·0	1·0	4·3	1·55	6·66	16
1874.									
January	87·0	75·5	81·0	8·0	0·7	3·6	1·35	6·86	19
February	86·0	75·5	81·8	9·8	1·0	4·4	5·01	12·00	16
March	87·0	77·0	82·2	9·0	1·5	4·8	1·00	3·00	13

Therefore although it is evident that the climate of Fiji is strictly tropical, yet owing to the prevalence of strong trade-winds during the greater part of the year, and its insular position, it is singularly healthy, and free from tropical as well as other diseases.

Dysentery is indeed the only malady which Europeans have to fear, and as it is neither epidemic nor chronic, and is stated to be in nowise peculiar to the climate, or local causes, there is every reason to believe that with a little care it may be coped with or guarded against with complete success.

The natives mark the seasons by the flowering of various plants as well as by the cultivation of the yam, their staple article of food, upon which they also chiefly found their calendar. The following interesting remarks and table, illustrating the Fijian computation of time, are extracted from Dr. Seemann's official report, dated 1861:—

"The names given by me, as well as their succession, do not quite agree with those given by Wilkes. This discrepancy is partly explained by Wilkes having taken down his list upon the lips of Europeans imperfectly versed in Fijian, and by his adopting a loose way of spelling. The names of the months may also be different in different parts of the group. The subject however requires still further investigation. If, as has been averred, the Fijians invariably commenced the months with the appearance of the new moon, there would soon have been a vast difference between the lunar and the solar year. To guard against the irregularity that would thus have been introduced into the seasons, and to make the lunar year correspond with the solar, it would have been necessary either to intercalate a moon after every 36th moon, or to allow a greater period of time for one of the eleven months into which the Fijian year is divided. The latter seems to have been effected by the Vula i werewere (clearing month). Hazelwood (Fijian and English Dictionary, Viwa, 1850, p. 180) allows four months, May, June, July, and August for it, but this cannot be correct, as it would derange the others. By restricting

CLIMATE.

it to two or thereabouts, June and July, a proper arrangement is effected. I place the Vula i werewere first in my list instead of the month answering to January, because it is in the spring of the year (June and July), and the commencement of the agricultural operations, and natural phenomena upon which the calendar is based.

"FIJIAN CALENDAR.

According to Seemann.

1. *Vula i were were* = June, July, clearing month; when the land is cleared of weeds and trees.
2. *Vula i cukicuki* = August; when the yam-fields are dug and planted.
3. *Vula i vavakadi* = September; putting reeds to yams to enable them to climb up.
4. *Vula i Balolo lailai* = October; when the balolo (*Palolo viridis*, Gray), a remarkable Annelidan animal, first makes its appearance in small numbers.
5. *Vula i Balolo levu* = November; when the balolo (*Palolo viridis*, Gray) is seen in great numbers; the 25th of November generally is the day when most of these animals are caught.
6. *Vula i nuqa lailai* = December; a fish called 'nuqa' comes in, in isolated numbers.
7. *Vula i nuqa levu* = January; when the nuqa fish arrives in great numbers.

According to Wilkes.

1. *Vulai were were*, weeding month.
2. *Vulai lou lou*, digging ground and planting.
3. *Vulai Kawawaka.*
4. *Bololo vava Konde.*
5. *Bololo lieb.*
6. *Numa lieb*, or *Nuqa lailai.*
7. *Vulai songa sou tombe sou*, or *Nuqa levu*; reed blossoms.

According to Seemann.	According to Wilkes.
8. *Vula ni sevu* = February; when offerings of the first dug yams (ai sevu) are made to the priests.	8. *Vulai songa sou seselieb*, build yam houses.
9. *Vula i Kelikeli* = March; digging up yams and storing them in sheds.	9. *Vulai Matua*, or *Endoye doye*; yams ripe. (N.B.—Vulai Endoye, doye, probably is meant for Vula i doi; the Doi is a tree (*Alphitonia zizyphoides*, A. Gray), B. Seemann.)
10. *Vula i gasau* = April; reeds (gasau) begin to sprout out afresh.	10. *Vulai mbota mbota*.
11. *Vula i doi* = May; the Doi (*Alphitonia zizyphoides*, A. Gray), a tree plentiful in Fiji, flowers."	11. *Vulai kelekele*, or *Vulai mayo mayo*; digging yams.

CHAPTER III.

THE NATIVES.

THE origin of the Fijians is lost in obscurity; everything however tends to show that though they approximate in many remarkable respects to the Papuan tribes, they are but a modified type of their fairer neighbours, the Samoans and Tongans, who exhibit many of the characteristics of the Malays, and are anthropologically classed as Polynesian Malays. The stature of the pure Fijian is large, above middle height, and muscularly developed.

His skin is dark, rough, and harsh, his hair black and copiously bushy, as is also his beard, the former being frizzled, and having an apparent consistency of half wool, half hair, resembling that of the Cafoozos of South America.

The Fijian is changeable in disposition, and regards lying as an accomplishment and a virtue rather than a fault. The early visitors to this lovely group seem never tired of dilating on the fact that here only man is vile; and innumerable instances are given of the cowardice, treachery, and ferocity of the inhabitants, as well as of their habits of pilfering and covetousness, which were also formerly notorious. Thus we find concentred in the aborigine of the past an uninviting picture of humanity such as is seldom to be met with elsewhere.

Happily matters in this respect, of late years have much mended, and contact with civilisation as well as missionary influence have done wonders for native character in Fiji. Their versatility is well evidenced in the quickness of their movements and the ever watchful restlessness of their countenances.

Their anger manifests itself by a sullenness of disposition rather than in words, and a chief when offended puts a stick in the ground, that he may not perchance forget the reason of his displeasure. When the stick is pulled up by the offended dignitary, it is a sign that he will allow peaceful feelings to prevail, upon the receipt of the propitiatory offerings, which on such occasions it is deemed politic to make.

Their mode of expressing pleasure or thanks is by clapping their hands together several times. The half-castes are as a rule robust, hardy, and active, their intellectual capacities being about equal to their fathers', and superior to their mothers'.

Here are some interesting remarks on them by Staff-Surgeon Messer, M.D.:—

"It is estimated that there are now in the Fiji Islands about 120 adult men, 200 women, and 250 children of the European or American half-caste race.

"Although congregated in colonies, such as at Levuka, Vanua Levu, &c., on the Rewa river, they are to be found more or less in all the chief islands of the group.

"More than one half of the men are employed as sailors, a considerable number as boat-builders and carpenters, and a few as planters and cattle rearers.

"In their tastes and manner of living they take more after the native race than the white, being looked up to by the former and despised by the latter. They associate and intermarry mostly among themselves or with the Fijians, except some of the women, who not unfrequently become the mistresses, and occasionally the wives, of white settlers.

"Although many of the half-castes are married, yet the number of their offspring is rarely above three or four in family, who, as far as we have been able to observe, are frequently much diseased, and poorly developed.

" Physically the men are a fine, well-grown race, but the females, although often good-looking, are inferior in this respect. The men are of a roving and unsettled disposition, rarely settling to any fixed occupation: they mostly become sailors, and man the numerous small craft which navigate the Fiji seas.

" Few of them embrace any particular form of religion, although they are, in most cases, nominally Christians, and, a sa class, bear but an indifferent character for sobriety or trustworthiness, being particularly fond of card-playing and gambling.

"They are also said to be very improvident, the women especially being careless and extravagant.

" Exceptions, however, to this not over perfect character are not wanting, for there are a few families who have turned their attention steadily to boat-building, and who are industrious, useful members of the community, producing well-built boats at very moderate prices, and laying by money, buying land, and educating their children."

On the whole, the Fijians possess perhaps a greater intelligence, and more physical and mental energy than any other South Pacific Islanders, and certainly more than the inhabitants of the adjoining archipelagoes.

The chiefs are in every respect a superior set of men to the commoners, which may be attributed to the fact that as leaders their mental and physical faculties are more continuously active than those of the classes over whose destinies they rule. They are distinguished from the commoners by the *sala*, or turban, and the maro. High chiefs also wear round the neck a single shell of the *Cyprœa Aurora*, or a valve of the red spondylus, or a collar of whales' teeth, &c.

The fashion of wearing the comb, or hair-picker is also an indication of rank. The king only may wear it in front; those next in rank a little removed on one side, and the lower orders behind the car.

The Fijians appear to be easily controlled by those acquainted with their traditions and customs, which will account for the influence generally exercised by Her Britannic Majesty's Consuls throughout Fiji, and which until a late date has enabled them to control the native population in the interests of order and civilisation.

Besides those mbures devoted to purposes of worship there are also others, termed mbure ni sa, which are especially devoted to sleeping purposes. As the evening approaches the men congregate in these, it being quite contrary to Fijian ideas of delicacy and etiquette that husbands should sleep during the night-time in the same house with their wives. In the morning the husbands again return to the bosoms of their respective families.

Connubial felicity is promoted by means of secret rendezvous, only known to husband and wife. Until publicly admitted into the society of adults, boys have a sleeping mbure to themselves.

Although the great bulk of the people has until within a comparatively recent date been merged in the grossest barbarism, yet there is observable in many of their manners and customs a degree of politeness and etiquette which one is unprepared to expect, and which should be noted as one of the pleasant characteristics of this peculiar people. A chief would be considered ill-mannered if he did not return the salutation of an inferior; equals salute each other, but all others whom a chief meets retire crouchingly out of his path, and lower their clubs.

On the occasion of a feast each person is seated according to his rank, and the posture assumed, though possibly not strictly in accordance with our ideas of what is *comme il faut*, is nevertheless easy and graceful; and is marked by an absence of that *gaucherie* which is often so incongruously noticeable in more civilised society.

Their feasts are given in the mbure, and a priest generally officiates as master of the ceremonies, a duty which may be said to consist, principally, in his assiduously ministering to his own gastronomical propensities.

Among all classes the toilet occupies a considerable portion of time, that part of the person which claims a superlative degree of attention being the head.

A fortiori it will be almost superfluous to observe on the necessary importance of the barber, a factotum without whom no Fijian establishment of any pretensions can be said to be complete. The more the hair is distended the greater the dignity of the barber, the pride of the chief, and the appreciation in which they are respectively held by their admiring countrymen.

Barbers are attached to the households of chiefs in numbers varying from two to a dozen, and their duties are held to be of such a delicate and sacred nature that they are tambooed from all other employment, not even being permitted to feed themselves.

The coiffure of a chief often occupies several hours, and includes the dressing of his moustachios and his beard, of which he is not a little proud. The latter often grows to a very respectable length. The process is as follows:— The hair is first saturated with oil, which is blackened by a preparation from the *laudi* nut. The barber next proceeds to twitch almost every separate hair with a long slender rod, generally made of tortoiseshell, and which has the effect of causing it to frizzle and stand on end. It is now singed trim and smooth, and finally enveloped in a turban or sala. The hair is not dressed, except when the sala (which is a fine species of *kapa*, or native cloth) is removed, which with the principal chiefs is a matter of daily habit, but when taken care of the sala will last for several weeks. Formerly an attempt to assume the sala by a commoner was punishable by death.

The hair of the boys is cropped close, but on attaining manhood's estate it becomes fashioned in shapes as manifold as they are peculiar. Usually some part of the hair is coloured red or brown, and the prevailing fashion is to have it cut round. A good general similitude to these uninviting coiffures would be a stiffish mop well infested by vermin.

The women in this respect are also attentive to their charms. The younger girls, pending the development of a romantic aspiration for chignon—an excrescence which has yet to attain maturity and become fashionable in Fiji—wear their hair quite long, *au naturel*, and when they wish to be *en grande tenue*, they effectively decorate it with flowers.

After marriage however such attractions are either not valued, or are considered imprudent or unnecessary, and accordingly, under the influence of the scissors, these virginal locks give way to a 'short clip,' which is either let be, or takes the form of a frizzled wig. Those who lack the necessary quantity of hair have recourse to *bonâ-fide* wigs, which are often so well made as to quite baffle detection.

From a laudable desire to promote cleanliness, the missionaries, we are told, have pronounced against long hair and the use of the sala; "but in doing so they have deprived the natives of a capital protection against the sun; the immense mass of hair, curled and frizzled to make it stand off many inches, and covered by a piece of snow-white tapa, must have kept the head cool. Now most of the Christian natives move about without any covering for their head, and with their hair cut short, which, in a tropical climate, cannot improve their intellect. The abolition of the old custom might have proved more beneficial if immediately followed by the institution of some kind of head-dress."

To cleanse their "mops" they use lime, and also a preparation made from the ashes of the bread-fruit tree. In Fijian *toilette* the face also is not forgotten, and undergoes daily a painting of black soot and oil, which is occasionally picked out in vermillion, artistically splotched or daubed on the nose, and one or two other favourite places.

Both sexes have their ears bored, the women only in one lobe, the men in both. They resort to various expedients for distending the punctures, and occasionally with such success that, it is stated, some have been known large enough to admit of a hand being passed through.

The women only are tattooed, which is due to a superstition that they cannot otherwise propitiate the gods, who are ready to receive them in another world. The men in this respect offer a marked contrast to their Papuan *confrères* of New Guinea, as well as to the other races of Polynesia, whose bodies are invariably profusely decorated after this fashion. The tattooing is usually performed by a woman, being applied to the corners of the mouth and those parts of the body covered by their scanty clothing. The skin is punctured by a sharp-pointed instrument, made of bone, over the device which has previously been marked out; on the completion of this painful part of the operation, a blue dye, which they obtain from a ground nut, is rubbed into the punctures. Some days elapse before the patient is able to move about.

The Fijians have many amusements, but the one most in favour is dancing, which is common to both sexes, and is regularly taught by professors of the art.

They have a peculiar method of sending messages by reeds or sticks, which are supposed to fix the memory. They are given separately to the messengers, and with each is delivered the message which it is intended to represent; also at a bargain or sale it is usual to make a small deposit, called *yaqona* (as an earnest that the transaction is mutually assented to), which consists of one of these reeds, or a piece of kava root, or any other article that may be acceptable. This giving of something to bind the bargain is, according to Fijian law, quite as certain in its operation as the 17th section of our own statute of frauds, and affords one more instance of the comparatively short span between barbarism and civilisation.

The belief which formerly prevailed, that the condition in which a person left this life would be also his condition in a future state, formed a powerful incentive to the hateful practices of strangulation and self-immolation.

Apart, however, from the desire which natives had to immolate themselves, or to be put to death by their friends to escape from decrepitude or deformity, they manifested a decided repugnance to the crippled and the maimed, who were nearly always destroyed, regardless of the cause of their misfortune.

The following is a suggestive description by Wilkes of an immolation:—

"It is among the most usual occurrences that a father or a mother will notify to their children that it is time for them to die, or that a son shall give notice to his parents that they are becoming a burden to him. In either case the relatives and friends are collected and informed of the fact. A consultation is then held, which generally results in the conclusion that the request is to be complied with, in which case they fix upon a day for the purpose, unless it should be done by the party whose fate is under deliberation. The day is usually chosen at a time when the yams or taro are ripe, in order to furnish materials for a great feast, *mburna*. The aged person is then asked whether he will prefer to be strangled before his burial, or buried alive. When the appointed day arrives the relatives and friends bring tapas, mats, and oil as presents. They are received as at other funeral feasts, and all mourn together until the time for the ceremony arrives. The person then proceeds to point out the place where the grave is to be dug, and while some are digging it the others put on a new maro and turbans. When the grave is dug, which is about four feet deep, the person is assisted into it, while the relatives and friends begin their lamentations, and proceed to weep and cut themselves as they do at other funerals. All then proceed to take a parting kiss, after which the living body is covered up, first with mats and tapa, wrapped round the head, and then with sticks and earth, which are trodden down. When this has been done all retire, and are tabooed, as will be stated in describing their ordinary funerals. The succeeding night the son goes privately to the grave, and lays upon it a piece of ava-root, which is called the vei-tala, or farewell."

Notwithstanding this, the Fijians are represented to be devoted to their parents, and they themselves are in the habit of adducing, as a proof of this affection, that none but the children are willing to perform this horrible custom.

Of their numerous ceremonials perhaps the most interesting and impressive are those attendant on the death and burial of a chief. Surrounded by followers, friends, and relations, when his last moments are approaching, two whales' teeth are placed in his hands to throw at the tree which is supposed to stand on the road to the regions of the departed.

The slender debt to nature paid, those that remain now raise their voices in lamentation, and mourn the dead.

The corpse is then washed and prepared for interment. Being first anointed with oil, the neck, breast, and arms are daubed with a kind of black pigment, after which the body is dressed as in life, and a club is placed in the right hand lying across the breast, to indicate in the next world that the deceased was a chief and a warrior in this. These offices having been completed, the chiefs of the various subject tribes assemble and present offerings to the departed. The female friends also approach and kiss the body, and if any of his widows desire to accompany him in this last long journey, where there are

" No traces left, the path direct to show,"

they here make an opportune request of some near relative to be strangled—a wish which is no sooner expressed than it is gratified.

The same persons who have washed the corpse prepare the grave, which should be near to the banks of some river or stream. The operation is inaugurated by two of the officiating Ambati, who, having marked out the dimensions of the grave, make various mysterious passes with reeds, repeating the words: "Fiji, Tonga! Fiji, Tonga!"

The last sounds of this invocation have not died away before the two gravediggers, who have already taken up their respective positions at the head and the foot of the grave, are busy plying their task, not forgetting the important preliminary of three feints, before striking the ground with their staves.

The grave is made ready for the reception of the bodies by lining it with fine mats, along with which are placed the four reeds used by the Ambati at the ceremony.

On these the corpses are laid, having been wrapped up together in many folds of fine tapa. There at last lies the warrior chief, supported on either side by those faithful wives, who even in death have clung to him their lord and master. And then the closing of the grave concludes the mournful scene.

The common people are buried with far less ceremony. They are usually placed in a sitting posture just below the ground, wrapped in tapa cloth, and sometimes sprinkled with turmeric.

"Who's a prince or beggar in the grave?"

The funeral rites above described vary in minor details in different parts of the group. Thus while in some places it is customary to bury the chief in a grave, distinguished by the stone or slab which is placed over it, in other instances he is interred in a royal mbure, or tomb, formed of a series of slabs placed perpendicularly in the form of a square, the interior of which is filled with earth, the whole being covered in by a kind of shed. The day of death is celebrated by a feast called *mburua*, and on the fourth and tenth days there are also feasts respectively termed *boniva* and *boniviti*.

During the nine days preceding the last funeral feast, which also marks the time when the soul is supposed to leave the body, the women have a strange custom of striking the men with long whips, the lashes of which being knotted with shells, seldom fail to leave their mark.

The men, on the other hand, are by no means passive in this little game, and retort by flirting hard little balls of clay from pieces of split bamboo. All those who have been concerned in preparing the dead body, or in digging the grave, are tambooed persons; and at the conclusion of the funeral ceremony must cast off their old clothes, and rub their bodies over with the leaves of a plant called koaikoaia. During the tamboo, which lasts from four days to ten months, according to the rank of the departed one, the persons under its restriction are not only provided with food, but are actually fed by attendants. failing which they must eat from the ground: for while under tamboo they are not permitted to touch anything.

Placing a tamboo on a person is virtually to make him a temporary outcast. Its effect as regards provisions and the like (for it may be extended to anything) is to place them under a prohibition or veto, which can only be removed by a chief of high rank, accompanied by certain ceremonies; the principal feature of these, of course, consists in the usual presents to the ambati.

Outward signs of sorrow and mourning are manifested in cutting off the little finger and toe—a custom of which some few years since there was ample evidence in the numbers of dismembered joints to be seen. Women also denote their suffering of mind, and I should presume likewise of body, by burning blisters on various parts of their person. The least violent token of grief would appear to be a cropping of the hair or beard; an operation which is however of no trifling import, for they take long to grow, and are most highly valued.

The strangulation of wives at the funerals of their husbands, though generally done by their request, is not always voluntary, and notwithstanding what Seemann says to the contrary, reluctant victims have undoubtedly been compelled by interested relatives to render up their lives in this way. For by the death of the wife her connexions become entitled to the property of the husband; and thus, as a matter of fact, there is a stepping into 'dead men's shoes.'

Rarely however is such coercion necessary, and truly may it be said that never

> "Has Hindoo widow mounted the pile,
> And met her death with more placid smile,"

than do these misguided creatures resign themselves to their violent and untimely fate.

This desire to accompany their husbands in death is explained when we are told that " it is one of the cardinal articles of their belief, that in this way alone can they reach the realms of bliss, and she who meets her death with the greatest devotedness will become the favourite wife in the abode of spirits."

The mode in which the strangulation is performed is sufficiently simple and expeditious. Having expressed a wish to accompany her departed husband, the wretched victim, decked in her gaudiest apparel, seats herself on a mat, exclaiming, " Make haste to strangle me, that I may overtake my husband!" and those who are present applaud the while. Then, placing her head in the lap of some female friend, a cord is adjusted nooselike round her neck, and pulled tight by strong men until " death lies on her."

The cord is not removed, but is loosed when the friends of the husband present a whale's tooth, saying, " This is the untying of the cord of strangling!"

It is pleasant to note that amongst the great bulk of the population these practices have ceased, and enormities of paganism and idolatry have yielded to the powerful influence of that religion, upon which Penn says, men will venture their souls on trust, when they will not credit a synod about the goodness of half-a-crown!

The Fijian certainly possesses a considerable capacity for civilisation, but he forms, nevertheless, no exception to that apparently immutable law which decrees the wane of the savage upon contact with civilisation.

In the interior of Fiji scanty population, and the traces of ruined villages and abandoned cultivation which abound, must no doubt be attributed to the ferocious character of their frequent tribal wars, in which the victors were rarely satisfied with anything short of the extermination of their vanquished foes; but these influences only fail to account for the rapid depopulation which has proceeded in latter years.

In the year 1867 Her Britannic Majesty's Consul reports :—

"A very few years ago the island of Ovalau could send out 3000 fighting men, now it could only muster 500, by including the lads and old men. This is not a solitary example: the ruined and deserted villages throughout the country bear testimony to the disappearance of the race."

And thus co-equally with the advance of the white man's civilisation in Fiji is the decay of the aborigine, which is proportionately marked as its effects are manifested in his savage home.

CHAPTER IV.

THE LANGUAGE.

THE Fijian language is flowing, euphonious, and expressive, and belongs to that family of tongues known by philologists as the Polynesian-Malay, or Oceanic type. Those that are best acquainted with it state that its characteristics are boldness and originality; and its copiousness may be estimated from the fact of its furnishing distinctive names for every species of production yielded in the islands, including every kind of shrub or grass.

There are names for all the different kinds of yam, which amount to more than fifty; and there is a distinctive appellation for the different varieties of the cocoanut, as well as for each successive stage of its ripening.

The language not only contains words representing infirmity and disease, as well as every creation of the mind, but it is also sufficiently subtle to afford expression to the most delicate shades of meaning. Hence were it true, as asserted by some writers, that the language of a people may be considered a fair index to their minds, there would be indeed little left to desire in the character of the natives of these islands. Unfortunately we are aware that such is not the case.

Living in different islands, in which the climate is somewhat varied, want of intimate knowledge of one another, the partial assumption of a different national character, the adoption of different modes of life, and intercourse with the foreigner, are some of the many incidents which would perhaps help to account for the number of different dialects in Fiji, which we may reasonably suppose are the offspring of a parent tongue. While there is a considerable distinction between some of these dialects, of which there are supposed not to be fewer than fifteen, the particular genius of each is the same, and they are said likewise to agree in the same general idiom.

The missionaries are acquainted with no less than seven dialects, in four of which books have been printed. The most elegant of these is the dialect of Mbau, which is as much the Attic of Fiji, as those by whom it is spoken are the Athenians of the group. It is into this language that the Scriptures have been translated. The Fijian language, like other Malayo-Polynesian tongues, while rejoicing in liquids, nasals, and vowels, is remarkable for its excluding hissing and guttural sounds. As in Italian, in the pronunciation of words the penultimate syllable is generally most accentuated.

In many instances elementary alphabetical sounds obtain in one part of the group which are not found in others; thus the letter F is only heard at Lakemba and the other adjoining windward islands, where it has been introduced by the Tongans, and often supplants the letter V, while it is quite unknown throughout the rest of the Archipelago.

This supplies the etymology of the collective name of the group, which in the leeward islands is known as Viti and in the windward islands is known as Fiji. Those who may be further interested in this subject are referred to Mr. Hazlewood's Grammar and Dictionary of the Fijian Language, both of which are complete works of their kind, and valuable additions to linguistic science.

CHAPTER V.

MANNERS AND CUSTOMS.

FIJIAN domestic economy is of the most primitive description. Living in rude huts constructed of reeds, the natives congregate in 'koros' or villages, which if not more elaborately fortified, for defensive purposes are generally surrounded by a ditch.

In the absence of the white man's calico, which has not yet been generally adopted, their ordinary clothing consists of a plantain or cocoa-nut leaf, which they contrive to adjust to their persons with some skill and judgment. This simple garb is occasionally varied by another equally picturesque dress, called 'liku,' and which, fashioned from the fibre of various plants, consists of a number of fringes attached to a waistband. Men may wear these fringy screens of nature to any length, but they are more particular as regards the women, for whom shortness is etiquette, and is especially *de rigueur* amongst the young unmarried ones, for whom a fringe of three inches is the outside limit. As in those good old times when sumptuary laws prevailed, and " Jack " was not permitted to ape his master, when it was possible to distinguish a lady of rank from other *ladies* by her dress, so it is at the *present time* practicable in Fiji to discern a native lady from the plebeians of her sex by the style of her 'liku.' While with the former two, three, or more flounces, or layers of fibres—each one of which should be of a different colour—is of necessity *à la mode*, with the latter barely one layer is deemed sufficient.

Some of my readers unsophisticated in Fijian fashions may feel inclined to associate a certain amount of unchasteness and immodesty with such scantiness of apparel, but they must permit me to say that the imputation is unmerited. Amongst Fijian women immorality is the exception, not the rule, as elsewhere in Polynesia; and in these islands at least D'Urville found little necessity or opportunity for enforcing those singularly appropriate instructions which he received before assuming command of the French expedition to the Pacific in 1837—" d'apprivoiser les hommes, et de rendre les femmes un peu plus sauvage."

"Materials for the scanty clothing worn by the Fijians are readily supplied by a variety of plants, foremost amongst which stands the malo, or paper mulberry (*Broussonetia papyrifera*, Vent.), a middle-sized tree, with rough trilobed leaves, cultivated all over Fiji. On the coast the native cloth (tapa) and plaitings are gradually displaced by cheap cotton prints introduced by foreign traders, a fathom of which is considered enough for the entire dress of a man. In the inland heathen districts the boys are allowed to run naked until they have attained the age of puberty, and publicly assumed what may be termed their *toga virilis*—a narrow strip of native cloth (malo) passing between the legs, and fastened either to a waistband of string or to a girdle formed by one of the ends of the cloth itself. The length of the tapa hanging down in front denotes the rank of the wearer, the lower classes not having it longer than is absolutely necessary for the purposes of securing it to the waistband, whilst the chiefs let it dangle on the ground, and when incommoded by it in walking playfully swing it over their shoulder. In the Christianised districts of the coast a piece of tapa at least two yards long and one yard broad is worn around the loins, and distinguished persons envelope their body in pieces many yards long, and allow long trains to drag after them on the ground."*

* *Vide* Seemann's Official Report.

Like all savages, the Fijians keep their women in a state of great subjection, the only privilege they can lay claim to being a constant and attentive obedience to the capricious commands of their tyrannical 'lords and masters,' which is varied by carrying burdens, the weeding of yam and taro beds, and a strict performance of their household duties. And so it is, the lower we descend in the scale of civilisation, the lower is the estimation in which woman is ignorantly and, let it be said, inappreciatively held! They are not celebrated for their good looks, seldom being even comely, and indeed perhaps the only recommendation to be pleaded in their favour is the equanimity with which they bear their jealous exclusion from the mbures or council houses, and their serenely blissful ignorance of that social bugbear, "Woman's rights!"

Those circumstances, which concur in causing the social affections to assume a stronger influence over the mind, under the rule of a benign and enlightened government cannot fail to receive an impetus, which we trust will be soon manifested in the relaxation of that tyrannic sway by which the Fijian savage has hitherto so much debased himself and depressed the softer sex.

The spontaneous products of the soil, such as the yam, taro, cocoa-nut, and bread-fruit, furnish them with food *ad libitum*. They are also fond of fish, which abound in great quantity and variety, and which they are exceedingly expert in catching.

The women as well as the men are proficient in this sport, which they often indulge in at night-time on the reefs, by torch-light. One of these fishing parties, enlivened by the flitting torches and peels of merry laughter, forms a strangely weird and characteristic tableau, not often seen, nor soon forgotten.

Another method much practised of catching fish, is by nets and fences. The latter are constructed, both in the sea and river, with much care, and are never allowed to remain for more than a few days in the same place, for it is supposed that the fish become acquainted with their meaning, and avoid the cunning snare. In the rivers they are constructed zigzag, reaching to either bank, with a bamboo basket placed at every angle, in which the fish are caught. For netting the fish deep water is always selected. A circle of divers is then formed, which gradually concentrating, frightens the fish into the nets held to receive them. This novel mode of fishing is particularly practised by the men of the Soloira district, in Viti Levu.

One of the most common modes resorted to by them of catching the fish is by poisoning, or rather stupefying it, a custom as prevalent all over Polynesia as it is amongst the Indians of America, the materials employed by them for this purpose being " the square fruit of the vutu rakaraka (*Barringtonia speciosa*, Linn.) and the stem and leaves of the duva gaga (*Derris uliginosa*, Benth.), both plants growing in abundance on the sea-beach, just above high-water mark. As soon as these materials,—pounded to render them more efficacious,— are thrown into the water or drawn through it by means of a line or creeper to which they have been attached, the fish turn on their back and appear on the surface. They are perfectly stupefied, and are thus easily taken; but they soon recover their lost activity, and are believed not to die from the effects of the treatment they have received."

The national and intoxicating beverage is *kava* or *yaqona*. It is prepared from the root of the *Piper methysticum*, of which there are at least six different varieties, and it possesses the one recommendation, which is the Fijian's boast, that it does not make its devotees quarrelsome in their cups. Its taste has been compared to that of Gregory's mixture combined with soapsuds, and its appearance to that of dirty dish-water, which, coupled with the following description of its preparation, would in some degree account for the fact of its being considered by many to be an acquired taste. "In order to prepare the beverage, it is necessary to reduce the roots to minute particles, which, according to regular Polynesian usage, is done by chewing—a task in Fiji devolving upon lads, who have sound teeth, and who occupy a certain social rank towards the man for whom they perform the office. In other Polynesian islands it is done by young women."

Having been thus chewed, the root is placed in a large wooden bowl, upon which water is poured, while those present exclaim "Aisevu." Now commences the process of straining the liquid through the woody fibres of the *vau* (*hibiscus*), a sufficiently complicated operation, and which is thus minutely described by Mariner:—

"The man who manages the bowl now begins his difficult operation. In the first place he extends his left hand to the farther side of the bowl, with his fingers pointing downwards, and the palm towards himself; he sinks that hand carefully down at the side of the bowl, carrying with it the edge of the *vau*; at the same time his right hand is performing a similar operation at the side next to him, the finger pointing downwards, and the palm presenting outwards. He does this slowly, from side to side, gradually descending deeper and deeper, till his fingers meet each other at the bottom, so that nearly the whole of the fibres of the root are by these means enclosed in the *vau*, forming as it were a roll of above two feet in length, lying along the bottom from side to side, the edges of the *vau* meeting each other underneath. He now carefully rolls it over, so that the edges overlapping each other, or rather intermingling, come uppermost. He next doubles in the two ends, and rolls it carefully over again, endeavouring to reduce it to a narrower and firmer compass. He now brings it cautiously out of the fluid, taking firm hold of it by the two ends, one in each hand (the back of the hand being upwards), and raising it breast high, with his arms considerably extended, he brings his left hand towards his breast, moving it gradually onwards; and whilst his left hand is coming round towards his right shoulder, his right hand, partially twisting the *vau*, lays the end which it holds upon the left elbow, so that the *vau* lies thus extended upon that arm, one end being still grasped by the left hand. The right hand being now at liberty, is brought under the left fore-arm (which still remains in the same position), and carried outwardly towards the left elbow, that it may again seize in that situation the end of the *vau*. The right hand then describes a bold curve outwardly from the chest, whilst the left comes across the chest, describing a curve nearer to him, and in the opposite direction, till at length the left hand is extended from him and the right approaches to the left shoulder, gradually turning the *vau* by the turn and flexures principally of the wrist; this double motion is then retraced, but in such a way (the left wrist now principally acting) that the *vau*, instead of being untwisted, is still more twisted, and is at length again placed on the left arm, while he takes a new and less constrained hold. Thus the hands and arms perform a variety of curves of the most graceful description; the muscles both of the arms and chest are seen rising as they are called into action, displaying what would be a fine and uncommon subject of study for the painter, for no combinations of animal action can develope the swell and play of the muscles with more grace or with better effect.

"The degree of strength which he exerts, when there is a large quantity, is very great, and the dexterity with which he accomplishes the whole never fails to excite the attention and admiration of all present.

"Sometimes the fibres of the *vau* are heard to crack with the increasing tension, yet the mass is seen whole and entire, becoming more thin as it becomes more twisted, while the infusion drains from it in a regularly decreasing quantity, till at length it denies a single drop."

During this performance the people assembled are ranged, in sitting posture, in the form of a semicircle, in the centre of which is the chief operator. The ceremony is further enlivened by a sort of song, in which all join, and to which they keep time by repeating the motions of the kava strainer, and marking important stages in the process by a clapping of hands. Should the king be present, they are very particular that no one, except the cup-bearer, touches his cup. The first cup is always handed to the person of highest rank present, next to whom it is deemed a mark of honour to be served. The form of kava drinking is initiatory to and attendant on all Fijian ceremonies.

At Somo Somo the usage of the king drinking kava is peculiarly ceremonious:—

* " Early in the morning the first thing heard is the king's herald, or orator, crying out in front of his house, " Yango na ei ava," somewhat like a muezzin in Turkey, though not from the housetop. To this the people answer from all parts of the koro, " Mama " (prepare ava). The principal men and chiefs immediately assemble together from all quarters, bringing their ava-bowl and ava-root to the mbure, where they seat themselves to talanoa, or to converse on the affairs of the day, while the younger proceed to prepare the ava. Those who prepare the ava are required to have clean and undecayed teeth, and are not allowed to swallow any of the juice, on pain of punishment. As soon as the ava-root is chewed, it is thrown in the ava-bowl, where the water is poured on it with great formality. The king's herald, with a peculiar drawling whine, then cries, " Sevu-rui-a-na " (make the offering). After this a considerable time is spent in straining the ava through cocoa-nut husks, and when this is done the herald repeats with still more ceremony, his command, " Sevu-rni-a-na." When he has chanted it several times, the other chiefs join him, and they all sing, " Mana endina sendina le." A person is then commanded to get up and take the king his ava, after which the singing again goes on. The orator then invokes their principal god, Tava-Sava, and they repeat the names of their departed friends, asking them to watch over and be gracious to them. They then pray for rain, for the life of the king, the arrival of wangara papalangi (foreign ships), that they may have riches, and live to enjoy them. This prayer is followed by a most

* *Vide* Wilkes.

earnest response, "Mana endina" (amen, amen). They then repeat several times, "Mana endina sendina le." Every time this is repeated they raise their voices, until they reach the highest pitch, and conclude with "O-ya-ye," which they utter in a tone resembling a horrid scream. This screech goes the round, being repeated by all the people of the koro, until it reaches its farthest limits, and when it ceases the king drinks his ava. All the chiefs clap their hands with great regularity while he is drinking, and after he has finished his ava the chiefs drink theirs without any more ceremony. The business of the day is then begun. The people never do anything in the morning before the king has drunk his ava; even a foreigner will not venture to work or make a noise before that ceremony is over, or during the preparation of it, if he wishes to be on good terms with the king and people."

The Fijians are skilful doctors, after the Polynesian fashion, and their surgical and medical pre-eminence is acknowledged in the adjoining islands. Like many nearer home, they cunningly attach great importance to *faith*, and testimony can be adduced to some marvellous cures worked through the unpretending agency of bread pills.

Midwifery is a distinct profession practised only by women. They are said to be well-versed in the mysteries of their calling, and to perform many obstetrical operations with success. Procuring criminal abortion, which was formerly very prevalent, was the source of a lucrative employment to these creatures, who usually performed their office at the instance of the father. Of the various drugs employed for committing this unnatural offence the tikula (*Dracæna ferrea*) is held to be the most efficacious in its effects.

Seemann gives the following description of their medicinal plants:—

"The medicinal plants employed by the natives are as difficult, perhaps more difficult, to find out than the poisonous ones used for illegal purposes. Those who profess to be acquainted with their properties—often women, and answering to our herbalists—cannot be tempted by any presents to disclose secrets which to them 'prove a lucrative source of income for life. It is only the virtues of plants generally known that a casual inquirer has any chance of learning. The high estimation in which the oil of the dilo (*Calophyllum inophyllum*, Linn.) is held by the whole population, as an efficacious remedy for rheumatism and other pains. * * * * * The leaves of the Kura (*Morinda citrifolia*, Linn.), a middle-sized tree, with shining leaves and white flowers, not unlike those of the coffee-shrub, are heated by passing them over flame, and their juice squeezed into ulcers, whilst the leaves themselves are put on the wound, as a kind of bandage. The bark of the danidani (*Panax fruticosum*, Linn.), a shrub about eight feet high, and cultivated about the native houses on account of its deeply-cut, ornamental foliage, is scraped off, and its juice taken as a remedy for macake, the thrush—ulcerated tongue and throat. The properties of the sarsaparilla (*Smilax, sp*. . . . . .) as a means of purifying the blood are well-known. The creeper is found throughout the group, especially on land that has at one time been cleared, and might be gathered in quantities if there were any demand for it. In the London market it would at present be unsaleable. It belongs to that section of sarsaparillas distinguished by pharmacologists as the "non-mealy," the most valued representative of which is the Jamaica sort. Moreover, it has no "beard," or little rootlets. The natives of Ovalau, Viti Levu, and Vanua Levu name it kadragi and wa-rusi; those of Kadavu, "Nakau-wa," literally, "the woody-creeper." I met with it years ago in the Hawaiian group; it is said to be also common in the Samoan and Tongan groups, and prepared sarsaparilla occasionally imported to the two last-mentioned has found no market, the indigenous being preferred to the foreign production. Curious to add, in Fiji it is not, as with us, the rhizome that is used, but the leaves, which are chewed, put in water, and strained through fibre, like the yaqona or kava (*Piper methysticum*, Forst.), before being taken. Strong purgative properties reside in the vasa or rewa (*Cerbera lactaria*, Ham.), a sea-side tree, twenty-five feet high, with soft wood, smooth shining leaves, and white, scented flowers, used for necklaces by the natives. The aromatic leaves of the laca (*Plectranthus Forsteri*, Benth.), a weed abounding in cultivated places, and having purple bracts supporting pale blue flowers, cure, it is said, "bad eyes" and headaches on being brought in contact with the affected parts. It is also recommended for coughs and colds, in common with an acanthaceous herb, inhabiting swamps (*Adenosma* *triflora*, Nees.), which shares its aromatic properties. The people of Somosomo declare that the leaves of the vulokaka (*Vitex trifoliata*, Linn.), with which their beach is thickly lined, when reduced to a pulp by chewing, are employed by them for stuffing hollow teeth. The leaves and bark of another sea-side shrub, the sinu mataiavi (*Wikstroemia Indica*, C. A. Meyer), are employed for coughs, the bark alone for sores."

They believe in the immortality of the soul, and in another world, and in common with many other of the South Sea islanders, including New Zealanders, fix the point of departure to future bliss on the westernmost limits of their islands. They have traditions and a mythology of their own, distinctly differing from the neighbouring Polynesian races. They are polytheists, and have an enormous number of gods, duly superintended by priests, who are to be found in every village, and who harmlessly appropriate the food and other offerings perpetually made to the deities.

The sadly diminished number of sacred trees and groves afford sufficient indication of the operations of missionary zeal and of the white man's axe.

Dr. Seemann makes the following interesting remarks on these groves; he says:—

"They were not worshipped as gods, but, as in the Odin religion of our ancestors, looked upon as places where certain gods had taken up their abode. There were sacred stones on the same footing, and one near Bau, the abode of a goddess, gave birth to a little stone whenever any woman of rank was confined at the Fijian capital. The large stone was taken away at the introduction of Christianity to those parts, but the numerous little offsprings still remain in the once sacred spot to testify to the reality of Fijian mythology."

The tarawau (*Dracontomelon sylvestre*, Blume) does not seem to be regarded as a sacred tree in the light of those just mentioned, but it is held to be the business of the dead to plant it, and believed to grow not only in this world, but also in Naicobocobo, the Fijian nether world. Hence arose the expression, "Sa la'ki tei tarawau ki Naicobocobo,' literally, 'He has gone to plant tarawaus at' Naicobocobo,' i.e. he is dead. It is difficult to guess why these trees should have been deemed worthy of a place in the abode of their future state, where the souls amuse themselves with canoes and arms, and yams, taros, and all kinds of fruits are plentiful. The tarawau grows to a height of sixty feet, has flattish branches, pinnated leaves, insignificant whitish flowers, and a tough insipid fruit, only palatable to the natives. Fancy places Naicobocobo on the westernmost part of Vanua Levu, under water, where also the place of departure (ai Cibicibi) is situated."

In this custom of resorting for purposes of worship to these emblematic tabernacles of nature, fashioned by the great Architect of the universe, and hallowed by the inimitable impress of his handicraft, may be found an unconscious, though nevertheless a remarkable repetition of the idea conveyed by the *Mundus universus est templum solus* of those ancients who took the sun as the great symbol of the deity, and variously diversified by the Druids and the Indo-Germanic nations of the early ages, all of whom equally recognised the profanity of setting limits to the infinite of the Omnipotent. Here is a problem replete with interest for the philosopher and the ethnologist, how to account for this singular similitude and community of religious form between the pantheistic worshippers of *Isis* and *Osiris*, and the dusky devotees of *Ndengei* of Fiji. They have a legend, not unlike our own, of the origin of races, and also of a great flood, *Walavu-levu*.

What is the true solution of this universal tradition of a deluge, which we find repeated among so many peoples— which in the old world is rendered familiar to us in sacred history by the story of Noah and the ark, some of the features of which we detect later on incorporated in the tradition of the Thessalian flood, or Deucalion's deluge; which in the new world the Tamanacs—a tribe of Oroonoco Indians—reproduce in their legend of the sacred moriche

E

palm, the fruits of which, they relate, the only man and woman, who survived *their* deluge, cast behind them over their heads, and from which sprang men and women, who repeopled the earth; or which we find again in that period which the more civilized Mexicans refer to as " the age of water " ?

Do these traditions refer to that glacial period concerning the existence of which modern geologists are so well assured, or do they tend to advance the hypothesis that the Noachian deluge was really a universal one ? Or possibly may they not even refer to both of these supposed different cataclysms, for it has yet to be decided that they were not—though subject to different phases—due to the same original cause, and absolutely identical ?

The Fijians hold that all men are descended from the same parents. The first-born was the Fiji, but he misbehaved himself, and was black, with little clothing; next born was Tonga, who was not quite so bad, and was consequently whiter, and received more clothing; Papalangis, or white men, were born last, but did not sin, and were therefore quite white, and had many clothes. Their account of the deluge is that a great flood came which completely submerged the islands, but not before two large double canoes made a timely appearance, in which some of the progeny of the first man and woman along with Rokora, the god of carpenters, and Rokola, his head workman, took up their quarters, until the waters had subsided. Mbenga is supposed to be the place where the eight survivors of this inundation were landed, in virtue of which, and also of a tradition which relates that Ndengei first made his appearance here, the chiefs of this place take precedence in rank of all others.

Ndengei is supposed to be the chief of all the benign

gods, and though no one pretends to know his origin many assert that he has been seen by mortals. He is worshipped in the form of a large serpent, and is supposed to dwell in Nakauvandra, a western district in Viti Levu.

Next rank the two sons of Ndengei, Tokairambe and Tui Lakemba. These are supposed to act as mediators between the inferior spirits and their father, and for that purpose are said to be stationed at the door of his abode in the form of men.

Third in this mythological order are the grandchildren of Ndengei. Their name is legion, and their duties—the principal one of which is presiding over districts and islands—are as multifarious as they are indescribable.

A fourth class is made up of Ndengei's poor and more distant relations. They exercise a deputed jurisdiction over the different provinces, by whose priests they are respectively consulted. All the minor gods are collectively termed 'Kalou.' To Ndengei the spirit goes immediately after death for sentence or purification, whence it is again supposed to return and haunt the mbure in the vicinity of its former mortal abode.

It is not permitted to all to reach the tribunal of Ndengei, for an armed giant remains constantly on guard, endeavouring to wound those who would pass him.

Wounded spirits may not present themselves at the judgment seat, but are condemned to a perpetual wandering in the mountains. Those who escape being wounded are supposed to ascribe it to good fortune, but it really depends upon their conduct during life.

They also believe in devils or malicious gods, which are supposed to reside in *Mbula* or hell, underneath the world. The tyrant chief of devils, Lothia, rules despotically here, and lends fiendish countenance to his coadjutor *Samiualo*,

E 2

the destroyer of souls, who relentlessly precipitates the departed spirits of his victims, into a fiery cavern of plutonic misery and despair. This short notice of Fijian mythology, though deficient in minor details, nevertheless sufficiently describes those religious notions most universally prevalent throughout the group. At the present time the great bulk of the population have *lotued*, or profess Christianity.

The native priest or ambati, the office of which is usually hereditary, is an important individual, and is an essential appendage to the establishment of a Fijian chief. Besides being politically useful, they are occasionally employed by the chiefs when very much desiring the consummation of some particular wish or fancy, to act as mediators between them and the gods. They of course pretend to powers of predestination—an attribute which they take good care to exercise in harmony with the wishes of the chiefs. The office, being one of idleness and plenty, is much sought after when a vacancy occurs by death. To attain it, however, is no easy matter, for to pass through the public ordeal of preliminary initiation, involves the successful exercising of a simulation and deceit, calculated to tax the powers of the most consummate juggler. The principal test of a person being competent to exercise office, is a satisfactory exposition of the 'entering into him' of a *Kalou* or god. The proof of this is considered to lie in certain shiverings and contortions, in the producing of which, their own efforts are so violent, as to often cause a convulsive muscular action, which is really involuntary, and which to the ignorant and superstitious, must have every appearance of being the result of supernatural agency. On no occasion does the Fijian priest exercise his office without having been first propitiated by a suitable present; that which is most acceptable, being a root of kava and a whale's tooth. Failure is always attributed to the insufficiency of the offering, or its unacceptability to the gods. Besides these consultations of the gods through the ambati, there are certain stated religious festivals.

One of the most interesting of these, which however is only practised in the districts subject to Tui Levuka, takes place in the month of November. It lasts four days, during which period, work of every kind is strictly tabooed, and the women and boys are confined to their houses. The festival is inaugurated by one of the principal inhabitants of the koro, who at the hour of sunset, having gravely proceeded outside the village boundary, immediately in a loud voice lustily invokes the gods for favourable harvests, and many other equally desirable blessings. This is succeeded by a general hullabaloo of sticks, drums, and conchs, which continues for about an hour.

The men, who now are free, joyfully retire to the mbure, where they continually feast, and make merry during the remainder of the period, on a peculiar kind of salt-water worm, called 'balolo,' which makes its appearance for only one day in November, and from which that month takes its name.

The conclusion of the ceremony on the expiration of the fourth night, is heralded by the first streak of dawn, which is a signal for a wild scene of uproar and confusion, in the midst of which men and boys rush frantically about, knocking with clubs and sticks at every house door, and shouting out "Sinariba!"

The festival of *Batami mbulu* is a fitting sequel to the one just described, being a thanksgiving for good harvests and the fruits of the earth; it takes place at Ambau on

n of the in-gathering of the crops, &c., amidst
p and ceremony.

amy prevails, and unhappy is the Fijian who
placens uxor. The larger his harem, the greater
dignity; and his position in the social scale
may accordingly be fairly gauged by the number of his
wives.

The women look down with contempt on the man who can be satisfied with only one wife, and while they fail to appreciate our system of monogamy, seem in nowise to object to their husbands' affections, being indiscriminately distributed over a whole harem. The existence of polygamy is in a great measure no doubt due to the fact, that after child-birth husband and wife keep apart for two, three, and even four years, in order that the birth of another child may not interfere with the nursing of the first,—a process which with Fijians extends over a considerable period. Should a child be born before the customary nursing years have elapsed, the relatives of the woman are apt to look upon it as a direct personal insult, and to retaliate unpleasantly. Their marriages are sanctioned by religious rites, and are solemnized by the ambati with much form and ceremony.

A woman may not get married without the consent of her brother, even though she has her parents' permission.

The assent of the parents is marked by their acceptance of the presents, which must accompany the offer of marriage. Rejected presents and rejected addresses, are in Fijian courtship synonymous terms. Though the daughters of chiefs are generally betrothed in early life, many of their marriages are the result of *bonâ-fide* courtship and mutual attachment. Elopements occur.

Formerly the husband had an unreserved interest in the

person of his wife, whom he might have killed, and ate if so disposed. At present marital rights in this respect are considerably curtailed.

Here is a description by Wilkes of the marriage ceremony of a chief:—

"The ambati or priest takes a seat, having the bridegroom on his right, and the bride on the left hand. He then invokes the protection of the god or spirit upon the bride, after which he leads her to the bridegroom, and joins their hands, with injunctions to love, honour, and obey, to be faithful, and die with each other."

In fact were it not for the latter injunction, which in suggesting cremation would sound decidedly unpleasant in English ears, and the generally copious libations of kava, which in this, as in all other ceremonies, forms a festive, though an essential accompaniment to the scene, the main features of this giving and taking in marriage, are not unlike an English wedding.

The ceremonial amongst the commoners is much less complicated. Here the priest, having come to the nuptial house, cautiously proceeds, as a preliminary, to secure the inevitable present of a whale's tooth and kava, and anything else that in the joyousness of the moment he can piously secure, whereupon he briefly invokes continual happiness on the union; the bride's relations present to her a 'licolib,' or large petticoat, wherewith to hide her native charms and nakedness, and the ceremony is complete.

The barbarous practice of infanticide, which formerly prevailed to a frightful extent, is now extinct, except amongst the hill tribes, thanks to the continued earnestness of missionary toil.

So soon as a child is born it is named by some relative, and rubbed with turmeric, which is considered strengthening. If it be a first-born, a celebration feast takes place on the natal day, which is repeated on the succeeding fourth and tenth days respectively.

Cannibalism has been the chief objection to the country, but the wish for human food having of late years been discouraged, this revolting practice is now limited to the Kai Colos, and may be said to be on its last legs. These people inhabit the mountains only, and as their exact numbers are unknown, they are *safely* officially estimated as being from 10,000 to 20,000 strong.

The Fijians themselves are said entirely to repudiate this abominable practice, and have a tradition that in the first instance, they only had recourse to it as a kind of *dernier ressort*, against the incursions of the foreigner. If pressed, however, they freely admit that this distinction is ancient history, and was soon lost sight of. Though the constant human sacrifices, which formed a preliminary to all their undertakings, and enemies killed in battle, furnished a pretty constant means of satisfying the cannibal propensity, yet it is recorded, that even these sources of supply were often insufficient; for stratagem and violence were resorted to, to gratify these fearful appetites, and they banquetted on the bodies of their dearest friends.

Formal and informal human sacrifices were also made more frequent, and were multiplied, to indulge their taste for this loathsome food; and so highly did they esteem it, that the greatest praise they could bestow on a delicacy, was to say it was as tender as a dead man.

The flesh of women is preferred to that of men, and pieces of flesh from the thigh, and from the arm above the elbow, are especially looked upon as choice morsels and tit-bits. The return of victorious warriors laden with flesh for the oven is announced by the beating of the death-drum, *Rogorogo ai valu* (Reporter of war). If the distance be short to the town where the horrid feast is to be held, the bodies are dragged face downwards to the great oven by those warriors most distinguished and foremost in the fight; when the bokola has to be conveyed for any distance, it is lashed on to poles and carried on the men's shoulders. On approaching their town the warriors perform the war-dance, which consists in throwing their clubs aloft, brandishing their rude implements of warfare, firing off rusty muskets, and jumping wildly about. As they advance they are met by the people of the town, who throng round the bodies of the warriors, with loud shouts of exultation and triumph. There are particular ovens and pots in all the villages, set apart for cooking human flesh only, and which may not be used for any other purpose.

Here is an account of the manner of their sacrifices:—

"After being selected for this purpose, they are often kept for a time to be fattened. When about to be sacrificed, they are compelled to sit upon the ground, with their feet drawn under their thighs, and their arms placed close beside them. In this posture they are bound so tightly that they cannot stir or move a joint. They are then placed in the usual oven, upon hot stones, and covered with leaves and earth, where they are roasted alive. When the body is cooked, it is taken from the oven, and the face painted black, as is done by the natives on festal occasions. It is then carried to the mbure, where it is offered to the gods, being afterwards removed to be cut up and distributed, to be eaten by the people."*

The *bokola*, or dead man's flesh, is not eaten with the fingers, like every other kind of food, but with peculiar long-pronged wooden forks, which are much valued, and each of which bears some obscene or curious name, by

* *Vide* Wilkes.

which it is particularly known and distinguished. It is a common belief, that if the bokola comes in contact with a tender skin, and especially the skin of children, it is apt to generate cutaneous disease—an explanation which would fully account for this deviation from their ordinary mode of eating.

Perhaps one of the most remarkable incidents attaching to this cannibalism, is the circumstance that certain vegetables are always eaten with human flesh. Seemann speaks of it in these terms:—

"Human flesh, Fijians have repeatedly assured me, is extremely difficult to digest, and even the healthiest suffer from confined bowels for two or three days after partaking of it. Probably in order to assist the process of digestion 'bokola,' as dead men's flesh is technically termed, is always eaten with an addition of vegetables. There are principally three kinds which in Fijian estimation ought to accompany 'bokola,'—the leaves of the malawaci (*Trophis anthropophagorum*, Seem.), the tudano (*Omalanthus pedicellatus*, Benth.), and the boro dina (*Solanum anthropophagorum*, Seem.). The two former are middle-sized trees, growing wild in many parts of the group, but the boro dina is cultivated, and there are generally several large bushes of it near every bure (or stranger's house), where the bodies of those slain in battle are always taken. The boro dina is a bushy shrub, seldom higher than six feet, with a dark glossy foliage, and berries of the shape and colour of tomatoes. This fruit has a faint aromatic smell, and is occasionally prepared like tomato sauce. The leaves of these three plants are wrapped round the bokola, as those of the taro are round pork, and baked with it on heated stones. Salt is not forgotten.

"Besides these three plants some kinds of yams and taro are deemed fit accompaniments of a dish of bokola. The yams are hung up in the bure for a certain time, having previously being covered with turmeric, to preserve them, it would seem, from rapid decay,—our own sailors effecting the same end by white-washing the yams when taking them on board. A peculiar kind of taro (*Caladium esculentum*, Schott. *var.*), called 'kurilagi,' was pointed out as having been eaten *with* a whole tribe of people. The story sounds strange, but as a number of natives were present when it was told, several of whom corroborated the various statements or corrected the proper names that occurred, its truth appears unimpeachable. In Viti Levu, about three miles N.N.E. from Namosi, there dwelt a tribe known by the name of Kai-na-loca, who in days of yore gave great offence to the ruling chief of the Namosi district, and as a punishment for their misdeeds the whole tribe was condemned to die. Every year the inmates of one house were baked and eaten, fire was set to the empty dwelling, and its foundation planted with kurilagi. In the following year, as soon as this taro was ripe, it became the signal for the destruction of the next house and its inhabitants, and the planting of a fresh field of taro. Thus house after house, family after family disappeared, until Butuibuna, the father of the present chief Kuruduadua, pardoned the remaining few, allowing them to die a natural death. In 1860 only one old woman, living at Cagina, was the sole survivor of the Naloca people. Picture the feelings of these unfortunate wretches as they watched the growth of the ominous taro! Throughout the dominions of the powerful chief whose authority they had insulted their lives were forfeited, and to escape into territories where they were strangers would in those days only have been to hasten the awful doom awaiting them in their own country. Nothing remained save to watch, watch, watch the rapid development of the kurilagi. As leaf after leaf unfolded, the tubers increased in size and substance, how their hearts must have trembled, their courage forsaken them; and when at last the foliage began to turn yellow, the taro was ripe, what agonies they must have undergone! What torture could have equalled theirs?"

Williams, in his 'Fiji and the Fijians,' states:—

"The names of Tampakanthoro, Tanoa, Tuiveikoso, Tuikilakila, and others are famous in Fiji for the quantity of human flesh which they have individually eaten. But these are but insignificant cannibals in comparison with Ra Undreundre of Rakiraki. Even Fijians name him with wonder. Bodies procured for his consumption were designated *lewe ni bi*. The *bi* is a circular fence or pond made to receive turtles when caught, which then becomes its *lewena*, "contents." Ra Undreundre was compared to such a receptacle, standing ever ready to receive human flesh. The fork used by this monster was honoured with a distinctive epithet. It was named *Undroundro*; a word used to denote a small person or thing carrying a great burden. This fork was given by his son, Ra Vatu, to my respected friend the Rev. R. B. Lyth, in 1849. Ra Vatu then spoke freely of his father's propensity, and took Mr. Lyth nearly a mile beyond the precincts of the town, and showed him the stones by which his father registered the number of bodies he had eaten "after his family had begun to grow up." Mr. Lyth found the line of stones to measure two hundred and thirty two paces. A teacher who accompanied him counted the stones, eight hundred and seventy-two. If those which had been removed were replaced, the whole would certainly have amounted to *nine hundred*. Ra Vatu asserted that his father ate all these persons himself, permitting no one to share them with him. A similar row of stones placed to mark the bodies eaten by Nauugavuli contained forty-eight, when his becoming a Christian prevented any further addition. The whole family were cannibals extraordinary; but Ra Vatu wished to exempt himself."

Taken *cum grano salis*, or after any other fashion that we may wish, these figures are certainly big enough to speak for themselves, and we leave them to do so accordingly.

The practice of anthropophagism appears to date from the earliest periods. It is mentioned in the 'Odyssey,' in the story of Polyphemus; and Herodotus states that the Padai of India were in the habit of taking a shabby advantage of their relations, by killing and eating them when they fell ill.

In the Middle Ages it became the fashion to bandy the accusation between enemies, and accordingly during the Crusades we find Christians asserting that not only were Saracens ordinary anthropophagi, but that they were particularly fond of a sucking babe torn from the breast of, of course, a *Christian* mother. The Saracens, on the other hand, were not backward in attributing equally horrid practices to the Christians.

Even *friends* were in the habit of distinguishing their particular heroes, by the quantity of infidel flesh they were supposed to have devoured, which will in a measure account for the following lines, which we extract from the romance of 'Richard Cœur de Lion:'

> "King Richard shall warrant
> There is no flesh so nourissant
> Unto an English man,
> Partridge, plover, heron, ne swan,
> Cow ne ox, sheep ne swine,
> As the head of a Sarezyne."

Why the 'Slothful Knight' should be made to prefer the head does not appear; but it would certainly be interesting to know, as it happens to be one of those particular parts which the Fijian cannibal invariably rejects. Romances of this nature, and wild accounts of cannibalism, brought home by sailors in the sixteenth and seventeenth centuries, and circulated by credulous writers, caused a good deal of scepticism as to the existence of this practice, which has been entirely dissipated in latter years.

The origin of cannibalism remains yet to be accounted for; so far, I believe, no satisfactory explanation of it has been given.

CHAPTER VI.

INDUSTRIES.

It may be accepted as a general maxim, that in a country where there is little incentive to work there is necessarily but little industry; but when that country is peopled by savages who are not only immersed, in some respects, in the grossest barbarism, but whose few and simple wants are so bounteously satisfied by nature, as to render laborious exertion absolutely unnecessary, its truth becomes manifested in a very high degree. Under these circumstances it is indeed a matter of surprise, that the Fijian has not yielded to those influences arrayed against industry, somewhat more, and has not given himself up to the penalty of the fall, somewhat less. For he does certainly possess *some* industries, and in this respect is much in advance of other Pacific Islanders.

The people are expert canoe builders, and formerly drove a brisk trade in this industry with the Tongans. Their canoes are much superior to those of the other groups, and are constructed with great ingenuity and skill. They are usually built double, and with the small exception that one of the canoes, which serves the purpose of an outrigger, is always shorter than the other, on somewhat the same principle, though not quite for the same object, as Captain Dicey's twin ship, the *Castalia*. The two canoes are united by beams, on which a platform

INDUSTRIES.

is laid, which is several feet in width, and extends beyond the sides. The bottom of the canoe is formed of one single plank, to which the sides are dovetailed, as well as being further strengthened by lashings, while the joints throughout are made tight by gum. The depth of hold is usually about six feet, and they are often as much as 100 feet in length. When not sailing, they propel them by oars, about ten feet in length, with good broad blades. When rowing they stand up behind the oar, instead of sitting down to their work as we do. This method of propelling by oars or sculls is quite peculiar to the Fijians and the Tongans. In all the canoes there are small hatchways, with high combings at both ends, and when under way a man is continually employed in baling out the water.

The canoes of the chiefs, with their immense white sails, made of tapa, with royal pennants streaming from the yards, and profusely ornamented with *cypræa ovula* shells, present a singularly graceful and striking appearance. They sail with an almost inconceivable velocity, and any one who has seen them, cannot fail to have been surprised at the adroitness with which they are managed.

The employment next commanding consideration and respect is carpentery, an illustration of their proficiency in which, may be conveniently given by a description of one of their houses, which are constructed with considerable ingenuity. Though built of similar material, they differ from those of the other groups. The ordinary houses are usually of an oblong shape, about fifteen feet in height, and from twenty to thirty feet in length, by fifteen in breadth. The frames are made of bamboos, with two apertures, from three to four feet high, and as many broad, on opposite sides, which serve the double purpose of doors and windows. The roofs, which are very high-pitched, spring almost from the ground, and are serviceably thatched with grass or wild sugar-cane. The sides are neatly interwoven with cane, and mats are used for closing the doors. The exterior of these houses is not prepossessing, and is in decided contrast to the interiors, which are kept scrupulously neat and clean. The floors are sometimes strewn with mats, made of various kinds of grass or leaves, and at one or both ends there is a raised platform, which at night time is used for sleeping purposes, (for one of the peculiarities of these houses is, that there are no partitions,) and during the day as a daïs, on which the master or chief alternately lounges and receives visitors, dignitaries, and friends. Every house is provided with a fire-place, which consists of a pit sunk in one of the corners, and concealed by sundry logs of wood, behind which the cooking is carried on. If a person desires to have a house, he informs the king or chief of his wish, accompanying the same with a suitable present. Thus propitiated, the chief duly appoints a superintendent, who, if not dilatory in his commission, will run up a domicile, such as has been described, in an incredibly short time, which with care will last for at least twenty years. The workmen employed are also requisitioned by the chief, and their number varies, in a like ratio with the value of the present given, and the amount of work required.

The mbure, or council-house, in which strangers are entertained, and which corresponds in many respects to our town-halls, is a conspicuous structure, in every village in which they keep their sacred ornaments. It is also used as a temple or spirit-house by the priests, in which they keep their sacred ornaments, and where they resort for the worship of their gods. It is built on a raised walled mound with a peaked roof, from twenty to thirty feet in height, with a base of not more than ten to fifteen feet. The ridge-pole, which projects several feet at either end, is decorated with numbers of *ovula cypræa* (white shells), and it has two long spears crossing it, as nearly as possible at right angles. In other respects the Council House differs only from ordinary houses, in having the fire-place in the centre, and the sleeping-place screened off.

The following extract from Dr. Seemann's official report describes the favourite and lucrative occupation of plaiting sinnet:—

"Fibre used for cordage is derived from three species of vau (*Paritium tiliaceum, P. tricuspis,* et *P. purpurascens*), the cocoa-nut palm, the yaka, or wayaka (*Pachyrhizus angulatus,* Rich.), the kalakalauaisou, (*Hibiscus diversifolius,* Jacq.), and the sinu mataiavi (*Wikstrœmia Indica,* Meyer). Plaiting cocoa-nut fibre into 'sinnet,' afterwards to be made into rope, or simply used for binding material, and as such a good article of exchange in the group, is a favourite occupation of the men, even of high chiefs, when sitting in bures and discussing politics or other topics of the day. According to Mr. Pritchard, none of the Polynesians produce so great a quantity of this article as the Fijians, though the Tonguese excel them in colouring it. I have seen—he continues in the memorandum from which I quote—a ball of 'sinnet' six feet high, and four feet in diameter. Some heathen temples, Bure-ni-Kalou, used to be entirely composed of such plaiting, and their completion must have been a task extending over a considerable period, since a model of them, four feet high, ordered for the Museum of Economic Botany at Kew, could not be finished in less time than six weeks, and at a cost of £5. The fibre of the yaka or wayaka (*Pachyrhizus angulatus,* Rich. = *Dolichos bulbosus,* Linn.) is principally sought for fishing-nets, the floats of which are the square fruits of the vutu raka-raka (*Barringtonia speciosa,* Linn.). The sinu mataiavi (*Wikstrœmia Indica,* Meyer), a sea-side shrub, perhaps identical with the Sinu-ni-vanua, serves the same purpose, its bark, like that of other *Thymeleœ*, containing a readily-available fibre—a fact also known, according to Mr. Pritchard, in the Samoan islands, where the plant is termed 'Mati.' Only a limited use is made of the fibre of the kalakalauaisoni (*Hibiscus*

[*Abelmoschus*] *diversifolius*, Jacq.), a plant abounding in swamps all over Fiji."

Formerly the trade in cocoa-nut oil was one of the most important in the islands, and at the present time is only second to the trade in cotton. It will be of course understood that the large quantities exported in latter years have not been produced by the native process, which is of the most primitive description.

A singular evidence of the quasi-civilisation of this peculiar people, is afforded in the manufacture of a rough species of native pottery, which amply suffices for their domestic necessities. It is carried on to a considerable extent, but is solely confined to the women.

" The manufacture of native cloth is entirely left to women of places not inhabited by great chiefs, probably because the noise caused by the beating out of the cloth is disliked by courtly ears. The rhythm of tapa-beating imparts therefore as thoroughly a country air to a place in Fiji as that of thrashing corn does to our European villages. The masi-tree is propagated by cuttings, and grown about two or three feet apart in plantations resembling nurseries." *

They also make their tapa from the paper mulberry, *Broussonetia papyrifera*, which is likewise cultivated with considerable attention and care. The art of manufacturing cloth from the bark of this tree is well known throughout Polynesia, but in Fiji only do we find any knowledge of printing it in different colours and patterns.

Whence has this knowledge proceeded. Has it been obtained from China, where it is said to have been discovered in the middle of the tenth century, by one Foongtaon, a minister of state, but where it has probably been practised from the earliest times; or is it of endemic growth?

* *Vide* Seemann's Official Report.

CHAPTER VII.

POLITY.

THE people of Fiji consist of not less than forty different tribes, all more less or independent, and often hostile to each other; of these Mbau is the most powerful, and from its superior influence has been for many years the centre of political power, whilst its supremacy has been virtually acknowledged in all other parts of the group. Those next in importance are Rewa, Somo Somo, Verata, Naitasiri, Macuata, Mbua, and Lakemba. Each tribe is divided into five classes, which clearly denotes the marked distinctions of rank which exist.

They are,—1, Kings; 2, Chiefs; 3, Warriors; 4, Landholders; and 5, Dependents. The latter class, though nominally supposed to exercise a very minor degree of influence in the State, occasionally by force of numbers prevail, as was the case at Mbau not many years since, when the people rose *en masse*, and deposed the ruling chiefs.

The following statement gives a rough estimate of the native population of Fiji in March, 1874:—

Mbua	7,000
Macuata	7,000
Cakaudrove	15,000
Carried forward	29,000

Brought forward	29,000
Lau	8,000
Kandavu	10,000
Central	8,000
Tai Levu	10,000
Naitasiri and interior	20,000
Rewa	5,500
Serua	5,000
Namosi	7,000
Nadroga	20,000
Ra and Yasawas	18,000
Total native population	140,500

Though in many instances the rule exercised by the chiefs is undoubtedly despotic, the real power of the state resides in the landowners, who on the death of a ruler must proceed to the election of a successor from among the various members of his family. So long as those thus elevated to chieftainship carry out the wishes and policy of the electors, they are loyally supported in their dignity; but should a chief prove intractable and attempt to play the despot, he is generally brought to reason and a proper sense of his position, by a judicious stoppage of supplies.*

Councils, which are composed of the influential persons of the tribe, and therefore representative, meet for deliberation on questions of moment and importance, and the manner in which they are conducted is often marked by considerable intelligence and skill. In these assemblies an unsound argument or a crude suggestion, though made by a leading chief, would be at once ridiculed and rejected; here knowledge and wisdom are appreciated and commended, whilst rank or position of themselves wholly fail to command influence. It is therefore clearly

* *Vide* 'How about Fiji.'

an error to suppose that the people live in a condition of absolute despotism, and are debarred from all voice in the state.

Each tribe has its principal chief or *Tui*, or *Turaga levu*, to many of whom the theory and the advantages of divine right are not wholly unknown.

The laws of succession in Fiji are not unlike those of 'the faithful,' laid down in *El-Koran*. On the decease of a chief he is succeeded by his next brother, and failing him by his eldest son, should the chief have no eldest son of his own to fill his place. This rule however is not always strictly followed, and there are various circumstances, such as the rank of the mother, &c., which may cause a deviation from it. The ceremony of induction to regal office, is initiated by copious libations of *yaqona* by the king elect and the leading men of the tribe, and by a dash of red paint—in the absence of *Sainté-Ampoule*—the new-fledged monarch is anointed, and the coronation is complete.

Amongst the numerous insignia of chieftainship, which include various ornaments, and a peculiar kind of staff, *matana-ki-lagi* (point-to-the-sky), is found the royal sunshade, or umbrella, of African and Oriental nations.

The administration of the government is carried on by the chiefs, assisted by various officials, of which perhaps the *Mata-ni-vanuas* ("the eyes" or face of the land) are the most important.

"They are the legitimate medium of communication between the chiefs and their dependencies, and form a complete and effective agency. Taking the kingdom of Lakemba as an instance, the system is worked thus: in each island and town under the rule of Lakemba there is an authorized *Mata-ki-Lakemba*, 'Ambassador to Lakemba,' through whom all the business of that place and the seat of government is transacted.

"Then again at Lakemba there is a diplomatic corps, the official title of each individual of which contains the name of the place to which he is messenger, and to which all the king's commands are by him communicated. When on duty these officials represent their chief, after the manner of more civilised courts, and are treated with great respect.

"When they have to take several messages, or when one communication consists of several important parts, they help memory by mnemonical sticks or reeds, which are of various lengths. The *mata* having reached his destination, lays down one of these before him, and repeats the message of which it is the memorial. He then lays down another, proceeding in the same way, until the sticks are transferred from his hand and lie in a row before him, each message having been accurately delivered. I have seen men of this class practise their lesson before setting out, and have heard them give the answers on their return. In some parts there is one of the *matas* who is more immediately attached to the person of the king, and is styled *ona mata*. It is his business to be in attendance when tribute or food is brought to the sovereign, and to go through the customary form of acknowledgment, to receive and answer reports of all kinds, doing so in the king's presence, and under his direction, and to officiate at the *yaqona* ring, with other similar duties. Besides the *mata* there are other officials of various duties and degrees of importance. All these, except in extreme cases, go about their duties most deliberately, as every appearance of haste in such matters is supposed to detract from true dignity. A careful observance of established forms is deemed very essential. In some parts of Fiji the *mata* holds his post for life; in others for only a few years. In the latter case, when tired of public life, he presents a large quantity of provisions to his chief, asking for permission to retire. In Vanna Levu the election of a successor has the appearance of being done by surprise. The leading men having assembled and consulted awhile, one of their number advances to the person chosen, and makes him their *mata* by binding a blade of the red ti-tree leaf round his arm between the shoulder and elbow. It is the fashion for the man just bandaged to weep and protest against his election, asserting his incompetency, and pleading low birth, poverty, indolence, ignorance of official phraseology, &c., all which objections are of course met by the others declaring their choice to be good. The feast on such an occasion is prepared with extra care." *

* *Vide* Williams' 'Fiji and Fijians.'

The position which the different districts and islands occupy in their relations with each other, as well as the degree of submission required from tributaries and dependents, are matters in Fijian polity which are well understood, and strictly acknowledged and enforced. The two kinds of submission recognised are known as quali and mbati; tributary towns or provinces owing mbati submision are freer than those owing quali; but, strangely enough, the quali, though liable to severer exactions than the mbati, are the more respected of the two. This peculiarly anomalous custom, the reason of which yet remains to be explained, has in times gone by been a constant source of awkward difficulty and irritation.

Here are some extracts from a memorandum by Mr. J. B. Thurston, which, besides further helping to explain the position occupied by the mbati and the quali, also set forth the relations at present existing between the chiefs and the people in connection with the ownership of land in Fiji:—

"The people of Fiji are divided into matanitus and qalis. The matanitu is sub-divided into qalis, the qali being subject to its particular chief, who, with their people, are subject to their superior chief, the head of the matanitu, the head of the tribe.

"From long and careful inquiry I am of opinion that the people hold their lands from superior chiefs, that is to say, from their father or their gods * * under a feudal system that has existed from time immemorial. The principle of this system recognises the supreme chief as the grantor of land, and leaves the usufruct only (subject to certain conditions) in the hands of the grantee, i.e., qali chiefs and people.

"In proof of this conclusion we have before us certain evident facts. All qalis owe either military or domestic service to their lord or chief. The former are known as Batis-Mbati; their service is purely military, and they enjoy special privileges among the people. The qali-taukei are most likely families of whom the head is descended from a branch of the ruling chief's own family, or in some cases a petty tribe, formerly independent, but, unable to so maintain itself amidst the convulsions of barbaric life (which is one of treachery and warfare), has been compelled to seek the protection of some powerful chief. It commended itself to some such chief by voluntary submission, the payment of tribute, and tender of personal service.

"The qali-lewe in Kuro are the descendants generally of common people, who have been placed upon conquered lands, lands from which the original occupants have been driven beyond hope of return, or have been wholly exterminated. The man of this qali is a mere *villein appurtenant*; his duty is to plant food for himself and family; but, above all, for his chief. He has charge of his chief's cattle, pigs, and poultry, and thus provides daily food for the chief's household, or, when ordered to do so, the materials for a public feast.

"In return he is protected from aggression, and receives a share of the property presented by other qalis to his master; he may also rightfully use all the land he requires or can cultivate."

It will be observed from a review of the foregoing facts that land tenure in Fiji is based on simple principles and well-defined law or custom, and having regard to our experience in New Zealand, if care and judgment be exercised, should not hereafter prove the cause of any difficulty with the natives.

The lands in the different islands primarily vest in the ruling chiefs of the various tribes, and are in turn held from them by either subordinate chiefs or vassals, subject to a service called 'lala;' this, in times of peace, consists in the payment of legitimate taxes in kind, besides an occasional rendering of labour; and in time of war it imposes a liability for military service for the benefit of the immediate or principal chief.

A notable feature of Fijian tenure is that occupants of lands cannot alienate their holdings without the consent of the ruling chief, nor can such lands be alienated by the ruling chief without the consent of the occupants, so long as they render those services required by the tenure.

The most characteristic, if not the most peculiar, of all Fijian customs is that one which confers special rights on certain privileged individuals, called *vasus* (i.e. nephews). Simple though this relationship undoubtedly is, there is in it in Fiji a virtue almost marvellous, for excepting the wives, home, and lands of a chief, there is nothing that a *vasu* may not successfully lay claim to and appropriate at his pleasure; no matter how powerful a chief may be, or exalted his rank, so far as his movable property is concerned, he is completely at the mercy of the *vasu*. Resistance is never thought of, and objection is only made in very extreme cases.

There are vasus not only to individuals and families, but to towns and states, and even to the gods; the power of the latter, however, is limited to the vasus assisting themselves to the food-offerings, made to these luckless deities—a privilege they do not hesitate to avail themselves of freely.

The degree of importance of a vasu is regulated by the rank of his mother; thus formerly when Verata was the leading state of Fiji, the sons of the Verata queens enjoyed the pre-eminence now accorded to the son of the Queen of Mbau over all other vasus.

The two most important kinds of vasus are the Vasu Togai, or Taukei, and the Vasu Levu, i.e., great vasu; the former title is given to those whose mothers are the wives of landowners, or subordinate chiefs, while the latter term is applied to the sons of women of rank, whose husbands are leading or principal chiefs. The difference between the two may be said to be practically nil.

"When the vasu-togai or vasu-levu of a town or district visits it, he is received with honours even greater than those paid to the chief who rules over it; all bow in obedience to his will, and he is received with clapping of hands and the salutation, 'O sa vi naka lako mai vaka turanga Ratu Vasu-levu.' (Hail! good is the coming hither of our noble Lord Nephew.)

"When the Vasu of Mbenga goes thither, honours almost divine are rendered him, for he is supposed to be descended in a direct line from the gods. Mbenga formerly played a very conspicuous part in the affairs of the group, but of late years it happened to get into difficulties with Rewa, in consequence of which Ngaraningiou attacked it, conquered its inhabitants, and massacred many of them. Since that time it has had little or no political influence."*

There is no principle better understood or more freely applied in Fijian polity than that of church and state. The native priests or ambati exercise an important influence on the masses of the people; and although they are sacredly respected and consulted by all, they do not fail as a general rule to act most religiously in concert with the ruling chiefs.

Even these savages appear instinctively to be aware that the wisest human laws are defective, as their operation is necessarily precarious; that they must often fail, owing to a want of knowledge, to strike where they would condemn; that they have no particular inner witness of conscience to assist them, nor are they mysteriously of another world,—impossible to grasp; and that above all, they wholly lack an adequate system of reward, which must clearly be of the essence of any code pretending to the regulation of human conduct.

It is to considerations perhaps more crude, but nevertheless not wholly dissimilar to these, that we should look, if we would account for the sympathetic connection which undoubtedly exists between a Fijian ruler and the instruments of his religion. But it is to be feared that the union between these native priests and chiefs is also due

* *Vide* Wilkes.

to personal interest and temporal advantage, rather than to any abstract religious principles; indeed the chiefs themselves admit that they use the priests merely for purposes of government—a state of affairs which the ambati do not fail to take advantage of, by practising their mummeries under the authority and protection of the powers that be, and consequently with less fear of exposure or detection.

Fijian law and justice is of the most primitive and summary description, might is right, and the *lex talionis* of the Scripture, "An eye for an eye, a tooth for a tooth," prevails in its fullest and most varied sense. Vicarious suffering is recognised, and it is not an uncommon occurrence for a culprit to be permitted to give his father up to 'justice' as a substitute for himself. Nominally all cases of dispute should be referred to the nearest chief for adjudication; virtually this seldom happens, for the parties concerned prefer taking the law into their own hands.

There are few crimes that are not punishable by death, which is inflicted by the musket, the club, or by strangulation. The other punishments are fines, forfeiture of movable property belonging to the culprit, the destruction of his house or his plantations, the forfeiture of his lands, termed *suabi*, which is signified by the sticking of certain reeds into the ground, bound together in the form of tripods; and among the minor punishments may be numbered the loss of fingers, noses, and ears.

Adultery is looked upon as a serious offence, and if detected in infidelity, the woman may be put to death or be condemned to servitude for life; the man is also liable to be treated in a similar manner, besides losing his wife, who may be appropriated by the aggrieved party, or by his friends for him. There are various other modes by which an injured husband may revenge himself, but which do not here admit of description.

The condoning of offences by peace offerings, called *soro*, i.e. atonement, or in other words the purchasing of the good-will of an injured party, or (should he be past propitiation) that of his friends, is a custom generally prevalent throughout the group, and is unfortunately the frequent cause of gross miscarriages of justice.

"There are five kinds of *soro*. 1. The *soro* with a whale's tooth, a mat, club, musket, or other property, is in request for every kind of offence, from stealing a yam to running away with a woman, or the commission of adultery. 2. The *soro* with a reed, called *mata ni gasau*. This is not commonly resorted to in private affairs, but by civil functionaries and small chiefs when accused or convicted of unfaithfulness to the duties of their position. It is more humiliating than the first. 3. The *soro* with a spear, *mati ni moto*, is used to secure forgiveness in cases of civil delinquency of a graver sort. It is still more humiliating than the second kind. He who presents the spear, generally some one of importance, will stoop or nearly prostrate himself; the whole act is supposed to imply that he and those whom he represents have deserved to be transfixed by a spear to the earth. 4. The *soro* with a basket of earth, a *kau vanua*, is generally connected with war, and is presented by the weaker party, indicating the yielding up of their land to the conquerors. Sometimes however the ceremony may be an expression of loyalty by parties whose fealty is suspected. 5. The *soro* with ashes, *bisi dravu*, belongs to an extreme case, involving a life or lives. A chief or mata-ni-vanua disfigures himself by covering his bosom and arms with ashes, and with deep humiliation intreats the aggrieved person will compassionately grant the life of the offender or offenders.

"On the part of the offerer the presentation of *soro* is a serious thing, and his faltering voice and trembling body testify the emotion within.

"When a *soro* is refused it is repeated, it may be five, or even ten times, until the property given or the importunity shown gains the desired point.

"Whatever may have been the origin of this custom, and however beneficial its right use might prove to the innocent, or the unintentional offender, its operation in Fiji seems too generally to avert deserved punishment from the criminal, and in many cases is but legalised corruption. No small proportion of the misdemeanours brought under the notice of the chiefs are deliberate acts, in which a balance has been previously struck between the fruit of the crime and the *soro* which must follow, and the commission of the act has been accordingly determined on."*

In this rude and simple state of society, existing in an archipelago of the Southern Hemisphere, may be found many of the characteristics of those ancient Germanic tribes, so accurately delineated by the masterly pen of Tacitus.

Not incapable of social order; influenced by sentiments of religion and morality—though that morality be not always very refined; with distinct ideas of property, and consequently an inequality of ranks; and with an established form of government,—the Fijian has advanced a considerable stage in the progress of society from that primary or patriarchal state, in which man is supposed first to have lived united, and of which we are told in authentic history.

At this stage, however, the Fijian appears to have rested long: certainly for many years, probably for many centuries. But this stagnation in Fijian society may be perhaps satisfactorily accounted for, and traced to the natural influences by which he is surrounded.

In these islands there may be said to have been hitherto, scarcely any incentives to exertion. Here man in his primitive state has indeed seemed to live for enjoyment only, and appears to have been but placed in circumstances where every appetite may be gratified, every

* *Vide* Williams' 'Fiji and the Fijians.'

desire fulfilled, and where without exaggeration it may be truly said that want has been a thing unknown.

From what has been stated it will already have been perceived that though Fijian civilisation is yet in a feeble state of infancy, the people are nevertheless possessed of certain defined laws and customs, which though unwritten —*lex non scripta*—are as firmly established and as strictly adhered to as if they had been engrossed on parchment, or engraven on tablets of stone. Their political society was also formed "in order to enable men to live, and it has continued to exist in order that they might live, happily," and though their peculiar code of polity may not be best calculated to attain these desirable ends, an acquaintance with it is yet indispensable, if we would be successful in the government of these islanders. But if we would fully confer on them the benefits without the evils of civilisation, we must also "hasten slowly" with this breaking into harness; always remembering that, digging and delving for a livelihood, and all laborious exertion, have been hitherto to them, unnecessary and unknown.

CHAPTER VIII.

AN ACCOUNT OF THE VARIOUS PROPOSALS FOR THE CESSION OF FIJI.*

IN the year 1858, harassed by a claim of $45,000—about £9000—preferred by Captain Boutwell, on behalf of the United States Government (for which, as Tui Viti, he had, under pressure, made himself responsible), and by the insupportable exactions and tyrannies of the Tongans, under the leadership of Maafu, Thakombau applied to the British Consul † in Fiji for assistance and advice.

The result of this application was the conditional cession of Fiji to Her Majesty the Queen, as set forth in the following documents, which, in Mr. Pritchard's care, reached this country in 1859.

PROPOSAL OF CESSION. No. 1.

"EBENEZER THAKOMBAU, by the grace of God, Sovereign Chief of Bau and its Dependencies, Vunivalu of the Armies of Fiji and Tui Viti, &c., &c., to all and singular to whom these presents shall come, Greeting.

"Whereas We, being duly, fully, and formally recognised in our aforesaid state, rank, and sovereignty by Great Britain, France, and the United States of America respectively, and having full and exclusive sovereignty and domain in and over the islands and territories constituting, forming, and being included in the group known as Fiji, or Viti ; and being desirous to procure for our people and subjects a good

* *Vide* 'How about Fiji.'
† Mr. W. T. Pritchard.

and permanent form of government, whereby our aforesaid people and subjects shall enjoy and partake of the benefits, the prosperity, and the happiness which it is the duty and the right of all sovereigns to seek and to procure for their people and subjects: and being in ourselves unable to procure and provide such good and permanent government for our aforesaid people and subjects; and being, moreover, in ourselves unable to afford to our aforesaid people and subjects the due protection and shelter from the violence, the oppression, and the tyranny of Foreign Powers, which it is the duty and the right of all sovereigns to afford to their people and subjects.

"And being heavily indebted to the President and Government of the United States of America, the liquidation of which indebtedness is pressingly urged, with menaces of severe measures against our person, and our sovereignty, and our islands and territories aforesaid, unless the aforesaid indebtedness be satisfied within a period so limited as to render a compliance with the terms of the contract forced upon us utterly impossible within the said period, this said inability not arising from lack of resources within our dominions, but from the inefficacy of any endeavours on our part under the existing state of affairs in our islands and territories aforesaid to carry out such measures as are necessary for, and would result in, the ultimate payment of the aforesaid claims; and having maturely deliberated, well weighed, and fully considered the probable results of the course and the measures we now propose, and being fully satisfied of the impracticability, by any other course and measures, to avert from our islands and territories aforesaid, and our people and subjects aforesaid, the evils certain to follow the non-payment of the sum of money demanded from us by the Government of the United States of America; and being confident of the immediate and progressive benefits that will result from the cession herein now made of our sovereignty and our islands and territories aforesaid.

"Now know ye, that we do hereby, for and in consideration of certain conditions, terms, and engagements hereinafter set forth, make over, transfer, and convey unto Victoria, by the grace of God, Queen of Great Britain and Ireland, &c., &c., &c., Her heirs and successors for ever, the full sovereignty and domain in and over our aforesaid islands and territories; together with the actual proprietorship and personal ownership in certain pieces or parcels of land as may hereafter be mutually agreed upon by a commission to consist of two chiefs from Great Britain and two chiefs from Fiji, the said commission to be appointed by the representative of Great Britain in Fiji, who, in cases of dispute, shall himself be umpire; the said pieces or parcels of land to be especially devoted to Government purposes, and to be applied and appropriated in manner and form appertaining to Crown lands in British Colonies, or as the local Government of Fiji, appointed by commission from the aforesaid Victoria, Queen of the United Kingdom of Great Britain and Ireland aforesaid, may deem fit, proper, and necessary for the uses and requirements of the said local Government.

"Provided always, and this cession of our sovereignty and our islands and territories is on these conditions, terms, and considerations; that is to say,

"That the aforesaid Victoria, Queen of the United Kingdom of Great Britain and Ireland aforesaid, shall permit us to retain the title and rank of Tui Viti, in so far as the aboriginal population is concerned, and shall permit us to be at the head of the department for governing the aforesaid aboriginal population, acting always under the guidance and by the counsels of the representative of Great Britain, and head of the local Government appointed by commission from the aforesaid Victoria, Queen of the United Kingdom of Great Britain and Ireland aforesaid; that the aforesaid Victoria, Queen of the United Kingdom of Great Britain and Ireland aforesaid, shall pay the sum of forty-five thousand dollars ($45,000) unto the President of the United States of America, being the amount of the claim demanded from us; procuring for us and for our people a full and absolute acquittance from any further liabilities to the said President or Government of the United States of America aforesaid.

"For and in consideration of which outlay, not less than two hundred thousand (200,000) acres of land, if required, shall be made over, transferred, and conveyed, in fee simple, unto Victoria aforesaid, Queen of the United Kingdom of Great Britain and Ireland aforesaid, the selection of which said land shall be made by the commission hereinbefore named and referred to, to reimburse the immediate outlay required to liquidate the aforesaid claim of the President and Government of the United States of America.

"And we, the aforesaid Ebenezer Thakombau, by the grace of God, Sovereign Chief of Bau and its Dependencies, Vunivalu of the Armies of Fiji and Tui Viti, &c., &c., &c., do hereby make this cession, transfer, and conveyance of our sovereignty, and of our islands and territories aforesaid, unto the aforesaid Victoria, by the grace of God, Queen of the United Kingdom of Great Britain and Ireland, &c., &c., &c., aforesaid, Her heirs and successors for ever; on behalf of ourselves, our heirs, and successors for ever; on behalf of our chiefs, their heirs, and successors for ever ; on behalf of our people and subjects, their heirs, and successors for ever :—hereby renouncing all right, title, and claim unto our sovereignty, islands, and territories aforesaid, in so far as is herein stated.

"In witness whereof we have hereunto set our hand and affixed our seal, this twelfth day of October, in the year of our Lord one thousand eight hundred and fifty-eight.

"(Signed)   Tui Viti (his × mark).

"Signed, sealed, and ratified by the aforesaid Tui Viti, and by him formally delivered, in our presence, unto William Thomas Pritchard, Esquire, Her Britannic Majesty's Consul in and for the aforesaid Fiji ; the said Tui Viti at the same time affirming and admitting to us personally that he, the said Tui Viti, fully, wholly, perfectly, and explicitly understands and comprehends the meaning, the extent, and the purpose of the foregoing document or deed of cession ; and I, the undersigned John Smith Fordham, formerly of Sheffield, England, but now temporarily resident at Bau, Fiji, aforesaid, do hereby solemnly affirm that I myself fully, wholly, and explicitly translated the said foregoing deed of cession unto the said Tui Viti, in the presence of the aforesaid William Thomas Pritchard, Esquire, Her Britannic Majesty's Consul in and for the said Fiji ; Robert Sherson Swanston, Esquire, his Hawaiian Majesty's Consul in and for Fiji aforesaid ; and John Binner, formerly of Leeds, England, but now resident at Levuka, Island of Ovalau, Fiji, aforesaid.

"In witness whereof we have, each and all, set our respective names and seals, this twelfth (12th) day of October, in the year of our Lord one thousand eight hundred and fifty-eight aforesaid.

"(Signed)   John Smith Fordham,
                   "Wesleyan Missionary.   (Seal.)
"John Binner,
                   "Wesleyan Mission. Trainer.   (Seal.)
"Robert S. Swanston,
                   "Hawaiian Consul, Fiji.   (Seal.)
"Will. T. Pritchard,
                   "Her Britannic Majesty's Consul.   (Seal.)

"Recorded in the archives of Her Britannic Majesty's Consulate, and designated 'Register No. 6, folio 14.'

"(Signed)   Will. T. Pritchard,
                   "Her Britannic Majesty's Consul."

PROPOSALS FOR THE CESSION OF FIJI.

RATIFICATION OF THE CESSION.

" We hereby acknowledge, ratify, and renew the cession of Fiji to Great Britain made on the 12th day of October, 1858, by Thakombau.

" In witness whereof we have hereto affixed our names this 14th day of December, 1859.

"(Signed) Rambithi, Roko Tui Dreketi (his × mark), of Rewa.
Giogi Nanovo (his × mark), of Nadroga.
Na Waqualevu (his × mark), of Rakiraki.
Yui Levuka (his × mark), of Ovalau.
Koroi Thokanauto (his × mark), of Bau.
Koroi Tumbuna (his × mark), of Tavua.
Naimbuka Koroikasa (his × mark), of Nakelo Ratu Isikeli, of Veiva.
Tukana (his × mark), of Notho.
Tumbavivi (his × mark), of Rakiraki.
Thuruitha (his × mark), of Korotumu Ra.
Sesembualala (his × mark), of Korolumbu.
Tundraw (his × mark), of Dravo Samisoni, of Vewa.
Na Galu (his × mark), of Namena.
Koroi Kaiy-anuyanu (his × mark), of Lasakau.
Dabea (his × mark), of Kuku (Viti Levu).
Komai Vunivesi (his × mark), of Nakelo.
Pita Paula (his × mark), of Vewa.
Tui Bua (his × mark), of Bua.
Thakombau (his × mark), of Fiji.
Retova (his × mark), of Mathuata.
Tui Thakau (his × mark), of Taviuni.

" We hereby certify that the foregoing chiefs signed this document with a full understanding of its meaning, in our presence, this 14th day of December, 1859.

" I have, &c.
"(Signed) H. CAMPION,
"Commander R.N., H.M.S. *Elk*.

"(Signed) WILL. T. PRITCHARD, H. B. M. Consul.

" We hereby certify that we translated the foregoing document to

the chiefs who have signed, and they thoroughly understand its meaning. "(Signed) W. Collis,
"Wesleyan Mission Training Master.
"(Signed) E. P. Martin,
"Wesleyan Mission Printer.
"I hereby certify the foregoing to be a true copy.
"(Signed) Will. T. Pritchard.
"Consul.
"*December* 31, 1859."

The desirability of accepting the sovereignty of these islands, thus proffered, was generally recognised, not only by those in high office, but by all who were capable of forming an opinion on the subject. An occupation of the group had already been recommended by many naval officers well conversant with the question; notably by Admirals Sir Edward Belcher and Washington.

In order further to remove any obstacles in the way of of the cession, Captain Towns, a patriotic citizen of Sydney, offered a cheque for the indemnity claimed by the United States, and on the motion of Mr. McArthur, the Legislative Assembly of New South Wales voted an address to the Queen in support of the proposed annexation.

It appeared necessary to the Government, however, that they should be more fully supplied with information on the question, and accordingly, with this object, in the early part of the year 1860, Colonel W. J. Smythe, having been duly appointed Her Majesty's Commissioner in that behalf, proceeded to Fiji under instructions from the Duke of Newcastle.

The following extracts from Parliamentary Returns relate the views entertained on the question by Her Majesty's Government and the result thereof.*

* In my pamphlet, 'How about Fiji,' will be found Colonel Smythe's Report, in which the reasons for the rejection of the cession are stated at length.

PROPOSALS FOR THE CESSION OF FIJI.   85

The DUKE OF NEWCASTLE *to Governor* SIR JOHN YOUNG, BART.

"*Downing Street*, 26*th March*, 1862.

"With reference to my Despatch to your predecessor, marked 'Separate,' of the 4th September, 1860, enclosing copy of a correspondence which had passed between this department and the Foreign Office, relating to the proposed cession of the Fiji Islands, and also to certain unauthorised measures adopted by Mr. Consul Pritchard, which had been brought under the serious consideration of Her Majesty's Government, I transmit, for your information, a copy of the Report which was furnished by Colonel Smythe on his return to this country, together with copies of the communications which passed with the Foreign Office upon the receipt of that Report.

"You will learn from these documents that Her Majesty does not intend to assume the sovereignty of those islands.

"Lord Russell considers that, from your position as Governor of New South Wales, you are the most fitting person to assume the direction in the inquiry to be instituted, and the proper medium for communicating to the chiefs of Fiji the regret of Her Majesty's Government that the sovereignty intended cannot be accepted."

Extract from a Despatch from Governor the Right Hon. SIR JOHN YOUNG, BART., *to the* DUKE OF NEWCASTLE, *dated Government House, Sydney*, 21*st May*, 1862.

"I have the honour to acknowledge the receipt of your Grace's Despatch, No. 15, of date 26th March, 1852, with numerous enclosures and papers with regard to the Fiji Islands.

"I have lost no time in communicating with Commodore Seymour on the subject, and he has made arrangements for the early despatch of Her Majesty's ship *Miranda* on this special service, and Captain Jenkins, the officer commanding, will communicate to the chiefs the decision of Her Majesty's Government with regard to the sovereignty of these islands."

Governor the Right Hon. SIR JOHN YOUNG, BART., *to the* DUKE OF NEWCASTLE.

"*Government House, Sydney*, 10*th October*, 1862.

"MY LORD DUKE,—With reference to your Grace's instructions, directing me to communicate to the chiefs of the Fiji Islands the decision of Her Majesty to decline the proffered sovereignty of those Islands, I have now the honour to forward a communication which I have received from Captain Jenkins, of Her Majesty's ship *Miranda*, showing the manner in which that service was performed.

"2. Captain Jenkins has addressed a communication giving full details on this subject to Commodore Burnett, who is now absent on an expedition with Governor Sir George Bowen, for the purpose of selecting a site for the foundation of a new settlement on the north-eastern coast of Queensland. I presume that on his return Commodore Burnett will forward Captain Jenkins' report to the Admiralty.

"3. In my former Despatch, No. 58, of date 20th June, 1862, I forwarded copies of the message which I addressed to the various chiefs. From an enclosure to Captain Jenkins' communication to me, your Grace will perceive that Commodore Seymour seems to have added a message of his own, which I have not seen, but which will, I have no doubt, be duly transmitted to your Grace through the Admiralty.

"I have, &c.,
"(Signed)   JOHN YOUNG.
" *His Grace the Duke of Newcastle,*
" *&c.   &c.   &c.*"

CAPTAIN JENKINS to SIR JOHN YOUNG.

"*H.M.S. 'Miranda,' Hobson's Bay, Port Philip,*
"*27th September,* 1862.

"SIR,—In reply to your Excellency's letter of the 23rd instant, requesting me to furnish you with a report in reference to your message communicating to the chiefs of the Fiji Islands the determination of Her Majesty to decline the proffered sovereignty of those Islands, I have the honour to enclose extract from my Letter of Proceedings, No. 33, of the 30th August, to Commodore Burnett, C.B., showing the manner in which those messages were read and delivered to the several chiefs of the Fiji Islands.

"I have, &c.,
"(Signed)   ROBERT JENKINS, Captain.
" *His Excellency the Right Hon. Sir John Young, Bart., K.C.B.,*
" *Governor-in-Chief, &c. &c. &c. Sydney.*"

Extracts from CAPTAIN ROBERT JENKINS' *Letter of Proceedings of the 30th August,* 1862, *to* COMMODORE WILLIAM T. BURNETT, C.B.

"On the 7th July I arrived at Levuka, Ovalau, Fiji. I immediately communicated with Her Majesty's Consul, and requested him to summon Thakombau, and other chiefs who signed the cession of Fiji to the Queen, to a formal meeting on board the *Miranda*.

"On the 10th, at 3.45 p.m., Thakombau Vunivalu Tui Viti (principal chief of Fiji) came on board, he having arrived from Urban in compliance with my request. I received him with a guard of marines, and thanked him for his promptitude in coming to meet me. He had been very ill with dysentery, and before going away said that he came to an English man-of-war, but that he was not really well enough to leave Urban, and would not have done so but for an officer of the Queen of England; I requested him to come on board on the following day, that I might deliver a message with which I was intrusted. Before leaving he said he wished to say one word more to the captain—' I have always received from British naval officers a uniform treatment of consideration, kindness, and respect. I have found that British officers have always sought to do good to me and to my people; hence it is that I am pleased and honoured in meeting you to-day, and why I so promptly left Urban to comply with your request.'

"To which I replied, ' Wherever the British uniform is, which is all over the world, there is honour and justice. It must be so, otherwise an officer would lose his rank.' Saluted him with seventeen guns on his leaving the ship.

"On the 11th, at a formal meeting in 'full dress,' His Excellency Sir John Young's message, declining, on the part of Her Majesty's Government, the acceptance of the sovereignty of the Fiji Islands, was read, interpreted, and delivered to Thakombau, Vunwaka Tui Viti, Tui Duaketi, chief of Rewa (the two principal chiefs who attended), in the presence of Tui Levuka, Roli Visawanka, and other chiefs, after which I read Commodore Seymour's message, to which I added an address.

"On the 1st August I arrived off Lakemba; called on Tui Nayau; read Sir John Young's message, also Commodore Seymour's and my own.

"On the 4th, from Fawn Hailor, I sent to Tui Thakau (who is a prisoner in the hands of the Tongans at Lauthala) Sir John Young's message, with the Commodore's and my own.

"On the 8th, at Mathuata, I read Sir John Young's message to the Vumbalu (son of Ritova), a copy of which was given to him directed to his father, Ritova; to Katonivere (son of the late Bete Tui Mathuata); Bonavendorgo, and Ritanki; to whom also the Commodore's and my message was read.

"On the 9th, 4.30 a.m., sent cutter with the Rev. Jonas Calvert to take a copy of Sir John Young's message to Katomvin, addressed to the successor of the late Bete Tui Mathuata.

"I arrived at Sandalwood Bay at 2.15 p.m.; read and gave a copy of Sir John Young's message to Tui Mbua; also read the Commodore's and my message to him.

"On the 10th, being at Levuka, I sent a copy of Sir John Young's message to Tui Levuka.

"On the 14th, at Muku Muku, Wakaiakuraudnadna came on board; read and gave him a copy of Sir John Young's message; also read the Commodore's and my own.

"On the 16th, at Rantavu, Tui Tavuki, Tui Mamalata, Tui Bui, Tui Yalu, Garanivalu, and Thangi Levu, came on board; read to them Sir John Young's message, as well as the Commodore's and my own.

"I then gave to William Pritchard, Esq., Her Majesty's Consul, copies of Sir John Young's message for transmission to the persons named in Enclosure 18.

"I have, &c.
"(Signed)   ROBERT JENKINS, Captain."

"Copies of His Excellency SIR JOHN YOUNG's Message, declining the Sovereignty of the Fiji Islands, sent through Her Britannic Majesty's Consul, to—

"Kowi Thoananto, } of Bau.
Kowi Kaiyamyanu, }
Kowi Tumbuna, of Tarna.
Naimbuka Koivikasa, ⎫
Ragata, - - - - - ⎬ of Naketo.
Komai Vunioise - - ⎭
Ratu Isikeli, ⎫
Samisoni, - ⎬ of Vuava.
Peta Paula, - ⎭
Tukana, of Notho.
Lesembualala, of Kontuba.
Tundran, of Dravo.
Na Galu, of Nanuna.
Dalca, of Kuku Veti Leon.
Roko Tui Verkau, of Namaru.
Ko-mai Malaiovea, of Namata.
Magala, - ⎫ of Verata.
Sewuloma, ⎭
Kno Ramsa, of Nakalowea.

PROPOSALS FOR THE CESSION OF FIJI.

Toro Druketi, of Totatska.
Kono Koyawamalo, of Cautata.
Geogi Nonoro, of Naprogo.
Na Wagaleon, }
Tambavioe, - } of Rakuaki."

I do not here purpose, aided either by the light of after events or hostile criticisms, to enter upon any discussion of the merits of Colonel Smythe's unfavourable Report, which was undoubtedly the cause of the ultimate rejection of the proffered cession; and this more especially as I am aware that the gallant General has since not only himself acknowledged his mistaken views, but has stated his belief that the annexation of the islands would be favourable to British interests.

Hence suffice it to say that this Report was directly opposed to the opinions of those who were equally in a position and competent to judge, and was probably biassed by the non-annexation views imparted to Her Majesty's Commissioner in New Zealand, which was then opposed to the cession, and was moreover at that time involved in a Maori war.*

Meanwhile various faithful and more encouraging accounts had been published by Dr. Seemann and others, which gave a considerable impetus to Fijian immigration.

With the increased influx of settlers came also an imperative necessity for the establishment of order and justice, and on a firmer and more satisfactory basis than could be possibly afforded by a consular jurisdiction, practically unsupported by other than moral force.

This unsatisfactory state of affairs, notwithstanding several attempts to "establish the first principles of

* New Zealand is now strongly in favour of the cession.

government," continued to 1869, when with the *approval of the American Consul* at Fiji, the following petition for annexation was made to the United States Government.

Extracts are also given from the correspondence which consequently ensued with the Home Government, and which sufficiently explain its fate.

The EARL OF BELMORE *to the* EARL GRANVILLE, K.G.

" *Government House, Sydney,* 23rd *November.*
" (*Received* 29th *January,* 1870.)

" I append an abstract from the ' Sydney Morning Herald ' of October 12, apparently copied from the ' Melbourne Argus,' in relation to the United States Government granting a protectorate over the Fiji Islands.

"FIJI AND THE UNITED STATES.

" The Melbourne papers publish the following ' Petition ' to the President of the United States, asking that the Fiji Islands may be annexed to or placed under the protection of the United States:—

" ' Fiji, 1869.—To the Honourable the President of the United States of America.

" ' SIR,—1. You are aware of the political and social condition of the group of Fiji Islands, the residents of which, many of them American, but most of them British, begin to feel the want of the protection of some powerful nation, as well for the purpose of maintaining their position with the native authorities, as for outward security in their trade and commerce. 2. It has been mooted, in turn, that France, Prussia, and America contemplated annexations of these islands; and the consequent excitement and doubt tend materially to retard our progress. 3. It is the desire of some of us to govern ourselves in conjunction with King Thakombau, under the sole protection of America, and of others under the joint protectorate of the three Powers above-named, and England. 4. The connection which has hitherto existed between the native authorities and America, although from the nature of its creation distasteful to the former from the anxieties it has caused, has nevertheless been advantageous, enabling King Thakombau, from the prestige attending your care of him, to keep down native disturbances. The period is, however, arriving when you will no longer on your own account require to keep an eye to the country. 5. We therefore, the undersigned subscribers, being composed, firstly, of residents in the group, and, secondly, of others who have identified our fortunes with it, earnestly pray that you will, at an early date, announce to the world your resolve to extend the protection of your flag to these islands and waters permanently. 6. The geographical position of the group in the South Pacific Ocean points to it as being a suitable naval and coaling station in American interests. 7. The line of steamers projected to run between San Francisco and Australia, on the opening of the railway from the former place to New York, will necessitate the creation of a coaling station near to Australia, and these islands possess the advantage of being equidistant from the latter place, in the direct track of the steamers, about the same number of miles as the Sandwich Islands are from San Francisco. 8. The exquisite climate of the Fijis, with their valuable productions, such as cotton (none finer in the world), sugar, cocoa-nut oil, &c., naturally leads reflecting and enterprising men to look forward to these islands as becoming a desirable residence for both Americans and Europeans; and the opening up of extended commercial relations between the United States of America and Australia point to their political connection with the former as being likely to be beneficial to both. 9. We therefore again earnestly express the hope that the prayer of this petition for the protection of the American flag (under our own system of self-government) may be answered in the affirmative.—We have the honour to be, Sir, your most obedient servants.'

"The United States consul at Fiji, in acknowledging the receipt of the petition, wrote :—' Among the seventy petitioners whose names are thereunto attached, I recognise men of respectability and property, who are *bonâ fide* residents of the country, and who, I doubt not, have the general good of Fiji at heart. I sincerely hope that the boon you ask may be granted and permanently secured, and would hail such a consummation of the efforts now being made by both the local government of Fiji and foreign residents as that most likely to consolidate the peace and progress of the social, commercial, and material interests of this country."

The COLONIAL OFFICE *to the* FOREIGN OFFICE.

"*Downing Street, 4th February,* 1870.

"SIR,—I am directed by Earl Granville to acknowledge the receipt of your letter of the 31st of December, respecting a petition addressed to the President of the United States, inviting the protectorate of the United States Government in the Fiji Islands.

"Lord Granville desires me to request that you will inform Lord Clarendon that, in his opinion, it is not desirable for this country to take the responsibility of the government of the Fiji Islands.

* * * * * * *

"I am desired to enclose a copy of a despatch from the Governor of Victoria, in which a transcript of the above petition (slightly altered) was lately communicated to this office."

"I am, &c.,
"(Signed)   FREDERIC ROGERS.
"*The Under-Secretary of State,*
    "*Foreign Office.*"

"*The* FOREIGN OFFICE *to the* COLONIAL OFFICE.

"*Foreign Office*, 16th *March*, 1870.

"SIR,—With reference to my letter of the 31st December last, I am directed by the Earl of Clarendon to state to you, for the information of Earl Granville, that his Lordship has reason to believe that the United States Government have no intention to establish a protectorate over the Fiji Islands.

"I am, &c.,
"(Signed)   CHARLES SPRING RICE.
The Under-Secretary of State,
    "*Colonial Office.*"

Extract from a Despatch from the EARL OF GRANVILLE, K.G., *to the* VISCOUNT CANTERBURY, *dated Downing Street, March* 24th, 1870.

"With reference to your Lordship's Despatch, No. 192, of 8th November, on the subject of a petition which had been addressed to the President of the United States by certain residents in the Fiji Islands, inviting the protectorate of the United States Government, I have to inform you that a Despatch has been received by the Earl of Clarendon from Mr. Thornton, stating that he has no reason to believe that the United States Government have any intention of acceding to the request.

* * * * * * *

"Mr. Thornton adds, that Mr. Fish denies that there is any intention on the part of his Government to establish a protectorate of the Fiji Islands."

The possibility of Fiji falling into foreign hands, and the consequences thereof, had at this time fully engaged the attention of our Australasian Colonists, who expressed their appreciation of the position in the following resolution, moved and adopted at a meeting of the Intercolonial Conference at Melbourne, 20th June, 1870:—

"*Friday, July 1st, 1870.*

* * * * * * * *

"'The question of the Fiji Islands was then discussed, and the members of the Conference agreed to the following determination:—

"'This conference, being of opinion that the geographical position of the Fiji Islands renders their protection of the very highest consideration as regards Australia and both British and Australian commerce,

"'Resolves, that it is of the utmost importance to British interests that these islands should not form part of, or be under the guardianship of any other country than Great Britain, and that a respectful Address to this effect be prepared for transmission to the Imperial authorities.'"

The subsequent endorsement of the above resolution by public opinion in Sydney and the New South Wales Cabinet, and the refusal of the Home Government to meet the views of the Colonists, is fully set out in the following correspondence, including some extracts from a petition by Dr. Lang:—

The VISCOUNT CANTERBURY *to the* EARL GRANVILLE, K.G.

"*Government Offices, Melbourne, August* 12*th,* 1870.
"(*Received, October 3rd,* 1870.)

"MY LORD,—With reference to my Despatch, marked in the margin, in which a copy of the Report of the Intercolonial Conference, recently held here, was enclosed, I have the honour now to submit to your Lordship a copy (herein enclosed) of a Memorandum submitted to me by the Chief Secretary, on behalf of himself and his colleagues, calling my attention to the resolution adopted at the Conference in favour of the establishment of a British Protectorate over 'the Fiji Islands,' and requesting me to bring this question under the early and favourable consideration of Her Majesty's Government.

"Your Lordship is well aware that, for some time past, the interest felt by the Australian Colonies in the development of the resources, and in the civilisation and security of the Fiji Islands, has been considerable and rapidly increasing.

"And I should state to your Lordship that, within the last few months, or I might even say weeks, new symptoms have been apparent of largely extended commercial intercourse with these islands.

"I may state that, in addition to many smaller trading vessels recently despatched hence for Fiji, a steamer of considerable tonnage, with a large cargo and numerous passengers, is about to be despatched thither; and the establishment by any foreign government of supreme authority there would naturally and necessarily be distasteful, and prejudicial commercially in time of peace to the Australian Possessions of the Crown, and might be dangerous to them in time of war.

"On the other hand, I beg to assure your Lordship that I am fully aware of, and that I believe that my Advisers also recognise, the fact that the establishment of a protectorate, such as that recommended in the Chief Secretary's Memorandum, involves questions scarcely capable of a satisfactory solution by any one power without communication with others; and that while the subject, which I have the honour to bring under your Lordship's notice, is one on which the interests and wishes of the Australian Colonies are clear and defined, there may be difficulties in the way of providing immediately and completely for those interests, and of gratifying those wishes.

"I have, &c.
"(Signed)   CANTERBURY.
" *The Right Hon. Earl Granville, K.G.,*
"*&c.   &c.   &c.*"

" MEMORANDUM *for His Excellency the* GOVERNOR.

" *Chief Secretary's Office, Melbourne,* 11*th August,* 1870.

" The Chief Secretary has the honour to invite your Excellency's attention to the following extract * from the proceedings of the Intercolonial Conference, having reference to the establishment of a British Protectorate over the Islands of Fiji.

Your Excellency will observe that the resolution contemplated the

* See *ante,* page 93.

preparation of an address to Her Majesty's Government; but, owing to some accidental circumstance, the address was not drawn up.

"It devolves, therefore, upon the Chief Secretary to inform your Excellency that the members of the Conference were unanimously of opinion that, looking at the geographical position of the Fijis in connection with Her Majesty's Australasian possessions, and in view of their future commercial intercourse; having regard also to the fact that numbers of Her Majesty's subjects, from these colonies, have already established themselves on the Islands; it is, on every ground, and for obvious reasons, desirable that Her Majesty should be moved to extend her protection over them. In that opinion your Excellency's advisers concur, and the Chief Secretary would therefore request your Excellency to be so good as to urge the subject upon the early consideration of Her Majesty's Imperial Government.

"I have, &c.,
"(Signed)   JAMES McCULLOCH.

"*His Excellency the Governor,*
"*&c. &c. &c.*"

The EARL OF BELMORE *to the* EARL OF KIMBERLEY, *dated Government House, Sydney, 7th September,* 1870.

(*Received, 7th November,* 1870.)

* * * * * * * *

"With reference to past correspondence on the subject of the Fijis, I enclose another article from the 'Herald' of the same date, on the subject of absconding defaulters, and particularly to the asylum offered them by the Fijis in their present state."

* * * * * * * *

"'*Sydney Morning Herald,*' 13*th August,* 1870.

"'A very serious fact is becoming more distinct in our commercial and social risks, as well as affecting that sense of responsibility which is often the substitute for honesty of principle. Within the last few months a succession of defaulters, some liable to charges for embezzlement, and others for carrying off the property of their creditors, have escaped from the Colony. At the late conference propositions were made for adjusting the law to this new difficulty.

"'With the aid of the telegraph, offenders could often be readily followed. Long before they arrived they would find waiting upon the wharf, or watching the boats, that very useful class of functionaries who bring malefactors to justice. But if legal formalities interpose to prevent arrest, they are unable to act, and meanwhile the foul bird escapes. Had there been an electric telegraph, and a prompt power of arrest, it is extremely probable that the distinguished swindler, Miranda, who carried off 20,000*l.*, would have been brought to account. The possibility of escape has often suggested it. There is a large proportion of mankind whose rectitude of conduct requires the aid of necessity. They walk in a straight line only when the road is well fenced in. It thus becomes necessary to strengthen the law, not so much in the severity of punishment, as in facility for detection and pursuit, and in creating in every man's mind a moral certainty—not only that his crime will be found out, but that it will be punished. We may expect, therefore, that every colonial legislature will remedy, as far as the law can afford it, any defects in the means of arrest ; of course, under those responsibilities which prevent the wanton exercise of power. We hope, indeed, that there are few examples of hardship such as were recorded in this journal the other day, when two young men were carried back to Melbourne to answer the charge of obtaining goods, of no great value, under false pretences. But supposing they themselves gave no reason to suspect the honesty of their intentions, the effect of hard cases would be rather to increase the formalities of a warrant for arrest than to withhold or abolish the power of detention.

"'Such an amendment of the law will not, however, meet the whole case so long as the Fijis are accessible. The dishonest creditor, or fraudulent employé, without much difficulty, can escape beyond the jurisdiction of the courts, and set up a new home within a few days' sail of the country he has quitted, and of the creditors he has pillaged. We understand an increasing number of this class of men are becoming settlers at the Fijis. A warrant, of course, only runs within the dominions of a regular government, and even the practice of extradition is rarely carried beyond the arrest of persons charged with felony. There is therefore no remedy possible, so long as there is no recognised government. The late conference pointed out the danger from the continuance of this condition of affairs. Not only does it impose the necessity of inflicting penalties by illegal methods, not only does it favour the establishment of slavery, by which we understand labour enforced by corporal punishments, but in every relation of society and of nations it is sure to produce embarrassment, and some time or other more serious consequences.

"'There are three courses open to the British Government and to the inhabitants of the Fijis, to accept the sovereignty of these islands, or some of them, and to recognise the sovereignty of the principal native Chief; or to confer some charter of incorporation which may contain the power of self-government on the European population, and which will make them amenable to laws administered among themselves. The Consuls of Egypt exercise some such powers, although many inconveniences are felt in this partition of authority between the Native Government and the representatives of foreign nations. At all events, this last method might be adopted without committing the English nation to any permanent occupation of the country, and thus a power might be established which should enforce order and obedience to the recognised law of all civilised nations.

"The difficulty in the Fijis is however only the beginning of such embarrassments. There are few persons who have any conception of the extent and importance of these islands of the Pacific. There are many indeed not at all adapted for Europeans, and unfortunately the new slave trade has disturbed that tranquillity which their special isolation once seemed to assure them. But there are many islands of great extent, capable of supporting large native populations, and of producing many articles of commerce constantly in demand by the trade of the world. As adventure and enterprise bring these within the circle of commercial operations, they will become asylums for persons who evade justice or defraud their creditors. Some are convenient places of abode, and enjoy salubrious climates. They will form an important appendage to the existing spheres of commercial adventure; but they will also extend that very danger of which we have had recently such striking examples.

"After all, modification in the universal system of trade is not unlikely to be enforced by the great changes which are everywhere transpiring. The whole world is becoming an opening track. From every point there are means of communication, and therefore of escape. Those who travel have no need to stop, and are therefore not easily overtaken. Every kind of property has its market, and may be turned into money. The swindler can choose from all the countries of the world a place of retreat, and carry with him his plunder; and we fear that we have had examples of the promptitude with which dishonest men will cover the retreat of others without losing their position. Such men may be expected to go the same road, when they have sufficiently provided themselves with a full purse at the expense of their neighbours. The transactions of commerce are indeed increasingly hazardous, so far as they are dependent upon credit; but the improvement of communication tends to shorten this credit, and in time will make cash transactions the rule rather than the exception."

"*To the Honourable the Legislative Assembly of New South Wales, in Parliament assembled: The Petition of* JOHN DUNMORE LANG, *Doctor of Divinity*,

"Humbly showeth,

"1. THAT the Fiji Islands, one of the groups of the Western Pacific Ocean, have for years past, but especially of late, been attracting much attention on the part of the inhabitants of the Australian Colonies, as being a peculiarly eligible field for commercial enterprises, as also for the settlement of a people of British origin, for the growth of intertropical productions, the land being exceedingly fertile and the climate highly salubrious.

* * * * * * * *

"5. That although the natives of these islands are generally well disposed towards white men residing among them, such a state of things as this condition of the islands implies must necessarily lead to occasional if not frequent acts of aggression, violence, and bloodshed, together with much lawlessness, social injustice, and irremediable wrong-doing, while it has actually given rise to an earnest desire, in both classes of the population, for the establishment of a regular government in the islands by some civilised nation.

"6. That Her Majesty's Government having declined, about ten years ago, although strongly solicited by the native chiefs, to annex the Fiji Islands as a British Colony, and being now still less likely to do so after the recent withdrawal of the Imperial troops from the Australian Colonies and New Zealand, these islands are liable at any moment to be seized and annexed by some sovereign power in Christendom other than Great Britain, proposals having been actually put forth by interested parties in the islands for their annexation either to the United States or to the North German Confederation.

"7. That the occupation of the Fiji Islands by any foreign power in Christendom would be exceedingly detrimental to British interests in the Pacific Ocean, as well as calamitous in a very high degree to this Colony, with which, from its geographical position and vicinity, as well as from the common origin of their European inhabitants, these islands will always be intimately connected.

* * * * * * * *

"13. That the annexation of these islands to New South Wales, and the setting up of a regular government in the group under the Commission of 1787, would not only be a measure of great commercial importance, but one of equity and justice to this Colony, as it is only through the expenditure of British money in New South Wales for the last eighty years and upwards that the colonisation of any islands in the Pacific Ocean has been rendered at all practicable for any power in Christendom.

"16. That the waste lands of the Fiji Islands, if duly administered by a regular government assuming the right of pre-emption over all future purchases of lands from the natives, and establishing a court of competent jurisdiction to investigate and decide upon all alleged past purchases, besides insuring a sufficient extent of eligible land for the natives, and protecting them in the enjoyment of their possessions against the cupidity and chicanery of unprincipled Europeans, would form an eligible field for the settlement of tens of thousands of the redundant population of the mother country, and serve as an ample security for whatever funds might be required in the first instance for their importation.

"17. That, in the estimation of reputable persons well acquainted with the present condition and prospects of the Fiji Islands, we, European inhabitants of these islands, would be both willing and able to defray the whole expense of a regular government, so as not to subject this Colony to a single farthing of expense either for the construction of such government or for its future maintenance.

"18. That the natives of the Fiji Islands, being scattered for the most part over a number of moderately-sized islands, under their respective Chiefs, are incapable of combining, like the Maoris in New Zealand, in any common effort against Europeans, and that there is therefore no likelihood of any war with the natives, especially under a government that would do them justice and recognise and respect their rights.

"Trusting, therefore, that your Honourable House will take this matter of extreme urgency into immediate consideration, and do whatever in your wisdom may facilitate the establishment of a regular government in the Fiji Islands, your petitioner, as in duty bound, will ever pray, &c., &c., &c.

"JOHN DUNMORE LANG, D.D.

"SYDNEY, *September*, 1870."

The EARL OF KIMBERLEY *to the* VISCOUNT CANTERBURY.

"*Downing Street,* 16*th March,* 1871.

"MY LORD,—Her Majesty's Government have had under their consideration your Lordship's Despatch, No. 132, of 12th August, enclosing a Memorandum submitted to you by the Chief Secretary on behalf of your Ministers, in which he calls attention to the Resolutions adopted at the intercolonial Conference in favour of the establishment of a British Protectorate over the Fiji Islands, and requests you to bring the question under the notice of the Home Government.

" Her Majesty's Government have carefully considered the Memorandum of your advisers. The state of affairs in the Fijis appears to have so far changed since 1860, when, after a full inquiry by Colonel Smythe, who was sent out for the purpose, Her Majesty's Government determined not to annex the islands, that there is now in the islands a much larger *European* community, and therefore able to protect itself, and to provide for its own government;* but, otherwise, the same difficulties remain.

" The islands are under the jurisdiction of several Chiefs ; and even if they all concurred in an act of cession to the Queen, the experience of other colonies shows that disputes would be sure afterwards to arise, especially as to the occupation of land by the settlers. It would be impossible for this country to undertake the responsibility of the government of the islands without a sufficient force to support its authority, and Her Majesty's Government are not prepared to station a military force for this purpose in the Fijis. On these grounds Her Majesty's Government cannot depart from their former decision, not to extend British sovereignty over the islands. It is not very clear what is intended by the proposal that 'Her Majesty should extend her protection' over the Fijis ; but if by this is meant something short of direct annexation, it seems to Her Majesty's Government even more open to objection ; as, while it would not really diminish the responsibility this country would incur, it would weaken and embarrass the exercise of British authority, and would be certain after a period, more or less protracted, of uncertainty, and possibly discredit, to end in annexation, in circumstances less favourable than the present.

" Her Majesty's Government are, however, ready to give such aid as may be in their power, through the Consul, for the maintenance of

* See Note, *post,* page 105.

order, until the *European* community can establish a regular government, and they are considering measures with a view to increase the authority of the Consul over British subjects, by conferring on him magisterial powers.

"I have, &c.,
"(Signed) KIMBERLEY."

"*Government House, Sydney, August 9th*, 1871.

"MY LORD,—Referring to your Lordship's Despatch, No. 24, of 18th March last, in which was enclosed the copy of one to Lord Canterbury, dated 16th, on the subject of the renewal of the decision of Her Majesty's Government not to extend British sovereignty to Fiji, I have the honour to inform you that these papers have been submitted for the consideration of my responsible advisers, and I now forward the copy of a letter from the Attorney-General, containing the views held by his cabinet on the subject, which he requests me to communicate to your Lordship.

"I see Sir James Martin estimates the European (by which term I think he means white) population in the Fiji group, as not exceeding 1500. Including American citizens, my own impression is that the white population is, or was lately, about 3000.

"I have, &c.
"(Signed) BELMORE.

"*The Earl of Kimberley,*
"*&c., &c., &c.*"

"*Attorney-General's Office, August 8th*, 1871.

"'MY LORD,—The Cabinet have had under their consideration Lord Kimberley's Despatch of the 16th March last, addressed to his Excellency the Governor of Victoria, in which the grounds are set forth on which Her Majesty's Government adhere to their former decision, not to extend British sovereignty over the Fiji Islands.

"'2. My colleagues and myself consider that the course which the Imperial Government has felt itself compelled to take in this matter is one very much to be regretted. By the Despatch in question it appears that Lord Kimberley and his colleagues are willing to recognise any regular government which the European community in the Fiji Islands may establish, but are not prepared, as British Ministers, to undertake the responsibility and incur the expense of converting these Islands into a British Colony or possession. We are not aware of any precedent for such an invitation as this, to a few Europeans resident in a part of the world where there is no government, to establish a separate nationality for themselves. Hitherto the right of British subjects to throw off their allegiance, and either alone, or in conjunction with foreigners, to form themselves into an independent state, has not, so far as we are aware, been recognised. The number of the European population of the Fijis is not known with any degree of accuracy, but it cannot exceed 1500, and is probably not so large. To what country these Europeans respectively belong, how many of them are British subjects, how many Americans, how many citizens of other civilised communities, we cannot say; but there can be no doubt that the white population of the Fijis is made up of persons representing several nationalities, British subjects being probably the most numerous. The establishment of a regular government by so small and heterogeneous a body of persons would in all probability soon lead to complications of such a character as to demand the interference either of the United States or of some European power. For although none of these powers might be prepared to assume the government of the Fijis, they would certainly interpose to protect their own subjects in those islands from the acts of local authorities not having the support of, or deriving their power from, a population sufficiently large and civilised to command or justify their recognition by other countries. Within the last few weeks the white residents in the Fijis have, acting it seems upon the views contained in Lord Kimberley's Despatch, framed a Constitution for those islands, or a part of them, and have commenced the transaction of some of the ordinary business of a government, with the concurrence of the most powerful native Chief. We are persuaded that this is a step which the British Government ought not to countenance in any way. The proposal of Lord Kimberley to increase the authority of the Consul over British subjects in the Fijis, by conferring on him magisterial powers, would, if carried out, be of no advantage. The conferring of such powers by the Imperial Parliament would itself be an act of sovereignty over the Fijis, and the exercise of such powers would be inconsistent with the recognition of the local authority now stated to be established. If Her Majesty's Imperial Government admit that the white inhabitants of Fiji have acted properly in establishing a government, they cannot, except by treaty with that government, give their Consul any jurisdiction in the new territory, but must leave their subjects resident in that territory amenable to the jurisdiction of its courts, in the same manner as they would be subject to the jurisdiction of the courts of any other foreign country in which they might reside. We venture to express the hope that the Imperial Government will not, by its refusal to interfere, leave British subjects and British property open to control of this description.

"'3. We are aware, from unofficial but reliable sources, that Her Majesty's Ministers in England are anxious to have this Fijian question settled in some way or other without delay. We have been informed that powers would in all probability be conferred upon this Colony, if we desired it, to annex Fiji or take it under our protection. We cannot see how such a scheme could possibly be carried out. This Colony could not hope to control the inhabitants of the Fijis, native or European, without a considerable armed force to cause its authority to be obeyed, and there is no reason to believe that the expense necessary to maintain such a force would be incurred. This Colony can have no motive sufficient to warrant it in taking upon itself such a burden. The establishment of a government in the Fijis, with a legislature and courts, and all the appliances necessary to keep order, preserve property, and enforce rights, would be a convenience, no doubt, to the inhabitants of all these Colonies, but in such convenience persons in other countries also would largely participate. A new and attractive field for colonisation would be opened up, mainly for the benefit of the more populous communities of Europe, but in a very minor degree for the benefit of this or any of the neighbouring Colonies.

"'4. The securing of such advantages is an Imperial question, and as such should, we think, be taken up by the Imperial Government, whose naval forces are already sufficiently powerful in these seas to protect, in its early stages of development, when alone such protection would be necessary, any government which under Imperial auspices might be created. Entertaining these views, we think it right to request that your Excellency will be pleased to communicate them to the Secretary of State for the Colonies, in the hope that the dangers arising from the assumption in the Fijis of legislative and executive powers by persons who can have no right to exercise such powers may be avoided, and a splendid country may be secured, while there is yet time, as a field for British capital and enterprise.

"'I have, &c.,
"'(Signed)   JAMES MARTIN.

"'*His Excellency the Right Honourable*
    "'*the Earl of Belmore.*'"

"*Downing Street, November, 3rd,* 1871.

"My Lord,—I have the honour to acknowledge your Lordship's Despatch, No. 128, of the 9th August, transmitting copy of a letter from Sir James Martin, embodying the views of your responsible advisers on the subject of the Fiji Islands.

"Her Majesty's Government have attentively considered the arguments of Sir James Martin; but they must decline to admit that, because a certain number of British subjects, proceeding for the most part from the Australian Colonies, have established themselves in the Fijis, the Imperial Government is called upon to extend British Sovereignty to these islands, in order to relieve such persons and their property from the risk which they may incur.

"Sir James Martin is mistaken in supposing that the conferring upon the Consul magisterial powers over British subjects would be an act of sovereignty over the Fijis. In barbarous countries, where there is no regular government, such powers have not unfrequently been conferred upon Consuls with the consent of the native Chiefs.

"As regards the Government which has recently been set up by the white settlers in the name of King Thakombau, I have in another Despatch informed you that as long as this newly-constituted Government exercises actual authority, you should deal with it as a *de facto* Government, so far as concerns the districts which may acknowledge its rule, but that Her Majesty's Government are not prepared to give any opinion as to the propriety of formally recognising it without much fuller information as to its character and prospects.

"Sir James Martin adverts to the suggestion that the Fijis might be annexed to New South Wales; and if the Colony were willing to undertake the responsibility of providing for the government of the islands, Her Majesty's Government would not refuse to entertain such a proposal, if it met with the concurrence of the native Chiefs.

"It is, of course, entirely for the Colony to determine whether such a scheme would be for its advantage; but as Sir James Martin affirms that the establishment of a regular government in the Fijis would be mainly for the benefit of European communities,* and in a very minor degree for the benefit of New South Wales or any of the neighbouring Colonies, I must observe that if this correctly represents the general opinion in the Australasian Colonies, the interest of Her Majesty's Government in the question would be greatly lessened, since in their

* As a field for colonisation; see *ante*, page 103.

view it is principally on account of the Australasian Colonies that the affairs of the Fiji Islands are a matter of concern to this country.

"I have, &c.,
"(Signed) KIMBERLEY.
" *The Earl of Belmore,*
" &c. &c. &c."

During the period which elapsed between the rejection of the Petition for Annexation to the United States, and the date of the foregoing Despatch from Lord Kimberley to the Governor of New South Wales, the settlers in Fiji had not been idle; the necessities for the protection of life and property had not diminished; the white population had increased. In this exigency they determined upon issuing the following Address, in which their case is stated with moderation and intelligence.

The EARL OF BELMORE *to the* EARL GRANVILLE, K.G. ; *dated Government House, Sydney, May* 18*th*, 1870.

"(*Received July* 15*th*, 1870.)

"I enclose, for your Lordship's information, a pamphlet, addressed 'To the White Residents of Fiji,' by a number of settlers there, which has been forwarded to me by Mr. March, Her Majesty's Consul in Fiji.

"'To THE WHITE RESIDENTS IN FIJI.

"' GENTLEMEN,—We, who hereafter subscribe our names, are addressing you on a subject the importance of which, with regard to the safety of your lives, and of your families and property, we hope to make clear to you in this circular.

"' In the first place, we call upon you to consider the security which you now hold for the protection of your rights, and do feel sure that any intelligent mind is capable of understanding its insignificance.

"' Secondly, we will ask you to consider what means we are able to adopt in order to increase this security, by depending upon the protection of any European or American power, and to weigh well how small a chance there is of any of these powers bettering our position.

"' Thirdly, we will ask you to consider whether, relying upon ourselves, and trusting to the support which we can mutually accord to each other, we may not strengthen our position by forming an independency whose members will renounce their reliance on the protection of any other power, and will swear allegiance to the community proposed to be formed. This is the principal object of the circular, and of the meeting which we propose to convene in order to discuss the subject.

"'Fourthly, we beg to give you some idea of the plan we recommend for the formation of the government of such a community, and for procuring the means to afford protection to the white settlers who join the association.

"'Lastly, we will propose the day upon which shall be held this meeting, urging upon all of you who have the real interests of the white settlement in Fiji at heart to use your best endeavours to be present upon such an important occasion, and to deliver there, for the first and last time, the views which you hold and the measures which you are ready to adopt.

"'(1.) Many offers have been made to the British Empire, soliciting it to add these fertile islands to its possessions. These have all been scouted.

"'It appears to us, who have tried to obtain the best information on the subject, that the policy of the British Government is to get rid of such of its dependencies as entail a cost to the Crown, and yet are able to dispose of their produce in any market the colonists may think fit. It holds that, whether countries are cultivated under their flag or not, they will equally come to the English markets, if such markets will pay best to the importers of produce.

"'It does not consider that any advantage is to be derived from interfering in colonial politics.

"'Such being the case, it is very unlikely that it will spend British money upon any new dependency, such as this would be.

"'The American Government holds views very similar to the British Government, and though anxious to protect trade and enterprise of every legitimate kind, is unwilling to weaken itself by having to protect positions so far removed from the centre of its government.

"'The French have obtained possession of some of the most fertile islands in the South Seas, whose commercial and military positions are unrivalled, whose harbours cannot be surpassed for the use of warlike fleets, or ports for merchant shipping. Thus it is not likely that their Government will incur further expense by taking possession of these islands; nor is it certain that it would be desirable that the strong, and perhaps arbitrary, measures adopted towards the natives and original holders of the soil in New Caledonia, would be such as would be most beneficial to a white population settling in Fiji.

" 'The other Continental Governments, we know, have their hands full, and are not likely to be able to lend us any extraordinary assistance towards securing our properties in the group.

" 'It must thus appear that we are in an excessively unprotected state, far from our native homes, having brought with us our families and fortunes; and although we have made more room for those we have left behind, we not only receive no thanks, but we also receive no assistance in the somewhat perilous career which most of us have undertaken.

" 'The Consuls have their hands tied by their Governments, and are thus unable to afford us any practical protection. The promise that they will see into any affair which may arise between ill-disposed savages and ourselves when a man-of-war arrives, is but poor consolation to the man whose wife has been assaulted, whose children have been injured, whose property has been destroyed, and who, after several years of labour in a tropical climate, for the good not only of himself and family, but of Europeans in general, finds himself injured, wounded, and penniless, and, to add to the sum of his evils, slighted by his Consul, and offered a passage home as a destitute subject.

" 'On this head it is only necessary to add that the respect hitherto partially shown by natives towards white men is daily decreasing. The time has come when it behoves all of us to consider well our precarious position, and to take such steps as will enable us to offer a better security to all commercial people in the Colonies, and to secure for ourselves permanently the advantages and profits which must accrue from cultivating, under proper auspices, those lands which we have rightfully acquired.

" '(2.) We can soon expect answers to the numerous petitions that have been sent to different Governments; and, considering their answers, find out whether we may not decline, with thanks, receiving any more of their insignificant protection; and it will be well to ascertain whether foreign powers will not show more respect to us as an independent community, well regulated in its internal government, and observing justice to all natives and outsiders, and strictly looking into the commercial integrity of those trading in this group.

" 'The public are informed, on fair authority, that the commanders of American war-vessels would recognise and respect any self-governed community professing the same principles of liberty and justice which are now respected in the United States; and we have no doubt that, though the community proposed to be constituted will consist of the sons of many nations, the American eagle will spread its protecting wings over a body of honest, resolute, and enterprising men.

"'(3.) Under the third head we announce the most important part of the proposed plan, and begin by stating the probable result of advanced steps being taken by the community. We have been led to believe, and we hope rightly, that there are some 2300 white inhabitants of this group. We are sure that from this number 1000 can be found worthy of the name of men, in the highest acceptation of the word; men who have come here bent upon making a pleasant but honest livelihood, and acquiring properties which they will be able to leave in a flourishing condition to their successors, and which they may feel sure shall be secured to them by their present toil and energies. Amongst this 1000 men we may hope to find persons suitable, and commanding zeal enough to be chosen to form a governing committee, uninfluenced by pecuniary motives, and for whom, having been duly elected, the community will show all allegiance and all proper obedience, without allowing private affairs or personal jealousy to interfere.

"'If such a committee, with a universally balloted-for president, were elected, should a wrong or an outrage then be committed upon anyone, who, relying upon the integrity of the community, has signed allegiance to its governing power, let him then appeal for protection and redress to that governing power; and it will, having satisfied itself of the facts of the case, call together a sufficient number of the community, bounden to obey its orders, and proceed at once, at public expense, to redress the wrongs of the applicants.

"'The president, with the approval of the committee, will appoint a suitable person to take command of such an expedition, whose duty it will be to control those under his orders, at his own responsibility, and to inflict such punishment as he may deem fitting, after reviewing the nature of the offence on the ground where the outrage has been committed.

"'Having so far, in this preliminary appeal to your assistance, stated the self-protectory object we have in view, we may give you our ideas of the capability of 50 or 100 men to punish any aggressor, be he a powerful or a petty Chief in Fiji. In all cases a large preponderance of natives will always be on our side; and it is not to be doubted that, though a failure attended the principal attempt on the part of a small British force to avenge injuries sustained by their fellow-countrymen, fifty gentlemen conversant with the habit of Fijians, and acquainted with the manner of their tracks and fortifications, would have no difficulty in expelling them from their most secure strongholds.

"'Much also might be effected without violence by the mere presence of determined and well-armed white men. There can be no doubt also that less bloodshed would ensue by a strong though inoffensive militia being always ready and at hand to support their own just rights, as well as those of the persons who will join with them in the cost and risk of self-protection.

" '(4.) It will be proposed to you at the general meeting that a capitation tax of 2*l.* per annum be levied by this community to defray expenses. We believe that, taking into consideration the number of white residents, this subscription will be found amply sufficient to cover the cost of boats, munitions of war, stores, &c., necessary for use in order to quell any disturbance which might arise, and to defray the expenses of calling and mustering the force required. It will also be understood that every person seeking the protection of this community will be bound to supply any boats or other articles wanted by the committee for an expedition of the sort alluded to above, the committee compensating the owner of such property at the current rate.

" '(5.) Lastly, we propose that Thursday, the 14th of April, 1870, be appointed the day for the general meeting to be held at Levuka, to which all people, whether desirous of furthering these views or not, are requested to attend, that men in different parts of the group, who by peculiar and extraordinary circumstances may be unable to be present, will authorize such of their friends (as they may think fit, and who are coming), by written and attested authority, to sign for them any document agreed to by the majority. As such a large gathering of white men might alarm the natives, who would not understand its object, we think it advisable that you bring with you your personal arms in as unostentatious a manner as possible.

" '(Signed)   * * * * &c.' "

Whether the meeting thus convened in the last paragraph of the preceding Address ever came to pass does not appear; but that it was not productive of unanimity of purpose, one of the good results expected and looked for, is evidenced from the following Charter, granted by Thakombau to the *residents at Levuka only.*

An opinion on this Charter by Sir James Martin, Q.C., then Attorney-General to the New South Wales Government, is also given:

Her Majesty's Consul, Fiji, *to the* Earl of Belmore.

"*British Consulate, Fiji, Ov dau, February* 24*th*, 1871.

"Dear Lord Belmore,—A Charter, of which the enclosed is a copy, has been granted by the native Chief, Thakombau, to the European residents at Levuka, authorizing the formation of a 'Body Corporate,' to frame and pass 'police, municipal, and other regulations; with power to levy and recover such taxes, imposts, &c., as may be necessary for the carrying on of such corporation.'

"It is very probable that among the residents at Levuka many would resist the execution of these powers, and I should therefore feel extremely obliged to your Lordship if I could have the benefit of some advice on the bearing of the relations which would arise in such a case.

* * * * * * * *

"I beg, &c.,
"(Signed)   Edward March.

"*The Right Hon. the Earl Belmore,*
"*&c. &c. &c., Sydney.*"

"Copy *of* King Thakombau's *Charter, granted by him to the European Residents at Levuka.*

"'To all to whom these presents shall come, I, Epeniza Cakobau, King of the Bau Dominions, send greeting:

"'Whereas it has been represented to me that in consequence of the large number of European settlers in Levuka, which number is rapidly increasing, and for the preservation of the good feeling that has always existed between European settlers and my own subjects, the effecting of sanitary and other improvements for the public good, it would be advisable to confer some special powers on the said European community settled in Levuka: Now know ye that I, Epeniza Cakoban, King of the said Bau dominions, do hereby authorize the said European community, inhabitants of Levuka, to elect annually seven house or landholders, by ballot or otherwise, to form a body corporate to frame and pass such police, municipal, and other regulations as may be deemed necessary and expedient for the public good; and also to pass, levy, sue for, and recover such rates, taxes, and other imposts as may be necessary for the carrying on such corporation, and any improvements by them deemed advisable; Provided always, that no regulation or regulations shall be lawful that may be antagonistic or contradictory to the spirit of the present constitution or any future amendment thereof.

"'In witness whereof I have hereunto set my hand and seal this the 21st day of November, 1870.

"'(Signed)   CAKOBAU, × his mark. (Seal.)
            "'Na Vuni Valu.

"'Signed, sealed, and delivered by the said Epeniza Cakobau, in the presence of—
    "'(Signed)   F. HENNINGS.
                JOSEPH NETTLETON.
                J. C. SMITH.
                S. C. BURT.
                TH. GROVER.
                G. L. GRIFFITHS,
                G. R. B. TOWSON, Solicitor, Levuka.'"

LORD BELMORE *to* HER MAJESTY'S CONSUL *at Levuka*.

"*Government House, Sydney, March,* 31st, 1871.

"DEAR MR. MARCH,—I have received your letter of the 24th February, 1871, enclosing a copy of a Charter which has been granted by the native Chief, Thakombau, to the European residents at Levuka, authorizing the formation of a body corporate for certain purposes, and requesting some legal advice on the bearing of the relations which might arise, should the execution of the powers conferred be resisted.

"2. At my request, Sir James Martin, Q.C., the present Attorney-General, has been kind enough to furnish me with an opinion, a copy of which I enclose.

"3. I propose to send another copy to the Secretary of State by the next Suez mail, for the information of Her Majesty's Government.

                                    "I have, &c.,
"*E. March, Esq.,*   "(Signed)   BELMORE.
"*Her Majesty's Consul at Fiji and Tonga.*

"OPINION *of* SIR JAMES MARTIN, *Q.C., Attorney-General, with respect to the Charter granted by* KING THAKOMBAU *to the European Residents at Levuka.*

    "'*Attorney-General's Office, Sydney, March* 31st, 1871.

"'MY LORD,—In reference to your Excellency's inquiry touching the proposed incorporation of European residents at Levuka, in Fiji, by a

Charter under the hand and seal of the native King or Chief of that place, I have the honour to state it as my opinion that the right to enforce obedience to bye-laws or regulations of such an incorporated body is one which cannot be maintained. There is nothing in the law of nations to prevent the aboriginal inhabitants of any of the islands in the Pacific Ocean establishing for themselves, or acquiescing, by general consent, in the adoption of any form of government whatever; but foreign nations would not admit the coercive power of such governments over their subjects, unless there was that amount of fairness, force, and certainty which generally characterises the administration of affairs in civilised communities.

"'Forty-three years ago, when the Act 9 Geo. 4, c. 83, commonly known as the New South Wales Act, was passed, the Imperial Parliament did not consider that any of the islands in the Indian or Pacific Oceans which were not subject to any European State were capable of adopting or enforcing any form of government, for by that Act offences committed in such islands by British subjects were made triable in New South Wales. Some of these islands have since become British Colonies, some are subject to France, and some have become sufficiently civilised to establish regular governments of their own; but most of them are still in much the same state, so far as their capacity for government is concerned, as they were in 1828. Where that is the case, any coercion amounting to assault or imprisonment, or the forcible seizure of property in any of these islands by British subjects resident there, would render such British subjects amenable to prosecution in the courts of this Colony, and I believe in the courts of any of the neighbouring British Colonies also. I am disposed to think that Fiji has not yet advanced in civilisation to that state which would entitle the charters or decrees of any of its Chiefs, in the constitutions adopted by its inhabitants, to be recognised by other countries. It has not yet, I think, entitled itself to be enrolled in the family of nations, and British subjects taking the property, or restraining the freedom of any person under the authority of the laws promulgated by any Fijian Chieftain would, I think, be liable to prosecution under the Act to which I have referred. I do not know what steps Mr. March can take, beyond letting British subjects know, as far as he can, the position in which they may probably place themselves by joining in coercive acts under the authority of the Charter which King Thakombau has promulgated.

"'For any trifling exercise of authority under this Charter, which may be convenient for the preservation of the public peace, neither the action of the courts here nor the interference of the Naval authorities would, perhaps, be invoked. But any serious injury to individuals would, I think, compel the Naval authorities to interfere with a view to a prosecution in some one or other of the Australian Colonies.

"'I have, &c.,
"'(Signed)   JAMES MARTIN.
"'His Excellency the Right Honourable
"'The Earl of Belmore.'"

At this period of the Colony's politico-governmental mishaps, it was given to a Mr. Woods, in combination with some other Fijian residents, to initiate both settlers and aborigines in *arcana imperii*.

Unfortunately, without that experience recently afforded to us at home, of the unadaptability of the British character to, at least one, of foreign institutions, these gentlemen, we are told, initiated their constitutional scheme by a *coup d'état*. Under such inspirations as these a cabal was formed, which in turn developed itself into a Constitution and a Parliament, which sat in 1872 and 1873.

Notwithstanding the auspices under which the government was thus established, it did not appear to enlist the sympathies of either the whites or the natives, who gave a somewhat unconstitutional expression to their feelings by reserving to themselves the right of disowning, or dissolving, the government whenever they thought fit.

The chief characteristic of this government is naïvely described by Her Majesty's Commissioners, as consisting in a "continued want of *frankness* in *financial matters* on the part of the ministers."

It appears that latterly, though, affairs have not been so mismanaged; nevertheless, a debt of 87,000*l.*—incurred in less than two years—and a strong feeling on the part of the Colonists that *misera est servitus ubi jus est vagum aut incertum*, still exist.

I

Fully indorsing the latter sentiment, the *last* proposal 'to hand' for the cession of Fiji is given without further preface.

It is related of a great man, that, when overshadowed by the seriousness of death, he was heard to say, "*Je vais quérir un grand peut-être*" (I am going to resolve a great doubt). Well might King Thakombau have also similarly expressed himself—were, indeed, such a contemplation possible to his savage intellect—when in the act of dispossessing himself of his kingdom. Of the resolution of Rabelais' doubt beyond the grave, we know nothing; of the resolution of the '*grand peut-être*' of Fiji, in the hands of Her Majesty's Ministers, we are assured that it will be satisfactory!

THE LAST PROPOSAL FOR THE CESSION OF FIJI.

(*Translation.*)

"*On board Her Majesty's Ship 'Pearl,' Levuka,*
"*March 21st,* 1874.

"*To* COMMODORE GOODENOUGH *and* CONSUL LAYARD, *the two Chiefs sent out by Her Britannic Majesty the Queen of Great Britain, to visit Fiji.*

"We, with the Chiefs of Fiji, have thought over your letter, which was brought to us by Mr. Thurston, on the 2nd day of the month of January; and after thinking the matter over, I now say to you, Sirs, that it is our minds to give the Government of our kingdom to the Lady the Queen of Great Britain; and let the document I told Mr. Thurston some time ago to prepare, be conformed to as document of promises to us.

"This is the extent, Sirs, of my words to you.

"I am, &c.,
"(Signed) CAKOBAU R.
"(Signed) HENRY S. MILNE, *Private Secretary.*
" JOHN B. THURSTON."

(Translation from the Fiji 'Gazette.')
"*The 'Pearl,' Levuka, March* 21st, 1874.
"*To* COMMODORE GOODENOUGH *and* MR. CONSUL LAYARD, *the Commissioners of the Queen of Britain.*

"We, and the Chiefs of Fiji. We have reconsidered your letter, which was brought, Sirs, to us by Mr. Thurston, on the 2nd of January last. And we now tell you, Sirs, that we desire to cede the Government of our kingdom to the Queen of Britain, and that the document which I formerly told Mr. Thurston to prepare, be the agreement of the cession.

"This is all, Sirs, we have to say to you.

"(Signed)   CAKOBAU R.
"(Countersigned)   HENRY T. MILNE, *Private Secretary.*
"J. B. THURSTON."

"CHIEF SECRETARY'S DEPARTMENT, FIJI,
"*April* 11*th*, 1874.

"GENTLEMEN,—In accordance with the tenor of the King's letter to you, signed on board Her Majesty's ship 'Pearl,' upon the 21st ultimo, and with his commands to me, I beg to inclose the conditions upon which His Majesty—for himself and people—offers to cede the government of his kingdom to Her Britannic Majesty.

"I have, &c.,
"(Signed)   JOHN B. THURSTON,
"*Commodore J. G. Goodenough, R.N.,*   *Chief Secretary.*
" *Commanding the Australian Station;*
"*Edgar Leopold Layard, Esq.,*
"*Her Britannic Majesty's Consul, Fiji and Tonga.*"

"*Offered Cession of the Kingdom of Fiji to Her Britannic Majesty.*
"*Conditions thereof.*

"'Article 1. King Cakobau to retain for life the designation of Tui Viti, and a pension of 2,000*l.* sterling per annum, payable at such times annually as may be directed by Her Britannic Majesty's Government.

"'The said pension (but not the designation) to be continued to and during the life of the eldest of King Cakobau's three sons, Epeli, Timoci, and Iosefa, who may survive him (the King), and after the death of such elder surviving son to the elder of the said remaining sons, or to either of them as may be then surviving, for his life; and if, after the death of such last named of the King's sons, the youngest of the three shall still be living, then to such youngest son for his life.

"'On the day of cession Her Britannic Majesty's Government to give King Cakobau, or his survivor as above provided, the sum of 1600*l.* sterling for the purchase of a vessel.

"'Art. 2. The last Article not to be affected by the death of King Cakobau before Her Britannic Majesty acquires (if the offer of cession is accepted) the sovereignty of Fiji.

"'Art. 3. In the event of the death of King Cakobau before cession, his eldest son and heir, Ratu Epeli Nalatikaio, to be the Chief with whom Her Britannic Majesty shall conclude the cession of Fiji, as herewith offered.

"'Art. 4. The King's heir, Ratu Epeli Nalatikaio to be the chief native executive officer over the island of Viti Levu, and the adjacent islands of Kadavu and Yasawas, subject to such future arrangements or changes as may, from time to time, be found necessary, with an annual allowance of 400*l.* sterling per annum.

"'Art. 5. Ratu Golea Tui Cakau to be the chief native executive officer over the islands of Vanua, Levu, Taviuni, and adjacent islands, subject to such future arrangements or changes as may, from time to time, be found necessary, with an annual allowance of 400*l.* sterling per annum.

"'Art. 6. Ratu Tevita-Ulu-i-Lakeba to be the chief native executive officer in the Province of Lau (as now defined), with an annual allowance of 300*l.* sterling per annum.

"'Art. 7. Ratu Savenaca to be the chief native executive officer in the Province of Central Fiji (as now defined), with an annual allowance of 300*l.* sterling per annum.

"'Art. 8. The following minor Chiefs to receive an annual allowance of 200*l.*, and to be the subordinate executive officers in their respective districts:

> "'The Chief of Rewa.
> The Chief of Naitasiri.
> The Chief of Nadroga.
> The Chief of Tai Levu.
> The Chief of Kadavu.
> The Chief of Rakiraki.
> The Chief of Ba and Yasawa.
> The Chief of Bua.
> The Chief of Macuata.

"'The following Chiefs to receive 100*l.* annually:—

The Chief of Namosi.
The Chief of Serua.

"'Every Chief hereinbefore written to be succeeded, upon death or removal from office, by his next of kin as hereafter provided.

"'Art. 9. Every native executive officer to draw the aforesaid allowances contingent upon the actual performance, in respect to Fijians, of the duties confided to him. Should any high native officer be removed from his post, his place to be filled by the next man of his family entitled to succeed him by Fijian law or customs.

"'Art. 10. The Government of Her Britannic Majesty to concede and preserve to the Chiefs and people of Fiji, under any form of British Government, an equitable share in the Councils of State; and, in the event of Fiji becoming a Crown Colony, to appoint not less than four Fijian Chiefs to seats in the Executive Council.

"'The Government of Her Britannic Majesty to confirm to the heirs of Fijian Chiefs the succession to the emoluments and official rank of such Chiefs, provided always that such heirs are capabable of fulfilling the duties pertaining to such official rank.

"'Art. 11. In the event of Her Britannic Majesty accepting the offered cession of Fiji, the Judges of the Supreme Court, holding commissions during good behaviour under His Fijian Majesty, to be compensated, according to the principles adopted in British Colonies in similar cases, for loss of position, and being so compensated to have no claim to office under Her Britannic Majesty. On the other hand, such functionaries or any of them shall not be bound to accept office if offered. In the event of accepting office the past services of such officers, under His Fijian Majesty, to be counted as service under Her Britannic Majesty's Government, and to be so reckoned in any future regulations for retiring allowances under British Colonial Government.

"'Art. 12. The Government of Her Britannic Majesty to assume the existing financial liabilities of Fiji, as stated in Schedule A.

"'Art. 13. The Charter granted by His Fijian Majesty, under the Order in Council, dated the 19th of August, 1873, to the Fiji Banking and Commercial Company, Limited, to be confirmed; and also all other contracts made or concluded by His Fijian Majesty, or his Government, excepting that with the Company known as the Polynesian Company of Melbourne, Victoria, the final settlement of which contract shall (in the event of cession) be assumed by Her Britannic Majesty's Government.

"'Art. 14. All Crown grants issued before the date of cession, to be of the same validity as grants of Her Britannic Majesty, or her representative, after cession.

"'Art. 15. The broad principle to be accepted, that the Fijian Chiefs and people, in changing their allegiance, retain all existing private rights, real and personal.

"'Art. 16. The ruling Chief of every tribe to be recognised as the owner of the lands of his tribe, and guardian of their rights and interests.

"'The people of the tribe to be recognised as tenants of tribal lands, with hereditary right of occupation, subject always to rental obligations, which shall and may be accepted by the Chief in money, labour, or kind, as may be agreed between Chief and people.

"'Art. 17. The offer of King Cakobau herewith made to cede the kingdom of Fiji to Her Britannic Majesty, shall remain open for a period of twelve months from the date of the offer being made, but no longer.

"'Art. 18. In consideration of the acceptance by Her Britannic Majesty of the foregoing conditions, His Majesty King Cakobau offers to cede and transfer to Her Britannic Majesty the full and absolute sovereignty of Fiji, with all its rights and privileges, maritime and territorial.

"'Art. 19. The Government of King Cakobau will transfer to Her Britannic Majesty the Crown lands and other assets, as set forth in Schedule B.

"'By command,

"'(Signed) JOHN B. THURSTON.

"'Compared with counterpart.

"'(Signed) CHARLES ST. JULIAN, C.J.,

"'*Chancellor of Fiji.*'

"RECOGNITION OF THE PROPOSED CESSION BY MAAFU.

"(*English.*) '*Pearl,*' at *Levuka, Fiji,* 12*th March,* 1874.

"'It is my wish that the Chiefs of Fiji give up the government of Fiji to Great Britain.'

"(*Tonguese.*)

"'Ko ho ku loto ke foaki ki Beletania.'

"(*Fijian.*)

"'Sa, zalogu méra solia na vanua Ko Viti Ko erà na Luraga ni Viti, vei Peritania.'

"'(Signed) MAAFU.

"'Witnesses: (Signed) W. WYKHAM PERCY, *Secretary.*

E. TURNER, *Interpreter.*'

"'Schedule (A).

"'Liabilities of the Fijian Government, as estimated by Messrs. Thomas Norton and Carl L. Sahl,

	£	s.	d.
upon 16th March, 1874	87,145	9	2
Deduct	1,291	1	4
	£85,854	7	10

"*Note by Commodore* Goodenough.

"'The mortgage on the Levoni lands having been foreclosed, the sum of 1291*l*. 1s. 4*d*. has to be deducted from this debt.

"'Schedule (B).

"'*Memorandum of National or Crown Lands in Fiji, estimated by* Mr. Thurston *at a Conference with the King, Chiefs, and* Mr. R. S. Swanston.

"'Viria and Neighbourhood, with part of Tai
Vugali	60,000
Upper Navua, Batiwai	10,000
Mogodro and Ba-i-colo	300,000
Wai-nu-nu-Vanua, Levu	30,000
Nadroga and Kadavu	10,000
Carkandrovi (at Natuva Bay)	10,000
South Viti Levu (west of Suva)	20,000
Lau	10,000
"'Total	450,000

"'The Government buildings and the lands pertaining thereto at Nasova Bay, Levuka, upon the Island of Ovalau;

"'The Government printing plant;

"'The provincial court-house, gaol, and the inclosed reserve, known as Totogo, situate within the municipality of Levuka;

"'All vessels, boats, furniture, and material of every description, in use or possession of the Legislature, Judicial and Executive branches of the Government;

"'All military stores as per return annexed.

"'Return of Arms, Ammunition, &c., in Use and in Store, April 9, 1874.

Description, &c.		In use.	In store.	Total Number or Amount.	Estimated Value.		
					£	s.	d.
Terry rifles . . . at 20s. each		7	4	11	11	0	0
Spencer „ . . . . „ 80s. „		..	1	1	4	0	0
Snider „ . . . . „ 80s. „		19	5	24	96	0	0
Sharp's Carbines . . „ 20s. „		..	9	9	9	0	0
Vic. A. C. rifles . . „ 20s. „		4	34	38	38	0	0
Henry „ . . „ 80s. „		..	1	1	4	0	0
Enfield „ . . „ 50s. „		100	11	111	277	10	0
Musket, percussion . „ 10s. „		884	66	950	475	0	0
„ flint . . . „ 2s. „		..	189	189	18	18	0
Revolvers . . . „ 15s. „		37	..	37	27	15	0
Terry carbines . . „ 40s. „		9	11	20	40	0	0
Ball cartridge . . „ 50s. per 1000		..	35,000	35,000	87	10	0
Enfield „ . . „ 80s. „		..	8,000	8,000	32	0	0
Terry „ . . „ 80s. „		..	1,700	1,700	6	16	0
P. F. revolver cartridge „ 120s. „		..	4,500	4,500	27	0	0
Gunpowder . . . „ 3s. per lb.		..	182 lbs.	182 lbs.	27	6	0
Percussion caps . . „ 5s. per 1000		..	52,000	52,000	13	0	0
Chinese frocks . . „ 5s. each		..	51	51	12	15	0
Iron pots . . . . „ 15s. „		28	1	29	21	15	0
Belts, pouches, &c. . .		..	..	..	100	0	0
Lead . . . . . at 4d. per lb.		..	380 lbs.	380 lbs.	6	6	8
Scales . . . . . „ 1l. 5s., 1l. 1s.		..	2 pr.	2 pr.	6	0	0
Total		..	..	..	1,341	11	8

"'(Signed)   FRED. P. BLACKMORE,
"'*Captain Commanding.*

"'*Nasova, April 9th, 1874.*

"'(Signed)   JOHN B. THURSTON,
"'*Chief Secretary.*'"

CHAPTER IX.

THE ANNEXATION.

SINCE the last chapter was written the '*grand peut-être*' of Fiji has been solved—and let us hope satisfactorily—by the unanimous and *unconditional* cession of the group by the Chiefs to Her Majesty the Queen.

Sir Hercules Robinson, to whom was intrusted the delicate mission of conveying to the Fijian Chiefs the wishes of Her Majesty's Government, arrived at Levuka on the 23rd of September, and was received in state by Thakombau on the following day.

Business was not however entered upon until the 25th, when Thakombau returned Sir Hercules Robinson's visit on board H.M.S. *Dido*, where he was received by a royal salute of twenty-one guns. On this occasion His Excellency explained that the conditions which accompanied the offer of cession, would, unless waived, render its acceptance impossible, and intimated that if the King was not prepared to trust in the generosity and justice of the Queen of England, the negotiation had better then terminate.

In reply to this the King said :—

"True, true, the Queen is right; it is not chief-like to make conditions. I was always opposed to it, but I was overruled. When the Commodore and Consul came here they took different ground to that which you have taken. They kept saying, 'Tell us what you want?' and pressing me to do so—hence the conditions attached to the offer of cession. If I give a chief a canoe, and he knows I expect something from him, I do not say, 'I give you this canoe on condition of your only sailing it on certain days, or your not letting such and such a man go in it, or your only using a particular kind of rope with it,' but I give him the canoe right out, and trust to his generosity and good faith to make me the return which he knows I expect. If I were to attach those conditions he would probably say, 'Bother your canoe, I can do very well without it.'"

Thus showing that in attaching these conditions to the offer of cession he had been acting under advice, and contrary to his own wishes, and that he well understood, it would be as impossible for the Queen of England to accept the offer on such terms, as it little consorted with his own dignity to propose them.

Having taken a day to deliberate, the King informed Sir Hercules Robinson, that personally he wished to cede his country unconditionally to Her Majesty, adding that he required peace and rest. "These," he said, "are our riches; tumult and strife are poverty. * * * Any Fijian chief who refuses to cede cannot have much wisdom. If matters remain as they are, Fiji will become like a piece of driftwood on the sea, to be picked up by the first passer-by."

With reference to the land question His Excellency informed Thakombau—

"That all lands which can be shown to have been fairly and honestly acquired by whites shall be secured to them; that all lands that are now in the actual use or occupation of any Chief or tribe, and as much land as may be necessary for the probable future support and maintenance of any Chief or tribe, shall be set apart for them; and that all the residue of the land shall go to the Government, not for the personal advantage of Her Majesty or the members of any Government, but for the general good, for the purposes of rule and order."

These provisions, which are virtually the same as some contained in a code of laws formerly framed by a confederation of chiefs—called the Lau Confederacy—in the Windward Islands, with whom Thakombau was once allied, gave the King great satisfaction, as they entirely accorded with his own views on the subject.

Also as regards the financial liabilities, debts, and engagements entered into, or contracted since 1871, His Excellency gave assurance that they would be carefully investigated, and would be equitably dealt with, in accordance with sound public policy, by Her Majesty's Government.

During the different interviews, whatever Sir Hercules Robinson said was interpreted sentence by sentence to the King, who before the next clause was entered on, always signified that he had quite understood ths gist of His Excellency's previous observations.

Throughout these negotiations, which continued for five days, Thakombau conducted himself with dignity and intelligence, and with a full knowledge of the important step he was taking. On the 28th, Thakombau held a council with the leading chiefs, and after a lengthy debate it was finally determined to surrender Fiji unreservedly to Her Majesty the Queen, reposing perfect faith in Her generosity and justice.

On the 29th Thakombau publicly signed the deed of cession; and the Chiefs, Ratu Abel, Tui Mbua, Ratu Savanaca, and Ratu Isikeli also attached their signatures. Sir Hercules Robinson then accepted the cession in the following terms:—

"I accept in the Queen's name the cession in the spirit in which it has been offered. I think that in this matter the King has acted the part of a great Chief in consulting as he has done only the interest of his country. From my heart I wish Fiji prosperity, and peace and happiness to her people."

Having thus satisfactorily concluded the mission so far as Thakombau was concerned, Sir Hercules Robinson now proceeded to Lomo Lomo, to receive the formal assent of Maafu to the cession.

On being apprised of the arrival of His Excellency, Maafu came on board H.M.S. *Pearl*, accompanied by Tui Cakau, Chief of Cakaudrove—who was on a visit with him—to pay his respects to the Queen's representative, and afterwards paid a visit to Thakombau, who was on board H.M.S. *Dido*.

In course of conversation Maafu intimated to the King, that he was of one mind with him respecting the cession, and that he was perfectly willing and desirous to sign the deed. To this Thakombau replied, " If you and I are of one mind we need not ask a second chief in Fiji."

On the following morning, 31st of September, Maafu and Tui Cakau met Sir Hercules Robinson and the King on board H.M.S. *Pearl*, and in their presence and that of the Commodore and the British Consul, and the members of His Excellency's suite, the deed of cession was fully interpreted to both chiefs. Having been questioned, they both said that they perfectly understood it, and concurred in its provisions; whereupon Maafu wrote his own name, and affixed his seal to the document in a most business-like fashion ; but Tui Cakau, less of a scribe, merely held the pen while his name was written. On the conclusion of this important ceremony the chiefs separated in a most friendly manner, having previously arranged to be present at the final cession of the islands at Levuka on the 10th of October.

Meanwhile Sir Hercules Robinson proceeded to Vanua

Levu, his object in making this trip to the different islands being to fully assure himself of the wishes of the principal chiefs as to the cession.

Nduri, the chief town on the Macuata coast, was reached on the 4th of October, when Thakombau informed the chiefs of what had already taken place, and then added:—

"I have but one object in view: I care neither for my position as a chief, nor for riches, European or Fijian. What I seek and greatly covet is the peace and welfare of my people and the firm establishment of a government in our land. Now I shake hands with you, and send you to your homes, try to carry out these principles. Have this as your object in all you do, and peace and prosperity will follow. I wish you all good-bye."

On Saturday, the 10th of October, the final scene of the drama was played out, and amidst much ceremonial and legal formality the Fiji Islands were ceded to the British Crown.

The proceedings were initiated by the King handing to Sir Hercules, as a present for Her Majesty the Queen, his favourite war-club, *Na Vu-ni-valu*, that is, 'the root of war,' covered with emblems of peace, in token of his friendly feelings to Her Majesty. This characteristic weapon, at once symbolical of the rule which has hitherto prevailed in those islands, and of the nature of its stalwart master, who has wielded it so often and so well, is now profusely adorned with silver ornaments, the handle being entwined with fern-leaves and doves in silver, and the top surmounted by a massive crown.

Sir Hercules Robinson having signified that he would have much pleasure in conveying the club to Her Majesty, Thakombau then signed a duplicate of the instrument of cession, and Maafu, Ratu Abel (or

Timothy), Tui Mbua, Savanaca, Roko Tui Dreketi, Ritova, Katonivere, Ratu Kini, Matanitobna, and Cagilevu also attached their signatures. The signatures of Tui Cakau and Isikeli, who were absent, were afterwards obtained.

His Excellency having also signed the deed in duplicate, then delivered the following address:—

"The legal forms for the transfer of the government of this country to the Queen have just been completed, and will be made public through the medium of the Gazette in the course of a few hours. It now therefore only remains for me to declare Fiji to be from this time forth a possession and a dependency of the British Crown. I fervently trust that this important step will tend to develop the great natural capabilities of these beautiful and fertile islands, and at the same time conduce largely to the contentment and happiness of all classes of the population. I hope too that past differences will henceforth be forgotten, and that all local animosities will this day be buried at the foot of the staff on which we are now about to hoist the British flag."

The ceremony was concluded by the royal standard of England being run up, amid the hearty cheers of those assembled, and a salute of twenty-one guns from H.M.S. *Pearl*.

Until such time as Her Majesty's pleasure shall be made known regarding the constitution and permanent administration of the Colony, a provisional government has been established, with Sir Hercules Robinson as Governor, with an executive Council consisting of the late British Consul, Mr. Layard, the Attorney-General of New South Wales, the late Premier, Mr. Thurston, Mr. T. Horton, and Mr. R. S. Swanston; Mr. Layard to act as Vice-President of the Council and Administrator of the Government in the absence of the Governor.

Thus after a period of fifteen years' continuous agitation, the leading incidents of which have been referred to in the preceding chapter, Fiji has at length been incorporated as a province of the British Empire.

The richest and most extensive group of Western Polynesia, in which it is centrally situate, at a distance of 2000 miles north-east of Sydney, and 1200 miles north of Auckland in New Zealand, the political importance of Fiji, viewed in connection with our Australasian Colonies, cannot be lightly valued or esteemed. Capable of affording shelter to the largest fleets, and offering a suitable place for coaling and taking supplies, its occupation by this country will be an essential set-off to the American and French possessions in the Pacific, which confer on those powers advantages which we hitherto have not possessed; while it will at the same time afford us a convenient centre from which to control the labour traffic in the South Pacific.*

In 1859 Admiral Washington pointed out that while Great Britain owned valuable possessions on either side of the Pacific Ocean—i.e. on the west coast of America and Australia—she did not possess an islet or a rock in the 7000 miles of ocean that separate them.

Considered then from a strategical point of view, Fiji may be looked upon, from its close proximity to New South Wales, Queensland, and New Zealand, as a maritime outwork of these colonies, and the possession of which in naval warfare would be to them a matter of almost vital consequence. But while dwelling upon the various advantages which we may reasonably hope for and expect from our New Colony, we can also afford to cast a lingering regret at that policy which has permitted Fiji to lie for so many years, indeed "like a piece of driftwood on the sea," exposed to the ambition and cupidity of the first

* *Vide* 'How about Fiji.'

Power that might feel inclined to pick it up; while its promoters, seeking to avoid the responsibility of rejecting previous overtures for cession,* made when Fiji was comparatively free from, and untrammelled by, those financial engagements with which she is now beset, would also impose upon others the obligation of recognising the wisdom of such policy, even at that moment when most fettered by its very infirmity.

The importance of this question to our Australasian Colonies is undoubted; and having regard to the considerable interest which they have necessarily taken in it, the vicissitudes by which it has been so long surrounded, and the remarkable *consensus* of opinion by which the policy of annexation has now been confirmed, it cannot but be to them a source of relief and congratulation that it has been thus satisfactorily disposed of and finally set at rest.

* *Vide* Letter, Nov. 3, 1871, *ante*, p. 104, from the Secretary of State for the Colonies to the Earl of Belmore, stating that while the Imperial Government did not care about extending British sovereignty to Fiji, there was no objection to New South Wales annexing the islands, should it so desire.

CHAPTER X.

PRODUCTIONS.

THE principal articles of colonial produce are cotton, sugar-cane, coffee, tobacco, indigo, arrowroot, and various spices; all spontaneous yields of the soil.

Nearly fourteen years have now elapsed since the well-known naturalist Dr. Berthold Seemann reported on the great capacities of these islands for the production of cotton. He said, "If I understand cotton aright, the Fijis seem to be as if made for it;" and again, "In fine, every condition required to favour the growth of this important production seems to be provided, and it is hardly possible to add anything more, in order to impress those best qualified to judge, with a better idea of Fiji as a first-rate cotton-growing country."

Since this expression of opinion the excellence of the Fijian cotton has become a matter of history.

All varieties of cotton grown in Fiji are perennial, not annual, as in America, where the plant is liable to be killed by frost, and otherwise injuriously acted upon by sudden variations of temperature. In Fiji, moreover, the plant bears ripe fruit without intermission throughout the year.

Sea Island is the most valuable variety grown, and in

1869 amounted to 95 per cent. of the total area then under cotton cultivation, viz. 5,000 acres.

Extract from Consular Report for 1869.

"Taking into consideration the spontaneous growth of the cotton plant in Fiji, the imperfect system pursued in the cultivation, and the large tracts of land lying waste over the numerous islands comprising the group, it is not too much to say that the movement is yet undeveloped, and that the cotton hitherto shipped is but an indication of the success which will follow upon a proper attention to the capacities of the soil."

Cotton, nevertheless, is undoubtedly an introduced plant, and is not indigenous in any part of the group.

Sugar-cane, of which there are several native varieties, also thrives well, and speedily promises to become an important article of trade and industry. The coffee-plant, which takes three years to grow, has been spoken of in the highest terms by planters from Ceylon who have visited Fiji, and there can be no doubt that, under proper management, these plantations will yield rich and remunerative harvests. There is also an indigenous variety of tobacco, but of an inferior quality. It is probable, however, that the numerous facilities which offer for growing good varieties will in future induce planters to turn their attention to its cultivation. Many of our so-called European vegetables are grown with success, and those which have hitherto failed would, in the cooler regions of the mountains, doubtless thrive well. Those generally cultivated are: the cabbage, the turnip, parsley, the shallot, and the tomato (*Lycopersicum esculentum*), which latter, as a tropical vegetable, grows in great perfection. Potatoes have not yet been cultivated with much success. The pea-tree (*Cajanus Indicus*), the seeds of which when young furnish a good substitute for green peas, has been introduced from the United States, and grows well. Indian corn also flourishes, though cultivated sparingly. Pumpkins, cucumbers, and large red capsicums grow in abundance. The indigenous kitchen vegetables are supplied by an innumerable variety of both cultivated and wild plants, of which the following are mentioned by Seemann:—

"The natives boil the leaves of several ferns, among them those of the *Litobrochia sinuata*, Brack., and in times of scarcity those of the balabala (*Alsophila excelsa*, R. Br.); those of the ota (*Angiopteris erecta*, Hoffm.), a species with gigantic foliage, are peculiarly tender, and their taste not unlike that of spinach. The common brake (*Pteris aquilina*, Linn., var. *esculenta*, Hook. fil.), though plentiful, does not seem to be used as it is by the Polynesian tribes of New Zealand. The leaves of the boro ni yaloka in gata (i.e., serpent's-egg-boro), our *Solanum oleraceum*, a spiny kind of herbaceous nightshade, serve as 'greens' to both the natives and foreigners. The young shoots of the vaulo of Viti Levu (*Flagellaria indica*, Linn.), known also, if I am not misinformed, by the names of tui, vico, turuka, and malava in different districts, after having been boiled, are eaten with taro and yams, but only by Fijians. Two kinds of purslane, termed 'Taukuku-ni-vuaka' in Taviuni (*Portulaca oleracea*, Linn., et *Portulaca quadrifida*, Linn.) are common weeds which, during my stay at Somo Somo, were frequently brought to table. The natives sometimes grow whole fields of the bete, or vauvau-ni-viti '(*Hibiscus* [*Abelmoschus*] *Manihot*, Linn.), an erect shrub attaining six or eight feet in height, bearing yellow flowers and lobed leaves, which, especially if not quite developed, are tender eating, relished even by Europeans. The boro dina (*Solanum anthropophagorum*, Seem.), a straggling shrub with glabrous leaves and scarlet or yellow berries, possessing a faint aromatic smell, and resembling tomatos in shape, has also edible leaves and fruit."

The bread-fruit tree flourishes in great perfection. There are at least thirteen different varieties, of which the two most common are *uto dina* and *uto buco*. Probably the largest and best tasting of these is the *uto buco*, which is an obovate obtuse fruit, apparently destitute of seeds, and with a smooth even surface when ripe.

The uto dina variety, however, is considered by most botanists as typical of the species, the correctness of which is borne out by the fact that the natives invariably attached to it the adjective 'dina,' meaning genuine or true.

These different varieties yield fruit throughout the year, but it is most abundant in the months of March and April.

There are various ways of preserving it, the commonest method being by burying it in pits underground, which when opened emit a most offensive odour, due to the fermentation of the fruit. When in this state the natives use it extensively for making 'madrai,' or native bread, as well as various sorts of puddings.

Bananas and plantains also flourish throughout the islands. There are at least eighteen different kinds, of which that kind known as the *vudi-ni-papalagi*, or foreign banana, is most esteemed. It is supposed to have been introduced into the Navigator Islands by the missionary John Williams — known as the Martyr of Eromanga — who brought it from the Duke of Devonshire's seat at Chatsworth. Having thus found its way to the South Seas, it was introduced into Fiji in the year 1848. These fruits are also spoiled by the natives, who pull them and bury them before they are ripe.

"Other edible fruits, some of delicious flavour, are met with throughout the group, either perfectly wild or in a state of cultivation. Most of them have been in Fiji from time immemorial, and only a few, such as the pine-apple, the papaw, the custard-apple, and the Chinese banana, have been introduced of late years. The most prominent place among the native fruits undoubtedly belongs to the wi (*Evia dulcis*, Comm., = *Spondias dulcis*, Forst.). The tree appears to be self-sown, and is met with in abundance about towns and villages. It is often sixty feet high. The bark is smooth and whitish, the leaves pinnate, glabrous, and of a dark green, forming a fine contrast with the yellow oval-shaped fruits with which the tree is heavily laden.

The fruit has a fine apple-like smell, and a most agreeable acid flavour, rendering it highly suitable for pies; indeed the wi is the only Fijian fruit which recommends itself for that purpose. At Rewa I weighed and measured several highly developed ones, and found the largest to be exactly one foot in circumference and 1 lb. 2 oz. in weight. The natives are as fond of wis as the white settlers, and quite content to make their dinner of taro and wis. The dawa (*Nephelium pinnatum*, Chamb., = *Pometia pinnata*, Forst.) is more plentiful than the wi; entire forests of it are frequently encountered, and there appears to be several varieties. It is sixty feet high, and shares with most Fijian fruit-trees the peculiarity of yielding a useful timber. The leaves are pinnate, the leaflets serrate, and when first opening display a brilliant red tinge, which at a distance looks as if the tree were in bloom. The flowers, arranged in terminal panicles, are whitish, and of diminutive size. The fruit, ripening in January and February, has rather a glutinous honey-like taste, and attains about the size of a pomegranate. The Fijians deem the dawa peculiar to their islands. It certainly does not occur to the eastward in a wild state, as the Tonguese are said to have obtained it from Fiji, but it seems to be quite common in all the groups lying westwards, the New Hebrides, New Caledonia, and others. A native of Were assured me it was plentiful in his island, and Dr. Bennett, of Sydney, found it cultivated under the name of ' Thav ' at Rotuma, a little island to the north of Fiji, as recorded in his 'Gatherings of a Naturalist.' I succeeded in carrying living plants to the botanic garden at Sydney, where they were left in charge of Mr. Moore, and whence they may perhaps find their way to the new colony of Queensland, and prove acceptable additions to the fruits of that country.

"The kavika or Malay apple (*Eugenia Malaccensis*, Linn.) abounds in all the forests. As in the Hawaiian and other Polynesian islands, there are two varieties, the purple (kavika damudamu) and the white (kavika vulavula). When the tree, which attains about forty feet in height, is in flower, the ground underneath is densely covered with petals and stamens, looking, especially if the two varieties grow together, like a fine Turkish carpet. I have often seen the natives gathering handfuls of them to strew on their heads. In their idea there is scarcely a finer tree than the kavika, and when in their fairy tales the imagination runs riot, and describes all that is lovely and beautiful, the kavika is rarely omitted. The Hawaiians, as I have stated elsewhere (' Narrative of the Voyage of H.M.S. *Herald*,' vol. ii. p. 83), thought this tree worthy of supplying materials for their idols, and thus, like the Fijians, recorded their veneration for it. A botanist, himself more than half a tree-worshipper, can fully sympathise with them. The fine oblong leaves, their smooth shining surface, the deep purple or pure white flowers, and afterwards the large quince-shaped fruits, with their apple-like smell and delicate flavour, are well calculated to justify much of the praise Polynesians bestow upon the tree. The ivi, or Tahitian chestnut, as it has been called by voyagers (*Inocarpus edulis*, Forst.), is one of the most common trees, and, when fully grown, has a most venerable aspect. I still see in my mind's eye a fine group on the banks of a rivulet between Wairiki and Somo Somo, diffusing a dense shade. Sixty, often eighty feet high, the ivi bears a thick crown of oblong feathery leaves, small white flowers emitting a delicious perfume, and kidney-shaped fruits which contain a kernel resembling chestnuts in taste. The kernel is either baked or boiled, and eaten without further preparation, or grated on the mushroom coral (*Fungia*), and made into puddings or bread (madrai). The stem is most singular. When young it is fluted like a Grecian column; when old it has regular buttresses of projecting wood. Ferns, orchids, and hoyas frequently take up their abode on the soft spongy bark. The roots of old trees appear above the ground somewhat like those of the bald cypress of North America (*Taxodium distichum*, Rich.). Thousands of seedlings are continually springing up around the old plants, and nothing save the dense shade of their parents, and the close proximity in which they grow to each other, exercises a check upon their engrossing all the adjacent ground. If the fruit of the ivi is compared with the chestnut, that of the tavola (*Terminalia Catappa*, Linn.) may be likened to the almond, both in shape and whiteness, though not in taste, the tavola having none of the flavour imparted by the presence of the essential oil of almonds; hence the name of 'Fijian almonds' given by the white settlers must be received '*cum grano salis.*' The natives are extremely fond of the tavola as a tree, and frequently plant it round their houses and public buildings. The branches, arranged in whorls, somewhat like those of pines, though perhaps not quite so regular, have a horizontal tendency, upon which the natives improve by placing weights upon them. The large obovate leaves are deciduous, and before falling off assume a variety of tints,—brown, red, yellow, and scarlet, such as one is wont to behold in a North American forest before the approach of winter. The flowers are white and small; the wood hard and applicable to a variety of purposes. A close ally of the tavola is the tivi (*Terminalia Moluccana*, Lam.), a timber tree, always growing on the sea-beach, and bearing seeds sometimes eaten by children. Like its congener, it changes the colour of its foliage, but the tints are neither so rich as those of the former, nor is the general habit of the tree so striking. The oleti or papaw-tree (*Carica Papaya*, Linn.) has been introduced in the early part of this century, and has spread with such rapidity that there is hardly a part of the group in which it is not to be found; neither the natives nor the white settlers (who sometimes will persist in calling it mamey-apple, a very different fruit!) seem to care much for it. Only a few seem to be aware that saponaceous properties reside in the leaves, which in the absence of soap may be, and in tropical America are, turned to advantage; that both the leaves and the fruit act in a hitherto unexplained way upon the animal fibre, and make the toughest meat tender, if either boiled with portions of them, or even wrapped up in the leaves; that the fruit is very good eating, either raw or boiled, and that the seeds, distinguished by a mustard-like pungency, are an efficacious vermifuge for children. The guayava (*Psidium Guayava*, Raddi) is another fruit of recent introduction, that has spread rapidly over the country, and is eaten either raw or made into sweetmeats. One of the custard-apples (*Anona squamosa*, Linn.) has not made such progress. I met a few trees on the Somo Somo estate of Captain Wilson and M. Joubert, of Sydney, and a few at Levuka in the garden of a French settler. The loquat (*Eriobotrya Japonica*, Lindl.) is of recent introduction, and seems to promise fair results. A number of healthy-looking plants grow in the garden of Mr. Binner of Levuka, where the grape-vine (*Vitis vinifera*, Linn.) and various other useful plants recently brought to the islands are also to be met with. The different species of *Citrus*, shaddocks, oranges, lemons, and Seville oranges, are known collectively as 'moli,' and distinguished from each other by additional names. The shaddock (*Citrus decumana*, Linn.), or moli kana (i.e., edible moli) is extremely common, and thickly lines the banks of rivers; as, for instance, that of Namosi in Viti Levu, where, during our stay in August, 1860, the stillness of night was frequently broken by the heavy splash of the falling fruits. There is a variety with white, another with pink flesh, both of which are much liked by the natives. The moli kurukuru (*Citrus vulgaris*, Risso) is equally common, but the Fijians do not make use of it as an article of diet. The moli kara or lemon (*Citrus medica*, Risso) was brought from Tahiti about 1823 by Mr. Vanderford, and is almost exclusively confined to the neighbourhood of present or former habitations of white settlers. The moli ni Tahaiti (*Citrus Aurantium*, Linn.) is the common variety of the orange, also derived, as the native name indicates, from the Society Islands, whence it was introduced simultaneously with the lemon by Mr. Vanderford. Like the other species of *Citrus* just mentioned, it succeeds well, and small cargoes of it have occasionally been shipped to New Zealand. The pomegranate (*Punica Granatum*, Linn.) is a recent acquisition. The pine-apple (*Ananassa sativa*, Lindl.), vernacularly termed ' Balawa ni papalagi,' or foreign screw pine, thrives well, especially near the sea. There is, besides the common variety, a proliferous one, having many different sprouts emerging from the top of the fruit. The water-melon (*Citrullus vulgaris*, Schrad.) is as plentiful as the vaqo, or bottle-gourds (*Lagenaria vulgaris*, Ser.), which supply the natives with vessels for their oil. Melons (*Cucumis Melo*, Linn.) have also found their way to the islands, and in common with indigenous cucurbitaceous plants are collectively called 'Timo.' There is besides a number of fruits eaten and even esteemed by the natives, but most insipid to an European palate."*

There are numerous varieties of the cocoa-nut, or *nindina* (*Cocos nucifera*)—the oil of which has long formed a valuable article of export—and which belt the coast-lines of most of the islands by their dense and stately forests. The young flesh is delicious eating, and the ripe nuts make capital puddings, besides being useful for various other domestic purposes. The yam, however, is the staple food of the Fijian, and is to him what corn is to the Englishman, what potatoes are to the Irishman, what the bread-fruit is to the Samoan, and the taro to the islander of Hawaii. Of this valuable esculent the natives distinguish various different kinds, all of which are known by the collective name of '*Uvi*.' Ordinary tubers weigh from five to ten pounds, but often attain much larger sizes; roots weighing even as much as one hundred pounds are occasionally produced.

The flowering of the drala (*Erythrina Indica*), which happens towards the end of July, is a general signal for all hands to busy themselves in the planting of the

* *Vide* Seemann's Official Report.

yam. In February the first yams begin to ripen, but during the months of March and April the principal crops are gathered in. They are eaten baked, boiled, or steamed, and when thus prepared can be consumed by the natives in startling quantities.

"There is another esculent root, the kawai (*Dioscorea aculeata*, Linn.), also planted on artificial hillocks, though not so high as those of the yam. The stem of this creeper is round, and full of prickles, but it is not accommodated with reeds as that of the last-mentioned species. It ripens about June; on the 27th of that month all the leaves were dead. According to the natives it never flowers nor fruits, and I looked in vain over many a field in hopes of being able to disprove the statement. It is propagated by planting the small tubers or roots, which, like the old ones, are oblong, of a brownish colour outside and a pure white within. When cooked the skin peels off like the bark of the birch-tree, as Wilkes expresses it. The root is very farinaceous, and when well cooked looks like a fine mealy potato, though of superior whiteness. The taste recalls to mind that of the aracacha of South America; there is a slight degree of sweetness about it which is very agreeable to the palate. Altogether the kawai may be pronounced one of the finest esculent roots in the world, and I strongly recommend its cultivation in those parts of the tropics still deprived of it."*

The taro, or dalo (*Arum esculentum*), is another most important article of Fijian diet, and is described by Mr. Calvert as his "'staff of life,' surpassing all his other esculents." It is either grown in taro beds, which require much labour and attention, and must be constantly kept irrigated, or in dry soil. It usually yields in from ten to twelve months from the time of planting. The root is oval in shape, of a purple-gray colour, and varies in weight from one to ten pounds. They are uncommonly good when roasted, or otherwise properly cooked, and the young leaves, served up like spinach, is a dish not to be despised.

* *Vide* Seemann's Official Report.

The aborigine prefers eating the cooked taro cold —a fashion which as yet has not found favour with the more unpractised European.

For local purposes, a practically unlimited supply of timber abounds in the large islands, easily obtainable, and excellently adapted for house and ship-building purposes.

Amongst the more valuable varieties should be mentioned the 'Kaurie,' or New Zealand pine, which grows in large forests. The knowledge that the gum which it exudes is a valuable article of trade, does not appear to have as yet extended itself to, or at all events to be appreciated in Fiji. The coral reefs furnish an inexhaustible supply of lime.

Here is a statement of the vegetable productions and resources of the Vitian or Fijian Islands addressed to his grace the Duke of Newcastle by Berthold Seemann, Ph. D., T.L.S.

General Remarks on the Flora of the Vitian or Fijian Islands.

Colonial Produce.

Sugar-cane (*Saccharum officinarum*, Linn.); Coffee (*Coffea Arabica*, Linn.); Tamarind (*Tamarindus Indica*, Linn.); Tobacco (*Nicotiana Tabacum*, Linn.).

Oils and Fats.—Dilo oil (*Calophyllum Inophyllum* Linn.); Candle-nut oil (*Aleurites triloba*, Forst.); Croton-oil plant (*Curcas purgans*, Med.); Castor-oil plant (*Ricinus communis*, Linn.); Cocoa-nut oil (*Cocos nucifera*, Linn.).

Starch.—Roro (*Cycas circinalis*, Linn.); South Sea arrow-root or Yabia (*Tacca*, sp. plur.); Cassava plant or Tapioca (*Manihot Aipi*, Pohl.); Niu soria or Sago (*Coelococcus Vitiensis*, Wendl.).

Spices.—Turmeric or Cago (*Curcuma longa*, Linn.); Ginger or Beta (*Zingiber Zerumbet*, Linn.); Nutmeg (*Myristica castaneafolia*, A. Gray); Bird's-eye pepper (*Capsicum frutescens*, Linn.).

STAPLE FOOD.

Edible Roots.—Yam or Uvi (*Dioscorea alata*, Linn.); Kawai (*Dioscorea aculeata*, Linn.); Tivoli (*Dioscorea nummularia*, Lam.); Kaile *Helmia bulbifera*, Kunth); Taro or Dalo (*Colocasia antiquorum*, var. *esculenta*, Schott); Via mila (*Alocasia Indica*, Schott.); Via Kau or Via Kana (*Cyrtosperma edulis*, Schott); Daiga (*Amorphophallus sp.*); Potato (*Solanum tuberosum*, Linn.); Sweet-potato or Kumara (*Batatas edulis*, Chois.); Masawe or Vasili Toga (*Dracaena, sp.*); Yaka or Wa yaka (*Pachyrhizus angulatus*, Rich).

Kitchen Vegetables.—Ota (*Angiopteris evecta*, Hoffm.); and other ferns. Boro ni galato ni gato (*Solanum oleraceum*, Dun.); Vaulo (*Flagellaria Indica*, Linn.); Taukuru ni vuaka (*Portulaca, sp. plur.*); Bete or Vauvau na Viti (*Hibiscus Manihot*, Linn.); Boro dina (*Solanum anthropophagorum*, Seem.); Tomato (*Lycopersicum esculentum*, Mill.); Cajan or pea-tree (*Cajanus Indicus*, Spr.); *Dolichos, sp.*; Sila ni papalagi or Indian corn (*Zea Mays*, Linn.); Cabbage (*Brassica oleracea*, Linn.); Turnip (*Brassica Rapa*, Linn.); Parsley (*Petroselinum sativum*, Linn.); Shallot (*Allium Ascalonicum*, Linn.)

Edible Fruits.—Banana (*Musa, sp. plur.*); Plantain (*Musa, sp. plur.*); Soaqa (*Musa Troglodytarum*, Linn.); Vudi ni papalagi or foreign banana (*Musa Chinensis*, Sweet); Uto or Bread-fruit (*Artocarpus incisa*, Linn.); Wi or Vi-apple (*Evia dulcis*, Comm.); Dawa *Nephelium pinnatum*, Chamb.); Kavika or Malay apple (*Eugenia Malaccensis*, Linn.); Ivi or Tahitian Chestnut (*Inocarpus edulis*, Forst.); Tavola or Fijian almond (*Terminalia Catappa*, Linn.); Tivi (*Terminalia Moluccana*, Lam.); Oleti or Papaw tree (*Carica Papaya*, Linn.); Guayava (*Psidium Guayava*, Raddi); Custard apple (*Anona squamosa*, Linn.); Loquat (*Eriobotrya Japonica*, Lindl.); Grape Vine (*Vitis vinifera*, Linn.); Shaddock (*Citrus decumana*, Linn.); Orange (*Citrus Aurantium*, Linn.); Seville Orange (*Citrus vulgaris*, Risso); Lemon (*Citrus medica*, Risso); Pomegranate (*Punica Granatum*, Linn.); Balawa ni papalagi or Pine-apple (*Ananassa sativa*, Lindl.); Water-melon (*Citrullus vulgaris*, Schrad.); Melon (*Cucumis Melo*, Linn.); Cucumber (*Cucumis sativa*, Linn.); Pumpkin or Squash (*Cucurbita Pepo*, Linn.); Tarawau (*Dracontomelon sylvestre*, Blume); Kura (*Morinda citrifolia*, Linn.); Balawa (*Pandanus odoratissimus*, Linn.); Wa gadrogadroga or native raspberry (*Rubus tiliaceus*, Smith); Bokoi (*Eugenia Richei*, A. Gray); Sea (*Eugenia, sp.*); Nawanawa (*Cordia subcordata*, Lam.); Vutu kana or Vutu kala (*Barringtonia excelsa*, Bl.); Somisomi or Tomitomi (*Ximenia elliptica*, Forst.)

Vegetables eaten with Human Flesh.

Malawaci (*Trophis anthropophagorum*, Seem.); Tudauo (*Omalanthus pedicellatus*, Benth.); Boro dina (*Solanum anthropophagorum*, Seem.); Kurilagi (*Co'ocasia antiquorum*, Schott, var.).

National Beverages.

Yaqona or Kava (*Piper methysticum*, Forst.); 'Water' of Cocoa-nut (*Cocos nucifera*, Linn.); Matadra or Fijian tea (*Missiesya corymbulosa*, Wedd.).

Vegetable Poisons.

Strychnos colubrina, Linn.; Mavu ni Toga or Upas-tree (*Antiaris Bennetti*, Seem.); Kau karo or Itch wood (*Oncocarpus Vitiensis*, A. Gray; = *Rhus atra*, Forst.); Sinngaga (*Excoecaria Agallocha*, Linn.); Vutu rakaraka (*Barringtonia speciosa*, Linn.); Duwa gaga (*Derris uliginosa*, Bth.); Salato (*Laportea, sp.*); Salato ni coro (*Fleurya spicata*, Gaud. var. *interrupta*, Wedd.); Malawaci (*Trophis anthropophagorum*, Seem.).

Medicinal Plants.

Dilo (*Calophyllum Inophyllum*, Linn.); Kura (*Morinda citrifolia*, Linn.); Danidani (*Panax fruticosum*, Linn.); Wa rusi or Sarsaparilla (*Smilax, sp.*); Vasa or Rewa (*Cerbera lactaria*, Ham.); Laca (*Plectranthus Forsteri*, Benth.); Tamoli (*Adenosma triflora*, Nees); Vulokaka (*Vitex trifoliata*, Linn.); Sinu mataiavi (*Wikstræmia Indica*, C. A. Meyer); Kalakalauaisoni (*Hibiscus diversifolius*, Jacq.); Wakiwaki (*Hibiscus moschatus*, Mœnch); Siti (*Grewia prunifolia*, A. Gray); Wa Vuti (*Pharbitis insularis*, Chois.); Tikula or Tekula (*Dracæna ferrea*, Linn. var.).

Scents and Perfumes.

Yasi or Sandalwood (*Santalum Yasi*, Seem.); Macou or Cassia bark (*Cinnamomum, sp.*); Uci (*Evodia hortensis*, Forst.); Makosoi (*Uvaria odorata*, Lam.); Balawa (*Pandanus odoratissimus*, Linn.); Bua (*Fagræa Berteriana*, A. Gray); Makita (*Parinarium laurinum*, A. Gray); Leba (*Eugenia neurocalyx*, A. Gray).

Materials for Clothing.

Malo or Paper Mulberry (*Broussonetia papyrifera*, Vent.); Baka (*Ficus sp.*); Plantain (*Musa, sp. pl.*); Banana (*Musa, sp. pl.*); Vono

(*Alyxia bracteolosa*, Rich); Wa loa (*Rhizomorpha, sp.*); Vau dina (*Paritium tiliaceum*, Juss.); Vau dra (*Paritium tricuspis*, Cas.); Vau damudamu (*Paritium purpurascens*, Seem.).

MATERIALS FOR MATS AND BASKETS.

Balawa (*Pandanus odoratissimus*, Linn.); Voivoi or Kiekie (*Pandanus caricosus*, Rumph.); Kuta (*Elaeocharis articulatus*, Nees ab Esenb.); Niu or Cocoa-nut (*Cocos nucifera*, Linn.); Vaulo or Tui (*Flagellaria Indica*, Linn.).

FIBRES USED FOR CORDAGE.

Vau dina (*Paritium tiliaceum*, Juss.); Vau dra (*Paritium tricuspe*, Cav.); Vau damudamu (*Paritium purpurascens*, Seem.); Yaka or Wa yaka (*Pachyrhizus angulatus*, Rich); Kulakalanaisoni (*Hibiscus diversifolius*, Jacq.); Sinu mataiavi (*Wikstrœmia Indica*, Mey.); Cocoa-nut (*Cocos nucifera*, Linn.).

COTTON.

Kidney Cotton (*Gossypium Peruvianum*, Cav.); *Gossypium, sp. nov.*; *Gossypium Barbadense*, Linn.; *Gossypium arboreum*, Linn.; Nankin Cotton (*Gossypium religiosum*, Linn.).

TIMBER.

Dakua or Kowrie pine (*Dammara Vitiensis*, Seem.); Kau Solo (*gen. nov. Coniferarum.*); Gagali (*Podocarpus polystachya*, R. Br.); Kuasi (*Podocarpus elata*, R. Br.); Kau tabua (*Podocarpus cupressina*, R. Br.); Leweninini (*Dacrydium elatum*, Wall.); Nokonoko (*Casuarina equisetifolia*, Forst.); Velao (*Casuarina nodiflora*, Forst.); Dilo (*Calophyllum Inophyllum*, Linn.); Damanu (*Calophyllum Burmanni*, Wight); Tivi (*Terminalia Moluccana*, Lam.); Tavola (*Terminalia Catappa*, Linn.); Mulomulo (*Thespesia populnea*, Corr.); Mamakara (*Kleinhovia hospita*, Linn.); Marasa (*Storckiella Vitiensis*, Seem.); Sagali (*Lumnitzera coccinea*, W. et A.); Dogo (*Rhizophora mucronata*, Lam.); Vuga (*Metrosideros collina*, A. Gray); Yasi dravu (*Eugenia rubescens*, A. Gray); Tatakia (*Acacia laurifolia*, Willd.); Qumu (*Acacia Richei*, A. Gray); Vaivai (*Serianthes Vitiensis*, A. Gray); Vesi (*Afzelia bijuga*, A. Gray); Balabala (*Alsophila excelsa*, R. Br.).

PALMS.

Niu dina or Cocoa-nut (*Cocos nucifera*, Linn.); Niu sawa (*Areca ? exorrhiza*, Wendl.); Niu niu (*Ptychosperma filiferum*, Wendl.) Niu soria, sogo, or sago palm (*Calococcus Vitiensis*, Wendl.); Niu;

Masei, Sakiki or Viu (*Pritchardia pacifica*, Seem. et Wendl.); Balaka (*Ptychosperma Seemanni*, Wendl.).

SACRED GROVES AND TREES.

Grove near Bau; Grove at Na vadra tolu, near Mataisuva (Rewa); Baka (*Ficus, sp.*); Vesi (*Afzelia bijuga*, A. Gray); Tarawau (*Dracontomelon sylvestre*, Bl.).

ORNAMENTAL PLANTS.

Danidani (*Panax fruticosum*, Linn.); *Croton pictum*, Hort.; Kala buci damu (*Acalypha virgata*, Forst. ?) Variegated grasses *Panicum, sp.*; Kauti or Shoe-black plant (*Hibiscus Rosa-sinensis*, Linn.); Kaumoce or Mocemoce (*Cassia obtusifolia*, Linn.; et *Cassia occidentalis*, L.); Pride of Barbadoes (*Poinciana pulcherrima*, Linn.); White trumpet flower (*Brugmannsia candida*, Pers.); Balsam (*Impatiens Balsamina*, Linn.); Sweet William (*Quamoclit vulgaris*, Chois.); Scented Acacia (*Acacia Farnesiana*, Willd.); *Clitoria Ternatea*, Linn.; *Gomphrena globosa*, Linn.; *Vinca rosea*, Linn.; *Calendula officinalis*, Linn.; Four o'clock (*Mirabilis Jalapa*, Linn.); Princess' feathers or Driti (*Amarantus cruentus*, Linn.); Driti, damudamu, *Amarantus tricolor*, Linn.); Carnation (*Dianthus Caryophyllus*, Linn.); Roses (*Rosa, sp. pl.*); Dahlia; Honeysuckle (*Lonicera, sp.*)

Flowers for necklaces, &c.—Passion flowers (*Passiflora, sp.*); Bua (*Fagraea Berteriana*, A. Gray); Buabua (*Guettarda speciosa*, Linn.); Vasa or Rewa (*Cerbera lactaria*, Ham.); Sinu dina (*Leucosmia Burnettiana*, Benth.).

MISCELLANEOUS.

Wa lai (*Entada scandens*, Benth.); Sila (*Coix Lacryma*, Linn.); Diridamu, Qiridamu or Leredamu (*Abrus precatorius*, Linn.); Bitu or Bamboo (*Bambusa, sp. pl.*); Qauqawa, or Waukawa (*Piper, sp.*); Moli Kurukuru (*Citrus vulgaris*, Risso); Wa Roturotu (*Vitis saporaria*, Seem.); Vaqo or Bottle-gourd (*Lagenaria vulgaris*, Ser.).

CHAPTER XI.

TRADE.

Though commercial intercourse between Fijians and Europeans dates from a very modern epoch, probably from about 1806, their transactions in the barter trade with the inhabitants of the neighbouring groups must have extended much further back, that is to say, if any importance is to be attached to the indications we possess of such intercourse having taken place, between the Friendly Islanders and the Fijians, prior to Tasman's visit in 1643.

It is certain that the Tongans for upwards of 200 years have traded with Fiji, and even to the present day are they dependent on their less comely, but more intelligent neighbours, for their canoes and potteryware. In exchange for these articles they barter Tonga cloth, whales' teeth, axes, and often muskets, which latterly appear to have been in especial request. In the beginning of this century a considerable trade was done in sandalwood, and Bêche-de-mer, or Trepang, which was much in demand in the Chinese markets. The very limited supply of sandalwood (which was only yielded in a small district of Vanua Levu) soon became exhausted, and when Commodore Wilkes visited the group in 1840, he found considerable difficulty in obtaining even specimens of it for his botanical collection. This void however was soon supplied by tortoise-shell, which had been ascertained, by traders from the East Indies and America, to exist in considerable quantities. Latterly the traffic in these articles has been almost wholly carried on by American vessels from the port of Salem, and at a profit which may be fully estimated from the following extract taken from Wilkes' 'United States Exploring Expedition.'

The returns from five cargoes of Bêche-de-mer, obtained by Captain Eagleston, an American:—

"1st voyage, 617 piculs, cost $1,100, sales $ 8,021
2nd   „   700   „   „ $1,200,   „ $17,500
3rd   „   1,080   „   „ $3,396,   „ $15,120
4th   „   840   „   „ $1,200,   „ $12,600
5th   „   1,200   „   „ $3,500,   „ $27,000

"A further profit also arises from the investment of the proceeds in Canton. This same trader obtained also 4,488 pounds of tortoise-shell at a cost of $5,700, which sold in the United States for $29,050 net."

These sea-slugs still continue to be much sought after for the Chinese markets, and are annually picked in large quantities from the reefs off the north-west coasts of Viti Levu and Vanua Levu. They vary from six to twelve inches in length, but are considerably reduced in bulk by the process of curing, which they must undergo before they are ready for market. In this state they have much the appearance of dirty, undersized, ill-shapen, half-baked bricks, of a "dun-duckety" mud colour, and with a consistency of such a nature, that in England they would probably be considered a bad substitute for solid india-rubber. Chinese epicures, however, are of a different way of thinking, and much value this uninviting delicacy, which they extensively use for making soups. Of the various varieties found, the black slug is held most in esteem.

The first consular return on the trade of Fiji was furnished in 1859, and was principally to the effect that the oil exported during the year amounted to fifty tons only. Prior to that date, however, some idea of the commerce done with the Islands may be arrived at from the following extract from a report by Consul Pritchard on the trade prospects of the group:—

"SYDNEY AND SOUTH SEA ISLANDS.

"To convey any idea of the extent of the trade already carried on between Sydney and the South Sea Islands, I have collected the accompanying returns from the 'Statistics of New South Wales, from 1848 to 1857,' presented to the Colonial Parliament by command of his Excellency the Governor-General.' Though these returns include *all the islands of Polynesia*, the chief seat of trade is Fiji and the groups immediately surrounding it. In examining these returns it should however be remembered that there are many vessels fitted out from Sydney for trading voyages among the islands which are cleared at the customs for other parts, and not for the islands, in order to deceive rival traders. The exports from Sydney to the islands are therefore actually greater than shown by the returns. With regard to the imports, much of the merchandise from Sydney is sold among the islands for cash, which, not appearing on the ships' manifests, is not included in the returns. If business to such an extent as is shown by these returns is carried on under the present system of insecurity, and in the total absence of law, the result of the establishment of British authority in the finest and largest of these groups may readily be predicted.

" IMPORTS.

"*Return of the Value of Imports into the Colony of New South Wales, from the year 1848 to 1857, inclusive, from the South Sea Islands.*

Year.	Amount.	Year.	Amount.
	£		£
1848	2,642	1853	29,702
1849	3,202	1854	47,065
1850	31,827	1855	59,334
1851	6,771	1856	59,029
1852	4,501	1857	41,804

FIJI.

"EXPORTS.

"*Return of the Value of Exports from the Colony of New South Wales, from the year 1848 to 1857, inclusive, to the South Sea Islands.*

Year.	Amount.	Year.	Amount.
	£		£
1848	6,944	1853	10,928
1849	10,160	1854	61,025
1850	17,537	1855	26,373
1851	15,334	1856	53,624
1852	6,271	1857	42,436

"*Return of the Number and Tonnage of Vessels entered inwards in the Colony of New South Wales from the year 1848 to 1857 inclusive, from the South Sea Islands.*

Year.	Number.	Tonnage.	Year.	Number.	Tonnage.
1848	23	2,695	1853	24	3,676
1849	20	2,804	1854	57	9,814
1850	22	2,755	1855	46	6,884
1851	40	5,643	1856	33	4,307
1852	32	3,602	1857	28	3,437

"*Return of the Number and Tonnage of Vessels entered outwards in the Colony of New South Wales to the South Sea Islands.*

Year.	Number.	Tonnage.	Year.	Number.	Tonnage.
1848	31	5,316	1853	45	7,939
1849	25	3,706	1854	60	9,616
1850	27	4,018	1855	64	9,708
1851	32	5,513	1856	43	6,135
1852	27	3,872	1857	37	5,394

"*Present Trade.*

"I will refer for one moment to the present trade of Fiji. From September, 1857, to September, 1858, in American vessels only, the imports amounted to 100,000 dollars (about 20,000*l.*), and the exports to 160,000 dollars (about 32,000*l.*). The imports consist chiefly of dry goods and hardware, muskets and powder, while the exports are cocoa-nut oil, tortoise-shell, and bêche-de-mer. This information I obtained from the American Consul. Had there been anyone to note the imports and exports in British vessels during the same period, I am convinced, from data collected after my arrival there, that the amounts would at least equal the American trade. There is also a large business done by some German merchants in connection with Hamburgh. The quantity of cocoa-nut oil at present made by the natives is not one-fiftieth of what the trees already growing could yield. The quantity exported during the period before quoted, in American vessels only, was nearly 700 tuns. Under the same auspices over 4,000 pounds weight of tortoise-shell were collected (worth some 4,000*l.*), and 2,500 piculs of bêche-de-mer, valued in the American Consul's tables at $38,000 (equal to about 7,500*l.*) These are the local valuations."

In the following year, 1860, an important event was chronicled in the consular records at Levuka—it was the despatch to Manchester of the first 1,000 pounds of cotton from Fiji.*

The yearly 'Trade Returns,' since furnished by Her Britannic Majesty's Consuls, and herewith given without further comment, sufficiently exhibit the gigantic strides made in the development of trade, and the material resources of the country.

"*Report on the Productions and Commerce of the Fiji Islands, for the Half-Year ending June* 30, 1863.

"Although the archives of this Consulate do not afford me any statistical information as regards the commercial progress of these

---

* Amongst the consular reports we cannot find anything relating to trade and commerce in Fiji during the years 1861 and 1862, but the exports of the latter year are noticed in the report for the year 1864.

Islands during past years, yet, from my personal observation, I am enabled to state that the amount of exports has gone on steadily increasing, more particularly in the leading product of the group, namely, cocoa-nut oil.

"Other and newer resources of the country, such as cotton and coffee have also worked into encouraging existence.

"Two Australian companies, composed of merchants of wealth and position, have invested capital largely, and have founded extensive and important establishments in these Islands, one company alone having erected machinery for making oil from the nut at an expense of over 7,000*l*. In these works the nut is ground, sweated, pressed, and caked by steam machinery of the most improved description.

"The other company has it also (I believe) in contemplation to erect steam works for the same purpose.

"*Cocoa-nut Oil.*—The quantity exported for the six months ending 30th June is, as near as I can ascertain, 450 tuns. The price here, delivered at the water's edge, stood pretty steadily at 22*l*. per tun; there is no reason to anticipate any material advance or decline from this figure.

"Owing to a feeling of insecurity which has pervaded the Fijian native population with regard to a threatened invasion by the Tonguese, the healthful progress of this branch of industry has been somewhat checked of late, and until a definite understanding is come to between the chiefs of this country and King George of Tonga that feeling of insecurity will not abate. Notwithstanding this drawback, however, as I have previously stated, the oil-trade continues to reply to the increasing demand.

"*Bêche-de-Mer.*—The quantity epxorted this year may be estimated at 320 piculs. The average price is 48*s*. per picul of 140 pounds; this article shows a decline as regards quantity, caused in the first instance by the natives being in too much fear of the Tonguese to venture where the fish can be gathered; and, secondly from a cessation of the trade, owing to the recent disturbances in China.

"*Tortoise-shell.*—1,700 pounds will cover all that has left these Islands this year; the price has ranged from 10*s*. to 12*s*. per pound, and as 10*s*. has been and is the highest obtainable price in Sydney (the principal trading port with this group), operations in the article have been considerably checked.

"*Pearl-shell.*—1,250 pounds has been exported this year: the price here may be given as 4*d*. per pound.

"*Cotton.*—7½ tons have left this group since January, viz., 2 tons cleared, and 5¼ tons in the seed; the former realized in Sydney 1s. 6d. per pound, and the latter 7d.

* * * * * * * *

"*Shipping.*—Since the 24th of January (the date of my arrival here) fourteen vessels have entered the Port of Levuka, the aggregate tonnage of which amounts to 2,554 tons; these vessels are, with only two exceptions, regular traders from the Port of Sydney.

"*Freights.*—The rate of freight keeps steady at 80s. per ton from and 70s. per ton to Sydney.

"*Inter-Island Traffic.*—The number of small craft plying amongst the group may be estimated at fifteen, having an average tonnage of tweve tons.

"*Weights and Measures.*—English.

"Exports.

	£	s.	d.
"Cocoa-nut oil, 450 tuns at 22l.	9,900	0	0
Bêche-de-mer, 320 piculs (140 lbs.) at 48s.	768	0	0
Tortoise-shell, 1,700 lbs. at 10s.	850	0	0
Pearl-shell, 1,250 lbs. at 4d.	20	16	8
Cotton, clean, 4,480 lbs. at 1s. 6d.	336	0	0
Cotton in seed, 12,320 lbs. at 7d.	65	6	8
Tobacco, 1,100 lbs. at 6d.	27	10	0
"Total	£11,967	13	4

"Imports.

	£	s.	d.
"Wearing apparel and soft goods	4,825	0	0
Groceries	2,000	0	0
Hardware	950	0	0
Spirits	1,500	0	0
"Total	£9,275	0	0

"*Levuka, Fiji, July* 10, 1863."

"Report on the Trade of Fiji for the Year 1864.

"During the last three years these islands have advanced more rapidly in commercial importance than any other group in the South

Pacific. The following table shows the value of this year's exports, as compared with that of the two years preceding:

Articles.		1862.		1863.		1864.	
		Quantity	Value.	Quantity	Value.	Quantity	Value.
			£		£		£
Cocoa-nut oil	tons	450	9,000	500	11,000	600	13,200
Cocoa-nut fibre	tons	..	..	..	..	80	2,150
Cotton	,,	12	360	30	900	100	3,000
Tortoise-shell	lbs.	1,000	800	700	420	500	250
Bêche-de-mer	tons	50	1,920	20	640	25	960
Wool	lbs.	1,500	50	3,750	125	6,100	204
Total	£	..	13,030	..	13,085	..	19,764

"*Cocoa-nut Oil.*—The supply of cocoa-nut oil will continue to increase for some years to come, if the demand for it is as brisk as heretofore. A thousand tuns could be furnished by this group alone. To the natives it can hardly prove a profitable article, as their process of manufacture is tedious and laborious. In proportion as the cultivation of cotton engages their attention will the manufacture of oil be neglected by them.

"There is no reason to believe, however, that this will check the oil trade in the islands; but that, on the contrary, it will be the cause of its increasing in importance, as up to the present time, although machinery has been employed to extract the oil, the result was not as profitable as was generally expected by the introducers, who frequently found their labours brought to a standstill by the refusal of the natives to supply them with nuts in sufficient quantities. They looked with jealousy on an undertaking that threatened to deprive them of the means of purchasing cloth, knives, &c., from the traders; and the oil that each could personally make was the only article of barter they possessed. When they find that the cultivation of cotton requires less labour and gives greater profits, they will have no further objection to supplying the oil-mills with any quantity of nuts they may require.

"*Cocoa-nut Fibre.*—Cocoa-nut fibre can be supplied in any quantity should the demand for it continue. Hitherto it has been uncertain.

"*Cotton.*—The cultivation of cotton is at present occupying the attention of many in these islands, both native and European. Various sorts are grown, but that known as the 'kidney seed' is the most common, although by no means the most profitable, but as hitherto the want of gins has caused the cotton to be exported in the seed, and as it was freely purchased in that state by the traders at the rate of eight cents per pound, the increased weight of the seed in the kidney cotton was believed by the sellers to compensate for any minor disadvantages.

"*Sea Island Cotton.*—Among the more intelligent growers the sea island is held in great favour, and found to flourish luxuriantly. It bears a far larger quantity of pure fibre in proportion to the age of the plant than any other variety. As compared with the kidney cotton, its value in this respect is as five to one.

"The cotton-plant is here a perennial, and after the first outlay for cleaning and planting, the subsequent expense is trifling.

"The island of Kandava, and the banks of the Rewa river, are the positions most in favour with the European planters. The facilities that both these places offer for transport and communication have caused this selection. The Rewa river, so disproportionate to the size of the island in which it rises, is navigable for boats of twenty tons for more than forty miles from its mouth, and for seventy miles of its course rafts and flat-bottomed boats could be used to transport the cotton from the upper country, without meeting with any obstacles in the shape of rocks, cascades, &c.

"The fertility of the soil, the salubrity of the climate, and the supply of cheap labour that can be obtained will enable the cotton grower of Fiji to compete successfully with any other in the markets of Europe, as the quality of the fibre that can be produced here is considered by competent judges to be equal to any that can be supplied by the Southern States of America.

"The high charge for freight to Sydney is the most serious drawback that the island traffic suffers. For cotton, in the badly-pressed state it leaves Fiji, the freight amounts to 9*l.* per ton. Until the quantity of cotton exported shall be sufficiently great to allow of a direct trade with Europe, there is no prospect of any reduction in these charges.

"*Tortoise-shell.*—Tortoise-shell is at present little in demand, and at a reduced rate, which accounts for its falling off as an article of export.

"*Bêche-de-mer.*—Bêche-de-mer has decreased from fifty tons, exported in 1862, to five and twenty in the past year. This is to be attributed in the first place to the low demand for this article, and likewise to the unsettled state of the Macuata coast, where the fish abounds. At present the demand is increasing, and should the people be allowed to fish peaceably, the exports of this article will increase considerably next year. The price is good, 1,200 dollars per picul of 140 lbs.; inferior, 1,000 dollars per picul. The firm of Hemmings Brothers, who may be regarded as the creators of Fijian commerce, is anxious to reestablish the trade in this article, once the principal export, as large orders have been received for it from Manila, and should the fishing districts be restored to order—which the mere presence of a foreign ship-of-war can effect at any time—there is a prospect of this branch of trade being further developed.

"*Sugar.*—The sugar-cane is found throughout these islands, and the natives use it in their food. As yet no attempt has been made to cultivate it on an extended scale.

"*Coffee.*—Coffee has been introduced here from Tonga, and there are at present 20,000 trees in a flourishing condition; two-thirds of these will bear fruit next year. Hitherto the berries have been required for seed, as the trees so produced are found to be healthier and more productive than those imported. In the course of a few years we may hope that coffee will form an important export from the Fiji and Friendly Islands. In the latter group (Tonga) coffee-trees raised from seed will bear fruit the fourth year.

"*Arrowroot and Tapioca.*—Arrowroot and tapioca are found as troublesome weeds throughout the South Sea Islands. The tedious operations necessary to prepare these articles for a European market prevents the traders from exporting them. In all the Pacific islands the supply far exceeds the demand, and the price they fetch in the colonial markets seldom exceeds $2\frac{1}{2}d.$ per pound.

"*Tobacco.*—Tobacco grows well in these islands, but has hitherto received no attention from the European settlers, who are content to use it prepared in the native manner. A quantity sent to Sydney on trial was not approved of, but the general impression here is that the mode of curing it is defective. The leaves are large and fine, and I doubt not that with the assistance of Manilla men experienced in the art, a manufacture of cigars for the colonial market would prove a profitable speculation in these islands.

"*Whaling Trade.*—Throughout the year, but especially in the months of May, June, and July, large numbers of whales are found around the coasts of Fiji and Tonga. Spermaceti and humpbacks especially abound. Before the civil war broke out in the United States, Fiji was a favourite station for American whalers, as many as nine calling here in one season. They generally carried a variety of articles for native trade, and, if they had any spare room, filled up with bêche-de-mer, cocoa-nut oil, pearl-shell, or anything that would find a sale in the markets of Europe.

"*Minerals.*—Up to the present time the only minerals that have been found in Fiji are some specimens of malachite and graphite, both of fine quality. When the interior of the larger islands is better known some additions will probably be made to this number.

* * * * * * * *

"*Exports.*—Quantity and Value of Exports during 1866, compared with the two preceding years:—

Articles.		1864.		1865.		1866.	
		Quantity	Value.	Quantity	Value.	Quantity	Value.
			£		£		£
Cotton	cwts.	650	3,000	2,400	9,200	5,880	19,800
Cocoa-nut oil	tuns	600	13,200	500	11,000	450	9,000
Cocoa-nut fibre	cwts.	1,600	2,150	1,000	1,500	..	..
Bêche-de-mer	piculs	350	960	500	1,200	300	600
Tortoise-shell	lbs.	500	250	750	375	2,000	1,000
Wool	lbs.	6,100	240	10,120	400	8,396	320
Provisions	fruit	..	..	..	500	..	250
Total Value	£	..	19,800	..	24,176	..	30,970

"*Imports.*—The quantity of imports cannot be accurately ascertained on account of the irregular nature of the Island trade. The following is an approximate estimate of their value during 1866:—

	£
"Manchester goods	10,000
Ironmongery, cutlery	7,000
Wine, beer, spirits	3,000
"Carried forward	£20,000

" Brought forward	£20,000
" Ship chandlery	1,500
Groceries, provisions	2,000
Wearing apparel	500
Tobacco	500
Machinery, agricultural implements	700
	£25,200

"*Shipping.*—The following statement of the tonnage and shipping employed in the trade with Fiji during 1866 shows a slight increase on that of the preceding year:—

	1865.	1866.
Entered aggregate tonnage	3,326	4,024
Number of ships employed:		
British	23	27
Foreign (Hamburgh)	3	3

"Report on the Navigation, Trade, and present Condition of the Fiji Islands for the Year 1867.

" There has been a slight decrease in the aggregate tonnage of shipping visiting the ports of Levuka and Rewa during the past year.

" This can be partly accounted for by the withdrawal of one or two ships from the trade, and to their being replaced by vessels of less capacity, but better adapted for insular navigation.

" The trade of this group is at present entirely carried on by British vessels sailing from ports in the adjoining colonies.

" The following statement shows the number of ships and gross tonnage entered compared with last year:—

	1866.	1867.
British ships	27	24
Foreign „	3	1
Gross tonnage	4,024	3,797

"During the past year three small vessels have been built, measuring respectively 30, 40, 45 tons.

"The number of small craft, belonging chiefly to British residents, occupied in island traffic amounts, at the present time, to eighteen, measuring in the aggregate about 350 tons.

"As the cultivation of cotton and other products, now engaging the attention of the settlers, progresses, it will be necessary to build or purchase other small vessels for the purpose of collecting the various articles from outlying districts, where it would not be safe or expedient for a large ship to proceed.

"There is a prospect of an enterprising Sydney firm despatching a ship direct from this port to London or Liverpool during the coming year. Not having a recognised government at Fiji, there are no port charges, dues, on imports of any nature.

"The navigation of the group is open with safety from April until December, during which time the south-east trade-winds prevail. From January until April the winds are variable, frequently blowing with great violence from the north and north-west, attended with heavy rains.

"*Commerce.*

"The following comparative Table will indicate the progress this group has made during the past year:—

Articles.	1865.		1866.		1867.	
	Amount.	Value.	Amount.	Value.	Amount.	Value.
		£		£		£
Cotton . . . cwt.	2,400	9,300	5,880	19,800	7,586	34,004
Cocoa-nut oil . tuns	500	11,000	450	9,000	150	3,260
Bêche-de-mer . piculs	500	1,200	300	600	880	1,600
Wool . . . lbs.	10,120	400	8,396	320	496	134
Tortoise-shell . ,,	750	375	2,000	1,000	1,700	812
Coir . . . . tons	50	500	..	..	..	..
Pigs, fruit, &c. . ,,	..	500	..	250	..	159
		24,175		30,970		39,960

"In addition to the above returns are cash remittances, the amount of which cannot be estimated.

"The imports do not exceed, as far as I can ascertain, the estimate formed for the year 1866.

"However, during the past year many of the immigrants from the adjoining colonies are of a class possessing some means, and have imported a considerable amount of trade and barter on their own account. The total value of imports may approximate—by traders 26,000*l.*, by settlers 3,000*l.*, making a total of 29,000*l.*

"The satisfactory increase in the value of exports is owing to the success attending the cultivation of cotton. It will be observed by reference to the foregoing table that cocoa-nut oil, formerly the principal export, has in quantity fallen short of what might have been expected; this however can be explained.

"*Cotton.*—The expenses in shipping cotton to the Colonies is excessive, and has a depressing effect upon the planter, which can only be removed by direct communication with England. This effected, I venture to predict that Fiji will rapidly rise to a position of commercial importance. At the present time freight upon cotton to Sydney is from $\frac{5}{8}d$. to 1*d.* per pound, which is about the same rate charged for conveying it thence to England.

"The expenses on this article for ginning, packing, freight, and brokerage, now consigned to England viâ Sidney, amounts to $4\frac{1}{2}d$. per pound.

"The varieties of cotton cultivated in Fiji are three in number, viz., Kidney, Egyptian, and Sea Island; for the two former an average of 9*d.* and 10*d.* per pound has been obtained at this port, and for the latter 1*s.* per pound.

"To the present time no definite report has been made by the cotton brokers regarding the quality of Fijian cotton.

"Private advices speak highly of them, and place their value according to variety from 1*s.* 3*d.* to 3*s.* 6*d.* per pound.

"*Oil.*—The value of exports has been greatly reduced by the small amount of oil made compared with former years. Two years ago these islands suffered from a violent hurricane, the effect of which the cocoa-nut trees have not recovered. Intelligent natives state the trees require at least three years to regain their vigour after these severe storms.

"*Bêche-de-mer.*—The bêche-de-mer fisheries have been extended during the past year, particularly upon the Mathuata coast, situated upon the north side of Vanua Levu; the increase of value of export under this head has been large, and provided the exertions used to keep the petty chiefs from quarrelling are successful, will no doubt augment. The fish is sold here at per picul, = 140 lbs., and at an average price of 36s. per picul. The market prices of this article fluctuate very much, being sometimes as high as 40s. per picul, and as low as 24s. during consecutive months. It is shipped to Sydney, and thence to China.

"*Wool*.—This article as an export is becoming less every year; sheep-farming has hitherto resulted in disappointment to its promoters, the flocks being carried off by some disease for which the owners are unable to account. Notwithstanding the want of success hitherto attending this pursuit, large tracts of land have lately been bought by some sheep-farmers from New Zealand, who intend importing their flocks next May.

"The following Return will show the increase of a small flock of ewes, the increasing weight of fleece, and the gross weight of the clip during three years:—

Year.	Number of Sheep.	Station.	Weight of Fleece.	Weight of Clip.
			lbs.	lbs.
1863 . .	440	Nananu . .	2,625	1,150
1864 . .	559	Island . .	2,826	1,580
1865 . .	530	Viti Levu .	3,400	1,800

"*Tortoise-shell.*—Tortoise-shell is plentiful, the amount exported might be increased threefold if the Fijians were at all industrious. The value of this article has fallen greatly. A few years since it was worth 20s. per pound, now it brings in the colonial markets 9s.

"*Pigs, Timber, Fruit, &c.*—Very little has been exported under this head, owing to the influx of settlers during the year past. Everything the native producer could raise in the way of food, either animal or vegetable, has scarcely sufficed to meet their requirements. For the same reason no timber has been exported, the whole being used here for the numerous additions and improvements to the houses of the settlers. Some fruit has been exported, also maize; the latter grows very finely here, and is consumed chiefly by the servants and labourers on the various plantations.

* * * * * * * *

"REPORT ON THE TRADE OF THE FIJI ISLANDS FOR THE YEAR 1868.

"The aggregate tonnage of shipping entered at the Port of Levuka during the year 1868 has nearly doubled that of 1867, the comparative statement being as follows:—

Nationality.	1867.	1868.
British ships . . .	24	48
Foreign „ . . .	1	3
Total Tons . .	3,797	7,101

"Under the head of shipping and navigation little can be added to the report of last year. The fact most worthy of record is the establishment of a Marine Branch of the Pacific Insurance Company of Sydney, which has appointed H. Emberson and Co. its agents in Fiji.

"Owing to the absence of any regular means of checking the annual exports and imports of this group of islands, it has always been a matter of some difficulty to arrive at conclusions approximating the truth.

"With the influx of population, and the wider dispersion of settlers, these difficulties increase, and are further augmented by the fact that small vessels calling at the remoter parts of the group often ship thence to the colonies produce which otherwise would have arrived at Port Levuka.

"The reports upon the commerce of Fiji must necessarily be regarded as approximations only, until the establishment of a civilised form of government will, through its proper departments, ensure the accuracy required to invest these returns with an exact value.

"Up to the close of last year it was customary to include in the Tabulated Return of exports all the cotton on hand baled ready for shipment. Thus the amount exported showed the amount produced during the year; any cotton remaining appeared in the next year's account. This system, had the population of ports of shipment remained numerically the same, might have been continued, but the rapid increase of settlers, and the establishment of numerous trading posts and cotton depôts, render its continuance inexpedient.

"In the following table quantities actually shipped before the date of this report are alone shown :—

Articles.		1867.		1868.	
		Amount.	Value.	Amount.	Value.
			£		£
Cotton	cwts.	7,586	34,004	5,488	30,975
Cocoanut oil . .	tuns.	150	3,260	306	7,202
Bêche-de-mer . .	piculs.	880	1,600	575	1,030
Tortoise-shell . . .	lbs.	1,700	812	1,023	512
Wool	,,	409	134	..	..
Fruit	,,	..	150	..	200
Total . . .		..	39,960	..	39,919

"It is quite impossible to state the value of imports during the present year. Every new settler, storekeeper, and trading-vessel increases the supplies, and of late the port has been so overstocked that prices generally have been reduced to a slight advance on Sydney rates."

* * * * * * * *

" REPORT ON THE TRADE OF THE FIJI ISLANDS FOR THE YEAR 1869.

" *Shipping and Navigation.*

"*Shipping Trade.*—The following table gives the number of ships which have entered the Port of Levuka during 1869, as compared with the three previous years :—

Nationality.	Year.	Vessels.	Tonnage.
British . . .	1866	26	4,024
	1867	24	3,797
	1868	49	5,830
	1869	90	7,450
Foreign . . .	1866	3	290
	1867	1	130
	1868	3	730
	1869	3	450

"It will be seen from the above that the shipping movement continues rapidly increasing, and that, with an exception scarcely worth noticing, it is confined to the British flag.

"The small unregistered vessels built and trading in the group are not included in the foregoing table. They belong to British subjects, and measure in the aggregate about 400 tons.

"*Trade and Commerce.*

"*Imports.*—The imports consist chiefly of such articles as are required in a new settlement, where all but the bare necessaries of life are difficult to obtain, and the system of barter is still in use. Spirits of the worst description form a considerable item. Old muskets, bearing the Government mark of the Tower, are also sold in large numbers to the natives at the rate of 30s. each. Print, navy blue, cutlery, and hardware continue in demand, whilst machinery for purposes connected with cotton is beginning to swell the value of imports.

"The average profit on the sale of wares is about 80 per cent.

"The absence of all local supervision over vessels discharging their cargoes at points other than Ovalau renders it impossible to ascertain the quantities and value of the merchandise landed in the Fiji Islands. It is evident, however, that the trade has more than doubled within the last three years, and that the commercial relations between Fiji and the neighbouring colonies are becoming closer and more marked.

"*Exports.*—The following comparative Table exhibits the relative value of the export trade (of which it will be seen that cotton is the staple article) during the last five years:—

Articles.	1865.		1866.		1867.		1868.		1869.	
	Quantities.	Value.	Quantities.	Value.	Quantities.	Value.	Quantities.	Value.	Quantities.	Value.
		£		£		£		£		£
Cotton . . . cwts.	2,400	9,300	5,880	19,800	7,586	34,004	7,300	30,975	10,500	45,000
Cocoa-nut oil tuns	500	11,000	450	9,000	150	3,260	250	5,000	260	5,500
Bêche-de-mer piculs	500	1,200	300	600	880	1,600	168	300	40	75
Wool . . . lbs.	10,120	400	8,396	320	496	134	4,800	195	2,000	80
Tortoise-shell ,,	750	375	2,000	1,000	1,700	812	17,500	8,000	2,300	1,150
Coir . . . tons	50	500	..	..	..	..	20	197	25	215
Sundries . . .	..	500	..	250	..	159	..	500	..	2,000
Total . .	..	23,275	..	30,970	..	39,969	..	45,167	..	57,020

The above figures show the rapid progress made in the cultivation of cotton, and there is no doubt that if the present quiet of the country remains undisturbed, the ensuing year will be marked by much larger shipments of this staple article.

"REPORT ON THE TRADE AND COMMERCE OF FIJI FOR THE YEAR 1870.

"*Shipping and Navigation.*

"The following Table shows the movement of British shipping in Fiji during 1870 as compared with the four preceding years:

Year.	Vessels Entered.	Tonnage.	Value of Cargoes (Out).
			£
1866 . . .	26	4,024	30,975
1867 . . .	24	3,797	39,969
1868 . . .	49	5,830	45,167
1869 . . .	90	7,450	57,020
1870 . . .	167	15,490	98,735

"From which will be seen that the rapid development of trade already noticed in former reports continues in the same ratio as heretofore.

"With the exception of two American vessels the arrivals and departures were all under the British flag.

"*Imports.*—Approximate total of imports:

Articles.	Value.
	£
Cotton and woollen stuffs	27,000
Iron and steel (wrought)	12,500
Provisions and groceries	10,000
Spirits	4,000
Wine and beer	3,000
Ship chandlery	3,700
Horses and cattle	4,200
Timber and furniture	2,000
Firearms, gunpowder, &c.	1,200
Fancy goods, clocks, watches, &c. . .	1,000
Glassware and crockery	750
Tobacco	600
Medicines, drugs, perfumery . . .	600
Cotton gins and other articles . . .	1,400
Total	71,950

"Most of the articles were of English manufacture, and shipped from Australia and New Zealand.

"The imports from the latter place amounted to about 2,000 tons, and judging by the efforts there made to establish regular communication with the South Sea Islands, it is probable the present year will see the trade doubled, and competing successfully with that of Sydney, which port has hitherto supplied Fiji with the bulk of its requirements.

"*Exports.*—The value of exports in 1870 amounted to 98,735*l.*, of which cotton alone represented upwards of 90,000*l.*, or double that of the preceding year.

"The principal articles exported were—

Articles.	Value.
	£
Cotton, Sea Island	91,500
,, short staple	1,200
Cocoa-nut oil	4,950
Tortoise-shell	260
Cotton seed	250
Kauri gum	100
Other articles	475
Total	98,735

"This augmentation in the trade of Fiji is due to the increasing operations in cotton-planting and the continued immigration from the neighbouring Colonies.

"The passenger lists of the vessels reported at the Consulate show that the white population in these islands received an accession of 1,035 souls during the past twelve months.

"*General Remarks.*

"Now that the natives are beginning to realise the fact that their land once sold is lost to them for ever, they show less eagerness to part with the little that remains to them. They are being gradually but surely driven from the sea-board to the interior, and the patches of ground that served to raise their taro and yam are now the sites of cottages which, if not in all instances more elegant and comfortable than the huts of the aborigines, are at all events the homes of enterprising Englishmen, and the centres of large and flourishing cotton plantations.

"There has been much activity in the importation of Polynesian natives, no less than 2,300 engagements having been registered at the Consulate during the year 1870, involving bonds to the amount of

7,000*l.* to insure the due fulfilment of the agreements and the return of the natives to their homes.

"The Fijians are no longer indifferent to this movement. They regard the irruption as tending to destroy their own supremacy by strengthening the position of the whites, and there is no doubt that in the event of troubles with the aborigines, the settlers would find a valuable auxiliary force in their imported labourers." * * * * *

The following Returns have been made by the authority of the late Fijian 'Administration.'

"*Exports, Port of Levuka, Fiji, from October,* 1872, *to September,* 1873, *inclusive.*

Description.	Quantity.	Value.	Countries whither Exported.
		Dols. c.	
Bêche-de-mer	713 bags	16,260 00	Australian Colonies.
Cotton	3,495 bales.	366,975 00	Great Britain and Australia.
Cotton seed	35½ tons	2,162 50	Australian Colonies.
Copra	258 ,,	12,775 00	,, ,,
Candle-nuts.	16 ,,	450 00	,, ,,
Cocoa-nuts	65,150 .	650 00	,, ,,
Fibre	1,513 bundles	4,079 16	,, ,,
Kava	4 mats	90 00	,, ,,
Gum	1 case	10 00	New Zealand.
Maize	1,014 bushels	652 00	Australian Colonies.
Oil (cocoa-nut)	188 casks, 9 tuns, 39 barrels, 2 drums.	12,540 00	,, ,,
Skins and hides	11 bundles, 4 bales, 140 hides	259 00	,, ,,
Shell, tortoise	14 cases, 4 boxes	6,300 000	Great Britain and Australia,
,, pearl	1 bag	25 00	Australian Colonies.
Pea nuts	46 bags.	92 00	,, ,,
Sandal-wood	162 pieces	107 00	,, ,,
Wool	7 bales	513 00	,, ,,
Fruit	454 bananas, 3,000 oranges	73 00	New Zealand.
		421,013 16 = £84,802	

"*November* 13, 1873. (Signed) D. H. SMART, *Collector of Customs.*"

The imports for the same year amounted to £87,653.

Statement showing the number of Vessels Entered at the Port of Levuka, Fiji, between July, 1872, and December, 1873.

ENTERED.

Flag.	From or To—	July, 1872 to June, 1873.						July, 1873, to December, 1873.					
		Steamers.		Sailing-ships.		Total.		Steamers.		Sailing-ships.		Total.	
		No.	Tons.	No.	Tons.	No.	Tons.	No.	Tons.	No.	Tons.	No.	Tons.
British	Sydney	3	732	18	2,833	21	3,565	3	732	12	1,882	15	2,614
Do.	Auckland	1	175	18	1,436	19	1,611	5	825	5	296	10	1,121
Do.	Labor Cruize			18	727	18	727			15	430	15	430
Do.	Melbourne			1	157	1	157						
Do.	Tonga, Rotumah and Samoa			3	277	3	277			3	320	4	535
Danish	Ditto									1	215	1	208
British	San Francisco									1	208		
Do.	New Caledonia												
Do.	Clarence River												
Fijian	Labor Cruize			10	332	10	332			6	160	6	160
Do.	Auckland												
Do.	Sydney			1	85	1	85						
American	Labor Cruize			2	405	2	405						
Danish	Hamburgh			2	144	2	144						
Fijian	Norfolk Island												
						77	7,303					51	5,151

Entered . . . 128 vessels . . 12,454 tons.

(Signed) D. H. SMART, *Collector of Customs.*

March 16, 1874.

FIJI.

Statement showing the number of Vessels Cleared at the Port of Levuka, Fiji, between July, 1872, and December, 1873.

CLEARED.

Flag.	From or To—	July, 1872, to June, 1873.						July, 1873, to December, 1873.					
		Steamers.		Sailing-ships.		Total.		Steamers.		Sailing-ships.		Total.	
		No.	Tons.	No.	Tons.	No.	Tons.	No.	Tons.	No.	Tons.	No.	Tons.
British	Sydney	2	484	20	3,276	22	3,760	3	732	9	1,759	12	2,491
Do.	Auckland	1	175	17	1,583	18	1,758	5	825	6	385	11	1,210
Do.	Labor Cruize			20	763	20	763			17	577	17	577
Do.	Melbourne			1	86	1	86						
Do.	Tonga, Fotumah, and Samoa			4	148	4	148			3	331	3	331
Danish	Ditto												
British	San Francisco			1	85	1	85			1	30	1	30
Do.	New Caledonia												
Do.	Clarence River									6	149	6	149
Fijian	Labor Cruize			18	526	18	526				194		194
Do.	Auckland			1	72	1	72						
Do.	Sydney			2	144	2	144						
American	Labor Cruize												
Danish	Hamburgh			2	405	2	405			1	215	1	215
Fijian	Norfolk Island			1	72	1	72			1	23	1	23
						90	7,819					53	5,220

Cleared . . 143 vessels . . . 13,039 tons.

(Signed) D. H. SMART, *Collector of Customs.*

March 16, 1874.

Thus have the small beginnings noted in the first pages of this chapter begotten results in the year 1873 of which the contemporaneous history of the group would seem well-nigh to warrant the impossibility.

If then in these few years, under the obstructive influences of barbarism and strife, in the total absence of settled government, limited capital and ill-managed exertion have been productive of such a truly marvellous increase of commercial prosperity, it will not be too much to say (though without desiring in anywise to strain at logical conclusions) that as a British Crown Colony we may expect much from Fiji.

Communication between Fiji and the Australian colonies has hitherto been very uncertain and irregular. Those vessels engaged in the trade usually arrived about the same time, and during the remainder of the year the residents were dependent for the mails on any vessel that might touch there on her way to Samoa, Tahiti, &c. The average passage to Fiji from Sydney is twenty days' sail, but from Fiji to Sydney, on account of the favourable trade-winds, it seldom exceeds twelve days.

This serious drawback is at the present moment to a certain extent removed by the establishment of a line of steamers between San Francisco and Australia, with Fiji for their port of call; France is about to establish another line between Tahiti and New Caledonia, also touching at Fiji; and in the recently projected scheme for the development of trade in Polynesia—by Mr. Vogel, the present distinguished premier of New Zealand—another profitable opening will also, let us hope, be soon found for the commercial and trading industry of our new province. A cursory notice of some of the conditions of this enterprise, which has already received the sanction of the late

Governor of New Zealand, Sir James Ferguson, and which if carried out is likely to exercise no small influence on the future of Fiji, is here briefly deserving of notice.

Mr. Vogel proposes the formation of a powerful trading association, under the style of 'The New Zealand and Polynesian Company,' with a guarantee of five per cent. for forty years on the share capital, subject to the control of a managing director, resident in New Zealand, and to be appointed by the Government. The object of the company is the civilisation and opening up of profitable productions and trade connections with the South Sea Islands, which is proposed to be carried out by the establishment of factories, plantations, &c., on the different islands; a constant steam-communication between the same and New Zealand; and also the establishment of at least one woollen factory, one cotton factory, and one sugar factory in the latter colony, and with the final grand ultimate object of welding the numerous South Sea Islands into *one* great Pacific Dominion, with New Zealand as the 'head-centre.'

These are a few of the most prominent outlines of the dazzling prospectus held out in Mr. Vogel's scheme.

The advantages which would accrue from such an enterprise to New Zealand are undoubted, but in the absence of further information it would be difficult to estimate the precise effect of this proposed gigantic monopoly on the future prosperity of Fiji.

Auckland in New Zealand has hitherto been the natural depôt for the South Sea Island trade. It is one third of the distance nearer to Fiji than Sydney, and the prevailing winds are favourable to the transit both ways. Merchandise from Europe can be landed there at about the same cost as at Sydney, and while the outward voyage is not longer, the return voyage occupies a much shorter time. It is therefore to be hoped that in the interests of both colonies, and independently of all other considerations, a steam communication between New Zealand and Fiji will soon become an accomplished fact.

CHAPTER XII.

LABOUR.

WITH the constant advent of fresh settlers and increased capital, came also a more careful system of cultivation, over a more extended area of land, and therefore the necessity for an increased labour supply.

Prior to 1864, in which year it would appear that importation of foreign labour first commenced, the planters had found it impossible to obtain a *constant* labour supply in Fiji. The Fijian, like his nigger cousin, the 'man and brother,' in his emancipated state, will only work to gratify some pressing desire or immediate want, which having satisfied, he speedily relapses into his normal state of idle dignity. On the whole he may be said to be strongly of the opinion that "fleeting fast old time is only made for slaves." Under these circumstances, then, the settlers found it necessary to turn their attention to the importation of labour. This system, notwithstanding some flagrant abuses of it, which have unfortunately taken place (and which in one instance, yet recently, has unhappily resulted in a tragedy, the details of which are still fresh in the public mind—the murder of Bishop Patteson by the natives, Nukapu, in 1871), has on the whole worked well, and been attended with success. It is estimated that about seven-eighths of the imported labourers are brought from the New Hebrides, which are situated at a distance of 550 miles due west from Fiji. The remainder are imported from the Gilbert Islands, on the equator, and more distant than the Hebrides by 650 miles; but these do not bear such an industrious character as the more docile Hebrideans, and are consequently not held in such esteem. The wages they get vary per agreement from £2 to £6 per annum, and the term of service is from three to five years.

The total number introduced into Fiji, and engaged as labourers up to December, 1870, amounted to 1649.

There can be no doubt that the system appears not only capable of being placed on a perfectly sound and satisfactory footing, but is evidently replete with advantage both to employer and employé. That there exist ample facilities for inquiring into the *bonâ fides* of the contracts made with the immigrants, ascertaining their treatment during the term of their service, and otherwise exercising a supervision over their interests, is abundantly evident from the following extracts :—*

"The agreements between the labourers and planters is made in the first instance by the master of the vessel at the time of embarkation, the master thus acting as agent for the planters who have employed him. This is the usual way; but it is satisfactory to note that in some cases the master's position is quite independent of both the owners of the vessel and the planters, and that his remuneration is in no manner made conditional on his obtaining the required labourers. An instance of this was yesterday under my notice. The schooner *Lapwing*, of 35 tons register, arrived at Port Levuka with forty-eight labourers from Tanna. The master reported himself at the consulate, and with the usual ship's papers deposited a list of the natives, and the agreement under which they had embarked. This agreement I have the honour to enclose.

* Extract of letter from Consul March to the Earl of Clarendon, dated Fiji, December 17th, 1869.

"Every facility was then afforded me in case I wished to visit the ship or examine the men. Under present circumstances I confined my attention to the latter, and from the questions which I put to them through an interpreter, my impression is that the men had come of their own free will. They seemed contented and in excellent health. The master, apparently an intelligent man, assured me that he had no pecuniary interest whatever in the natives, that whether or not he succeeded in engaging them, his remuneration would in either case be the same, and that no force, deception, or other unfair means had been employed in procuring the men. I mention this to show the desire which I see is evinced to deal openly in this trade.

"The means possessed by Her Majesty's consulate for ascertaining how these immigrants are treated are the following:—

"On arrival of the immigrants in Fiji they enter into an agreement with the planters, the nature of which is as follows:—

"The natives on the one side agree to work for so many yam seasons, equivalent to years, and the employers on their part covenant to pay certain wages, to supply them with food, lodging, and medicine, and on the expiration of the term of service, return them home free of expense. These conditions are explained through an interpreter, and there are but few instances in which consular intervention has been needed to have them carried out. I have the honour to inclose an agreement of this kind. For safe custody and official information these documents are deposited with the consul. This appears to have been attended to by all settlers employing imported labour, irrespective of their nationality, upon the grounds that the natives, having been introduced in British vessels, are entitled to the protection of the consul. On one occasion a number of men were, by the above ruling, removed from the employment of an American citizen who had neglected his contract.

"At the expiration of their agreements, the labourers have been usually paid off before the consul, who, in order that he may question them and satisfy himself, has been furnished with a list of the articles given by way of payment.

"The persons importing and employing these labourers are chiefly British subjects. With five exceptions, the whole number of immigrants have been landed from British ships belonging to Sydney, Melbourne, and various ports in New Zealand. The exceptions were small vessels built in Fiji by British subjects, each averaging 25 tons, and not registered. They were employed by their owners in the first stage of the immigration; and their size and the number of the crew was so small that any attempt at kidnapping must have been effectually resented.

"In the course of time an influx of settlers from the adjoining colonies, with the continued exertions of those already established in Fiji, produced an increased demand for labourers, and masters of various colonial vessels, varying from 60 to 140 tons burden, embarked in the trade. It is beyond doubt that some of these men have at times cajoled natives on board, and carried them away against their wishes; but the only case of this sort substantiated was that of the *Daphne*, taken into Sydney by Her Majesty's ship *Rosario*.

"I have the honour to enclose a return of the number of natives imported to Fiji since the commencement of the movement.*

"No guarantee appears to have been given by settlers to the British consul for the due performance of their contracts, because its acceptance might have been construed into official sanction of the traffic. Such supervision as Her Majesty's consulate has exercised in this matter has been with the view to prevent abuses as much as possible. Settlers have offered to deposit pecuniary security, and in some cases the title-deeds of their Fijian and colonial properties with the consul, who has declined accepting them, preferring to depend, until instructed by your Lordship, upon his influence over settlers generally, who show the greater readiness to submit to consular dicta.

"From the archives of this office it is apparent that upon the whole good faith has been kept with the immigrants, so far as the planters are concerned. The worst feature in this trade is the absence of all control over the manner in which the natives are obtained.

"Several natives from the New Hebrides speak Fijian or English sufficiently well to enable the consul to examine immigrants from that group of islands ; but he has no official interpreter to reply upon.

"The manner in which the natives are treated while in Fiji can be ascertained in many ways. First, by the consul paying visits to the plantations during his official journeys through the various islands of his district. Secondly, by information given by missionaries, who consider themselves the guardians of all natives in the country. Thirdly, by natives themselves reporting their grievances to the consul, either personally or through any of their countrymen visiting Levuka. The majority of the settlers I have seen belong to a respectable class of men, and any cruel treatment would in all likelihood acquire notoriety."

* See Appendix.

These regulations,* drawn up by the British Consul, and evidently based on the 'Queensland Polynesian Labourers' Act, 1868,' were productive of much good; but inasmuch as Her Britannic Majesty's Consul had no legal authority to enforce them, submission by the planters was purely voluntary, and liable to be refused at any time.

Hitherto the impotent and *ultra vires* character of these regulations has been the great drawback to the importation of Polynesian labour into Fiji.

In Queensland, where a government exists capable of legally enacting and enforcing laws for the control of this traffic, no such difficulties have arisen, and there the system may be considered a success. Mr. Anthony Trollope, in his recent book, entitled 'Australia and New Zealand,' devotes an interesting and impartial chapter to the question, of which here are some extracts deserving of consideration:—

"Let us," he says, "have no slavery, in God's name. Be careful, guard the approaches. Defend the defenceless. Protect the poor dusky foreigner from the possible rapacity of the sugar-planter. But in doing this, know at any rate what you are doing, and be not led away by a rampant enthusiasm to do evil to all parties. Remember the bear who knocked out his friend's brains with the brick-bat when he strove to save him from the fly. An ill-conducted enthusiasm may not only debar Queensland from the labour which she requires, but debar also these poor savages from their best and nearest civilisation.

* * * * * * * *

"I have seen these islanders working under various masters and at various employments. No doubt their importance to Queensland mainly attaches to the growth and manufacture of sugar; but they are also engaged on wharves about the towns, in meat-preserving establishments, in some instances as shepherds, and occasionally as domestic servants. I have told how I was rowed up the river Mary

* These regulations have been omitted, and the 'Queensland Polynesian Labourers' Act, 1868,'—which now applies to Fiji—is included in the Appendix instead.

by a crew of these islanders. They are always clean, and bright, and pleasant to be seen. They work well, but they know their own position and importance. I never saw one ill-used. I never heard of such ill-usage. The question to my mind is whether they are not fostered too closely, wrapped up too warmly in the lamb's-wool of Government protection. Their dietary is one which an English rural labourer may well envy; as he might also, if he knew it, the general immunity from the crushing cares of toil which these savages enjoy."

This common-sense statement is not only valuable from its perfect disinterestedness, but also from the fact of its coming from one, who may be said to have devoted an observant lifetime to the eradication of abuses. But were any further confirmation of these views necessary, it is readily afforded in the subjoined official correspondence:—

COPY OF A DESPATCH FROM THE MARQUIS OF NORMANBY, GOVERNOR OF QUEENSLAND, TO THE RIGHT HON. THE EARL OF KIMBERLEY.

"(No. 69.) *Government House, Brisbane,*
"1st *September*, 1871.
"(*Received* 6th *November*, 1871.)

"MY LORD,—I have the honour, at the request of my Responsible Advisers, to forward to your Lordship the enclosed copy of an Executive Minute, dated 24th August, 1871, in reference to the Circular Despatches, dated respectively the 20th and 29th April, 1871.

"I have &c.,
"*The Right Hon. Earl Kimberley,* "NORMANBY.
"&c. &c. &c.

"*Extract from the Minutes of Proceedings of the Executive Council of Queensland; at the Government House, Brisbane, on 25th August, 1871.*

"'Present His Excellency the Governor in Council.

"'His Excellency the Governor, at the instance of the honourable the Colonial Secretary, submits, for the consideration of the Council, Circular Despatches, dated 20th and 29th April, 1871, addressed to the Governor of Queensland by the Secretary of State for the Colonies, respecting the costs of prosecutions in the Colonial courts of persons guilty of kidnapping natives from islands in the Pacific.

"'The Council deliberate. They are not aware, from anything that has transpired within their own knowledge, "that acts of violence and barbarity have been from time to time committed by British subjects, in various islands of the Pacific, which are calculated to bring discredit on the British name."

"'So far as Queensland is concerned, due precaution has been taken by the Government to check any abuses that might be supposed to exist amongst the South Sea Islands in connection with the introduction of Polynesian labourers, and the Council have reason to believe that the experiment of appointing paid agents to accompany ships employed in carrying such labourers between the islands and this colony has been attended with great success, and has in a great measure disproved injurious statements as to the manner in which these islanders were formerly procured.

"'In further proof of the readiness of the Queensland Government to prevent the evils arising from kidnapping, or decoying natives by fraud from islands in the Pacific, the Council are prepared to recommend, if necessary, that a sum of money be placed on the estimates to defray the cost of prosecutions of persons guilty of such offences before the Supreme Court, and in the meantime they are prepared to defray expenses in cases brought with their concurrence (previously obtained in each case) before the Supreme Court, provided the case arises in a vessel conveying islanders to a Queensland port.

"'The Council advise that his Excellency the Marquis of Normanby be requested to transmit a copy of this Executive Minute to the Secretary of State for the Colonies.

"'A. V. DRURY,
"'Clerk of the Council.'"

EXTRACT FROM A DESPATCH FROM THE MARQUIS OF NORMANBY TO THE RIGHT HON. THE EARL OF KIMBERLEY, DATED GOVERNMENT HOUSE, BRISBANE, 19th OCTOBER, 1871. (SEPARATE.)

* * * * * * *

"(*Received* 1st *January*, 1872.)
"(*Answered* No. 1, 10th *January*, 1872.)

"During my tour I lost no opportunity of seeing, and as far as possible speaking to the Polynesians on the various plantations I visited. It is, I admit, generally difficult to make them understand, but there is usually one or more on each station who has a better knowledge of English than the rest, and who is able to act to some extent as an interpreter. In no case could I make out that they made any complaints as to their treatment in Queensland, or as to the mode in which they were brought here. Many of them had been sent back to their own islands, after having served their time, and had again enlisted for a second period; while others expressed their intention of returning again as soon as they had visited their homes. They all seemed happy and contented, and are intelligent and quick at learning their work. Their masters uniformly spoke most favourably of their conduct, and assured me that they gave them no trouble whatever. They appear to be well supplied with food, and though I must confess that the amount of clothes that they wear is often somewhat scanty, this is caused, not from any want of clothes, which are supplied by the masters, but in consequence of the disinclination of the men themselves to wear them. With the limited opportunity I have as yet had of personally examining into this question I am of course not in a position to contradict the various statements which have been made upon the subject of Polynesian labour.

"It is quite possible that abuses may have been perpetrated by some of those who import these islanders, and there may have been cases where they have been ill-treated by their masters; as yet however I have failed to detect anything that is objectionable, and it is satisfactory to me to state that neither from the men themselves, from their appearance, nor from the police-magistrates, who are bound to keep a strict watch over the condition of all Polynesian labourers, could I learn anything which would lead me to believe that they were otherwise than well-treated, contented, and happy; and the best proof of this is, I think, the number who have already returned a second time to the colony. At the same time I can assure your Lordship that I shall not fail to keep a vigilant watch over the matter, and should any case of injustice come to my knowledge, I shall use my best endeavour to have the question fully investigated, and the perpetrator brought to justice. The question is one of vital importance, at any rate to the northern portion of this colony, as without a certain amount of black labour of some kind I fear all the bright anticipations of future wealth and prosperity which are entertained must necessarily fall to the ground, and the whole of that large district must remain an uncultivated wilderness, only suitable for cattle stations; as in that climate I believe that it is found quite impossible to grow sugar without the assistance of blacks; white men being unable to bear the heat in the fields. At the same time the employment of blacks, so far from diminishing the demand for white labour, positively creates it;

N

as I found on each plantation a large proportion of white men (probably about one-third) engaged at very remunerative wages."

* * * * * * *

Copy of a Despatch from the Marquis of Normanby to the Right Hon. The Earl of Kimberley.

"(No. 83.) *Government House, Brisbane,*
"*25th October*, 1871.
"(*Received* 1st *January*, 1872.)

"My Lord,—In reply to your Lordship's Despatch, No. 30, of 5th July, 1871, on the subject of the expenses of a commission proposed to be appointed for the purpose of examining into and reporting upon matters in connection with the introduction of Polynesian immigration, I have the honour to transmit, for your Lordship's information, a letter from the Colonial Secretary of Queensland, in which he states that he is unable to recommend that any provision should be made for the same out of the funds of this Colony; but should your Lordship decide upon the appointment of such a commission, the Queensland Government will render every assistance in their power in promoting the object of the inquiry.

"I have, &c.,
"(Signed) Normanby.

"*The Earl of Kimberley*
"*&c. &c. &c.*"

"'*Colonial Secretary's Office, Brisbane,*
"'*23rd October*, 1871.

"'My Lord,—I have the honour to acknowledge the receipt of a copy of a Despatch of the 5th July last, from the Secretary of State for the Colonies, having reference to a letter addressed by me, on the 11th April last, to the Administrator of the Government at that time, on the subject of the abuses alleged by the Aborigines Protection Society to have been practised in connection with the introduction of South Sea Islanders into Queensland.

"'In that letter I ventured to suggest the desirability of a commission being appointed by the Imperial Government for the purpose of examining into and reporting upon the whole subject of Polynesian immigration.

"'In allusion to this suggestion Lord Kimberley remarks, that if this

Government will make provision for the expenses, his Lordship would be willing to appoint such a commission.

"'I must however point out that the suggestion was made not from any misgiving on the part of myself or the Government as to the nature of the engagement or treatment in this Colony of Polynesian labourers, but to set the minds of the English public at rest, and to remove the misapprehension arising out of erroneous information that evidently existed at home on the subject; and as the question appears to be one of Imperial interest, it is reasonable that the expenses of a commission appointed in connection therewith should be borne by the Imperial Government, and I am unable therefore to recommend that any provision should be made for this purpose out of the funds of the Colony; but I may add that in the event of his Lordship deciding upon the appointment of such a commission, this Government will render every assistance in their power in promoting the object of the inquiry.

"'I have, &c.,
"'(Signed)   A. H. PALMER,
"'Colonial Secretary.

"'*His Excellency the Marquis of Normanby,*
"'*&c.   &c.   &c.*'"

COPY OF A DESPATCH FROM THE MARQUIS OF NORMANBY TO THE RIGHT HON. THE EARL OF KIMBERLEY.

"(No. 88.)   *Government House, Brisbane, 24th November,* 1871.
"(*Received* 29*th January,* 1872.)

"MY LORD,—I have the honour to inform your Lordship that a few days since the schooner *Lyttona*, Captain Winship, having arrived with Polynesians, I went on board for the purpose of ascertaining by personal observation the state she was in and the condition of the men. I found the vessel clean, and the men seemed healthy and perfectly contented and happy, nor could I ascertain that they had any complaint to make either as regards their treatment on board or as to the manner in which they had been obtained. During my visit I had a long conversation with Mr. Gadsden, the Government Agent on board, who is an intelligent, and I believe very respectable man. He informed me that they experienced no difficulty in obtaining the men they had on board, as they all came most willingly, and that many of them even swam off to the vessel for the purpose of engaging themselves. He at the same time, however, told me that there could be no doubt that a system of kidnapping was being carried on among the islands, not by Queensland, but by Fiji vessels.

"2. He informed me that they had during their voyage met several vessels from Fiji, and especially mentioned one, a small cutter of 25 tons, called the *Volunteer*, belonging to a man of the name of Blair, which arrived on the 14th September while they were at anchor at Black Beach, in the Island of Tanna. This vessel had sixty men on board, ten being natives of Lifou, and the remainder from the northern islands. Mr. Gadsden told me that from what he had heard he had no doubt that these men had been kidnapped. Blair has a plantation in Tanna, where he intended landing twenty-five men; the remaining thirty-five men were to be taken to Fiji. The ten Lifou men were anxious to escape on board the *Lyttona*, but the *Volunteer* sailed before they were able to do so.

"3. From the conversation I had with Mr. Gadsden, and from other circumstances that have come to my knowledge of late, I think that there can be no doubt that the state of things among the islands is at present very bad, and that gross atrocities are being committed against the natives. At the same time I have every reason for hoping that the vessels belonging to this colony are in no way implicated. Every precaution is taken, not only by placing an agent on board each vessel, but also by strict investigation on her arrival in port, and I feel sure that not only my Government, but the employers of labour themselves, would be most anxious to check any irregularities, and to bring the perpetrators to justice.

"4. Your Lordship will however see that this colony has no power of interfering with the evil practices of the Fiji vessels, and that it is only by Her Majesty's Government stationing cruisers in those seas that these depredations can be put a stop to.

"5. Unless a certain amount of black labour of some description can be procured, I believe that the cultivation of sugar, which now promises to be one of the most important industries in this colony would, at any rate in the north, be impossible. At the same time if it be found that the employment of Polynesians cannot be carried on without giving encouragement to kidnapping and outrages, that labour must be sought for in some other direction. I believe however that the presence of Her Majesty's cruisers in those seas would not only put a stop to the practices which now exist, but that it would secure the Queensland vessels from the imputations under which they now lie, and facilitate the engagements of labour by the legitimate trader.

"6. I would therefore venture to suggest to your Lordship whether the time has not arrived when it would be desirable for Her Majesty's Government to take steps to put a stop to any illegal practices which may be perpetrated, whether by Fiji or Queensland vessels. These islands are so numerous, and the area they cover is so great, that I fear the presence of one man-of-war would be of little use; but as no resistance need be anticipated, the service might very well be performed by gunboats, or even three or four small fast sailing-vessels, the expense of which would be less than that of one man-of-war.

" I have, &c.,
(Signed) " NORMANBY.

" *The Earl of Kimberley,*
" *&c. &c. &c.*"

Views such as these, considered in connection with the Act for the regulation of Polynesian labour in Queensland,* will do much towards the dissipation of those fears indulged in by many of our benevolent fellow-countrymen to whom humanity is so much indebted, and who with a vivid recollection of the uncontrolled abuses of the past, look askance on this immigration of labour. The considerations which attach to this question do not, unfortunately, rest here. It is a fact deserving of notice that natural selection is rapidly fulfilling its part in other islands of the Pacific besides Fiji, and that uncontrollable depopulation is there proceeding at a rate which, though not calculated to cause fears for the present, may, if not attended to, prove a possible source of anxiety in the future.

Without pretending in anywise to suggest a solution of this very important question, it may be safely indicated that the future labour mart of our colonial possessions in the tropics *should be* India. There all positive checks to population, famine excepted, may be said to have ceased; those powerful depopulisers of all barbaric, and

* *Vide* Appendix.

semi-barbaric, and maladministered countries—viz., petty civil wars, criminal abortion, infanticide, the whole train of ordinary diseases and epidemics, and plague, may be said to have disappeared, and under the benign rule of the 'Competition-wallah,' the unbridled passions and procreative tendencies of the mild Hindoo run riot.

Of the many causes that operate in the encouragement of prudential habits among the lower classes of all countries, the most effective next to civil liberty is unquestionably education. Without education, enlightened government can do but little to check population, and direct legislation perhaps less. Uneducated, the people let the present go by unheeded, and do not think of the future, and though security of property and a pure administration of justice—the attendant benefits of enlightened rule—undoubtedly do exercise some influence, it must nevertheless be conceded that without education these benefits can be but very imperfectly understood, and still more lamely taken advantage of. Therefore as in this country it has seemed to many advantageous that the three R's should be varied by a technical education, so I also would urge that in India, and especially amongst the sixty-four swarming millions of Bengal, it may be found useful to supplement those rudimentary elements, by what might be appropriately termed an emigrational education. For the rest, bearing in mind the very limited area in the South Seas with which we are here particularly interested, it will be reasonable and satisfactory to conclude, that on the question of labour we need have no present concern for Fiji.

CHAPTER XIII.

THE WHITE POPULATION.

The first settlers—if indeed they can be thus termed—in these islands were some desperadoes, who appear to have escaped from the penal settlement of New South Wales in the year 1804. They are supposed to have numbered twenty-seven men on their arrival, but encounters with the natives and sanguinary quarrels amongst themselves speedily reduced their ranks, and in 1840 only two remained.

The last survivor was one Paddy Connor, who, after leading a life of the greatest depravity and lawlessness, is stated in his latter days to have been only concerned about the rearing of his pigs and fowls, and the increasing of the number of his children from forty-eight to half-a-hundred. He had a hundred wives! Commodore Wilkes saw him in 1840, when he visited Fiji. He says:—

"One day, while at the Observatory, I was greatly surprised at seeing one whom I took to be a Fiji man enter my tent—a circumstance so inconsistent with the respect to our prescribed limits, of which I have spoken. His colour however struck me as lighter than that of any native I had yet seen. He was a short, wrinkled old man, but appeared to possess great vigour and activity; he had a beard that reached to his middle, and but little hair, of a reddish grey colour, on his head. He gave me no time for inquiry, but at once addressed me in broad Irish, with a rich Milesian brogue. In a few minutes he made me acquainted with his history, which by his own account was as follows:—

"His name was Paddy Connel, but the natives called him Berry; he was born in the County of Clare, in Ireland; had run away from school when he was a little fellow, and after wandering about as a vagabond, was pressed into the army in the first Irish rebellion.

"At the time the French landed in Ireland, the regiment to which he was attached marched at once against the enemy, and soon arrived on the field of battle, where they were brought to the charge. The first thing he knew or heard, the drums struck up a White Boy's tune, and his whole regiment went over and joined the French, with the exception of the officers, who had to fly. They were then marched against the British, and were soon defeated by Lord Cornwallis; it was a hard fight, and Paddy found himself amongst the slain. When he thought the battle was over, and night come on, he crawled off and reached home. He was then taken up and tried for his life, but was acquitted; he was however remanded to prison, and busied himself in effecting the escape of some of his comrades. On this being discovered he was confined in the black-hole, and soon after sent to Cork to be put on board a convict ship, bound to New South Wales. When he arrived there his name was not found on the books of the prisoners, consequently he had been transported by mistake, and was therefore set at liberty. He then worked about for several years and collected a small sum of money, but unfortunately fell into bad company, got drunk, and lost it all. Just about this time Captain Sartori, of the ship *General Wellesley*, arrived at Sydney.

"Having lost a great part of his crew by sickness and desertion, he desired to procure hands for his ship, which was still at Sandalwood Bay, and obtained thirty-five men, one of whom was Paddy Connel. At the time they were ready to depart, a French privateer, *Le Gloriant*, Captain Dubardieu, put into Sydney, when Captain Sartori engaged a passage for himself and his men to the Fijis. On their way they touched at Norfolk Island, where the ship struck, and damaged her keel so much that they were obliged to put into the Bay of Islands for repairs. Paddy asserts that a difficulty had occurred here between Captain Sartori and his men about their provisions, which was amicably settled. The *Gloriant* finally sailed from New Zealand for Tongataboo, where they arrived just after the capture of a vessel, which he supposed to have been the *Port-au-Prince*, as they had obtained many articles from the natives which had evidently belonged to some large vessel. Here they remained some months, and then sailed for Sandalwood Bay, where the men, on account of their former quarrel with Captain Sartori, refused to go on board the *General Wellesley*; some of them shipped on board the *Gloriana*, and others, with Paddy, determined to remain on shore with the natives. He added that Captain Sartori was kind to him, and at parting had given him a pistol, cutlass, and an old good-for-nothing musket; these, with his sea-chest and a few old clothes, were all that he possessed. He had now lived forty years among these savages."

"After hearing his whole story, I told him I did not believe a word of it; to which he answered that the main part of it was true, but he might have made some mistakes, as he had been so much in the habit of lying to the Fijians that he hardly now knew when he told the truth, adding that he had no desire to tell anything but the truth."

Paddy was one of those whites who had early settled at Rewa, and had per force of powder and shot much contributed to the importance of that place.

Charles Savage was to Mbau what Paddy Connel was to Rewa; with this exception, that he appears to have possessed many redeeming qualities of which the other was void, and was acknowledged by his own companions as their representative and leader. He was originally a Swede, and did not belong to the convict gang from New South Wales, but was wrecked in Fiji in the American brig *Eliza*, in 1808. He appears to have been of a more ambitious turn of mind than Paddy, and lost no opportunity of profiting by the favourable circumstances in which he found himself placed. He exacted all the honours paid to the most exalted chiefs, and numbered amongst his many wives women of the highest rank—daughters of the Fijian chiefs. As Savage's male offspring by these women would have been 'vasus,' and would consequently have supplied him with a means of exercising an unlimited despotism of power, the natives deemed it politic that all Savage's children should be still-born, a determination which was rigidly persisted in, notwithstanding that Savage appears to have done everything to avoid it. He finally met his death in 1814 in an affray with the natives off Vanua Levu, who, having cooked and ate him, made sail-needles of his bones, which were distributed among the people in token of the event, and as a remembrance of the victory gained on the occasion.

Of the various peculiar characters who from time to time have sought Fijian hospitality, one of the best known and most remarkable was an individual commonly known by the sobriquet of 'Harry the Jew;' he was thus described by Dr. Macdonald, who saw him when exploring the River Rewa, 1857:—

"When we arrived at the mbure-ni-sa of this town we saw the celebrated Harry, who from his long intercourse with savage life was evidently much embarrassed at seeing white faces once more. He was a small, thin, spare man, apparently in very ill-health, from the absence of those comforts which an Englishman's constitution demands. He wore a long beard, Fiji fashion, and until very lately, when he was enabled to obtain some clothing, he was obliged to adopt the masi, or native cloth."

His story is full of adventure.* Born in London, he was early apprenticed to many trades, but failed in them all, and went to sea instead. In this manner he arrived in the South Pacific, where, finding the climate and the manner of living followed by the islanders not opposed to his peculiar tastes, he speedily came to a conclusion unfavourable to sailoring and kicks and half-pence, and accordingly took an early opportunity of deserting his captain and his ship at Tongataboo. He thence made his way in a canoe to Fiji, where he no sooner landed than he was condemned to be baked; but fortune was not unpropitious, and he succeeded in making good his

* *Vide* Seemann.

escape to Rewa, in which place he remained some time with the other whites. Here however he soon got into trouble, and having artfully succeeded in 'palming off,' on his best friend, for valuable consideration, a watch that never went, except when carried, he decamped from Rewa on the strength and proceeds of the transaction, to which he afterwards owed his nickname. After other innumerable escapades and mishaps, during which he had in turn played with various success the part of lover, rogue, and fool, he awoke one morning to find himself an outcast among the newly-converted natives, for his nickname had been translated into Fiji, and they refused that hospitality which as heathens they would not have denied him, because he " belonged to a people who had killed Christ."

In this dire extremity he determined on proceeding to more heathen parts, and eventually found himself, with many misgivings, in the Namosi valley, then a wild and unexplored region of the interior, and a very stronghold of cannibalism. Here again fortune extended her favours to our friend simple John Humphrey Danford, and smiled on him plenteously, in the shape of many wives and other native luxuries. When last 'interviewed,' he had been raised to the dignity of a 'brother,' and having lost all reckoning in the midst of so many comforts, could not say whether he had been surrounded by them for fifteen or twenty years. The only at all reliable information which could be then extracted from him was his decided objection to Christians, and a preference for Fiji.

On the arrival of the first resident British Consul in Fiji, in 1857, the whites numbered thirty in Levuka, and ruffianism still prevailed. These lived with native women, and traded with the natives for bêche-de-mer, tortoise-shell, cocoa-nut oil, &c., which they disposed of for barter to the American whalers and other vessels which chanced to visit the islands. In course of time some of the more industrious formed partnerships in trade, and in 1842 the leading firm was Messrs. Whippy, Simpson, and Cusick. The head of the firm, David Whippy, an American, had then resided for upwards of twenty-years in Fiji, and had long been considered the principal man among the whites at Levuka; when Commodore Wilkes visited the group in 1840 he became acquainted with him, and testifies to his excellent character and prudence. Not long after this he was appointed to be the United States Vice-Consul at Fiji, a post which he has long creditably filled.

In the year 1844 a calamitous event befell the community of Ovalau. They had been induced in an unlucky moment to befriend one of the resident whites of Rewa, who had taken an active part against Thakombau in the wars which had raged between those states. Thakombau soon came to hear of it, and was so incensed that he determined upon ousting the whites from Ovalau. Tui Levuka had also found their supremacy irksome, and cordially joined with the Chief of Mbau in this oppressive measure, which, notwithstanding many efforts made to avert the disaster, soon resulted in their having to sacrifice years of hard toil and striving, and commence the world afresh. Their new settlement was at Solevu, in Vanua Levu, but it not being either healthy or convenient for trade, they soon longed to be back again at Levuka. After an absence of five years, and many earnest pleadings and propitiatory offerings to those in authority, their wish was at length gratified, and in the year 1849 they once more found themselves in Ovalau, which ever since has continued to be the principal white settlement in Fiji.

In 1860 Colonel Smythe states that the whites had augmented to about two hundred, principally by 'runaways' from vessels visiting the islands, and their social status did not appear to have much improved. Since that date the white population has steadily increased.

In the year 1864 the white population of both sexes in Fiji amounted to about 300; in 1867 the Consul reported:—

"The white population is steadily increasing; the following statement shows the number of residents subject to civilised authority:—

	British.	British Half-castes.	Total British.	American.	American Half-castes.	Total American.	Various Nationalities.
Men . . .	252	85	337	31	23	54	40
Women . .	45	63	108	1	21	22	1
Children . .	114	90	204	6	57	73	2
Totals	411	238	649	38	101	139	43

and again in 1868:

"The population has greatly increased during the present year, consisting chiefly of British settlers and their families from New Zealand.

"The following table represents as nearly as possible the proportion of British residents to those of other nationalities:—

	British.	British Half-castes.	Total British.	American.	American Half-castes.	Total American.	Various Nationalities.
Men . . .	491	95	586	42	26	68	50
Women . .	89	65	154	2	22	24	2
Children . .	174	114	288	8	64	72	4
Totals	754	274	1,028	52	112	164	56

"The total British, American, and other subjects amenable to civilised law and authority is, as shown above, 1,288 souls, against 831 of last year."

At the present time the population is estimated at 2,000, of whom 1,700 are British subjects, 70 American, 100 German, and the remainder of other nationalities.

"The class of people settling in Fiji has much improved of late years. They are chiefly British, and, as a body, bear a good reputation. Many arrive with capital of from 2,000*l*. to 3,000*l*., and it may be said all possess some means. Among the planters are some who have held commissions in the army and navy; and a few of the officers who have served, or are now serving, on the Australian naval station, have invested capital in the country. Others again have held public offices in the Colonies, such as those of mayor, alderman, magistrate, and director of railways. There are also squatters, farmers, professional men, and tradespeople, who, in the absence of any recognised form of government, submit for consular adjudication all the disputes and claims arising among themselves."*

Taking into consideration the great difficulties with which the settlers have had to contend hitherto in the total absence of any settled form of government, they may on the whole be said to be an orderly and respectable community.

This statement gives the present white population in Fiji:—

"Males beyond the municipality of Levuka . 1,066
Women and children 150
Ratepayers within municipality . . . 200
Women and children 150
Fluctuating population . 160

"Total . . . . 1,786"

* Extract from Consular Report, dated Fiji, December 17th, 1869.

CHAPTER XIV.

EMIGRATION.

FIJI being now incorporated as an integral portion of the British Empire, a certain amount of curiosity in connection with that interesting fact must necessarily attach to the question of emigration.

Land is still plentiful, notwithstanding that extensive tracts have already been sold, as well as many of the smaller islands, which were formerly in great request, from the fact of their natural limits rendering fencing unnecessary, and boundary disputes impossible. It has been officially reported that at the present time the lands not yet cleared include a great portion of the very finest soil both on the Rewa River and also on the Island of Taviuni, admirably fitted for sugar-plantations, and also other land well adapted for coffee and spices. The following table gives the approximate area of the lands in Fiji at present held or leased by settlers:—

District.	No. of Plantations	Area of Holding.	Area Cultivated.	Area Uncultivated.
		Acres.	Acres.	Acres.
Tai Levu	24	17,605	727	16,878
Ba	27	66,234	829	65,405
Korotubu	29	75,413	586	74,827
Yasawas	11	16,970	250	16,720
Carried forward	91	176,222	2,392	173,830

Aproximate Area held or leased by Settlers (continued).

District.	No. of Planta- tions.	Area of Holding.	Area Cultivated.	Area Uncultivated.
		Acres.	Acres.	Acres.
Brought forward.	91	176,222	2,392	173,830
Nadi and Vuda. . .	21	41,180	783	40,397
Navua	18	9,000	500	8,500
Nadroga.	38	34,315	502	33,813
Suva	79	15,490	366	15,124
Upper Rewa . . .	58	20,697	1,234	19,463
Lower Rewa . . .	36	9,363	85	9,278
Ovalau	18	22,641	447	22,194
Savu Savu	60	54,105	795	53,310
Mbua	26	71,590	378	71,212
Dreketi	25	42,753	156	42,597
Macuata	31	225,040	438	224,602
Natawa	27	64,822	350	64,472
Taviuni	68	42,804	3,353	39,451
Lau	30	17,129	4,560	12,569
Kandavu	22	7,805	185	7,620
Totals . .	648	854,956	16,524	838,432

All sales were formerly registered at the British and American Consulates, and those conveyances were held good, which were concurred in by the immediate owner as well as by the ruling chief; in this respect, however, material changes may be expected, for doubtless all future sales and purchases of land from the natives will assume the form of Crown grants, and will be consequently negotiable through the authorized government authorities only.

A very few years ago the value of land was merely nominal, and was obtainable even for as small an equivalent as a 1d. per acre, a price which was considered a full consideration, for such lands as the natives had no immediate use. Latterly, since the Fijis have become a field of

immigration, prices have risen considerably, varying from
6d. to 10s. per acre ; while as a fancy price 10l. per acre
has been offered and refused ; and at Levuka frontages
have realised as much as 4l. per foot.*

"The value of land, and the security felt in regard to its tenure, is shown by the fact that for two years past no land in Levuka can be purchased for less than 1l. per foot. The last transaction occurring this year was the sale of the Criterion Hotel, a long, low, weather-board built house, with detached billiard-room, and having a frontage of 265 feet, and depth of 132 feet. These premises, namely, the house and ground only, sold for 2,550l., one-third cash, and bills at six and twelve months."

All payments to the natives have hitherto been made
by barter, the articles most in demand being :—

"*Fabrics.*—Cotton prints, those known as navy blues, are preferred to all other ; blue dungaree, Turkey reds, unbleached calicoes, blankets (blue and red), red serge shirts, red worsted, cotton thread.

"*Hardware.*—Wedge axes, bench axes, hatchets, twelve and fifteen-inch butchers' knives, razors, scissors, muskets, flints, gunpowder, lead, fish-hooks, needles, vermillion, beads (small white Venetian).

"This includes every article that can be profitably sold among the natives of Fiji. It is a great mistake to enter into the trade without a knowledge of the particular caprices of the islanders. The neglect or ignorance of this fact has been the cause of serious losses to many embarking in this traffic."

The three great difficulties with which the Fijian planter
has so far had to contend have been the absence of sufficient
guarantees for the security of life and property, the want of
adequate courts of justice, and the lack of a remunerative
outlet or market for colonial produce : the labour question
has been elsewhere treated on. The two former have of
course, by virtue of the Cession, *ipso facto*, become eliminated, but the latter yet remains to be solved. Hitherto
the exports have nearly all gone to the colonies (mostly to

* *Vide* Report of Consul March, dated 4th March, 1870.

O

Sydney), paying a freightage of at least 70s. per ton, besides additional high charges for storage, wharfage, brokerage, &c. In this manner the settlers have been really at the mercy of Sydney traders, for produce sold on the spot has barely failed to secure remunerative prices, while returns from the home market, owing to the absence of a direct communication with England, have been tardy and small, and only realisable after the lapse of a considerable time from the period of the first outlay. There can be no doubt that now a settled government is established, the prosperity of the colony will be soon sufficient to warrant a direct trade with Europe, by which means it has been estimated that a saving of at least one half the cost of transmission will accrue to the colonial exporter, besides the considerable advantage of obtaining imports at much lower rates.

The want of roads has not yet made itself felt in Fiji, as up to the present time the settlers have been always able to find land of good quality and in a sufficiently large quantity, either on the sea-board or on the banks of the numerous navigable streams.

In the year 1866 it was authoritatively stated that the rivers of Fiji would suffice for all purposes of trade and internal communication for some years to come; but having regard to the period which has elapsed since this view was expressed, and the comparatively small intercourse which then existed with the interior, it is clear that with the increased exigencies which in this respect must be imposed under the new *régime*, some more certain means must be soon applied for developing the resources and material prosperity of the colony.

The value of facts and independent testimony will be a sufficient excuse for the following lengthy extracts from consular reports on agricultural prospects in Fiji:—

"AGRICULTURE.

"The year 1864.

"*Cotton.* — * * * In Fiji at present there are about one hundred acres planted with this staple: the principal difficulty is in getting the native population to gather it in, but the interest has taken root in the country.

"*Coffee.*—A few enterprising men have devoted their attention to the growth of this article; 12,000 trees are under cultivation, half of which are expected to bear next year.

"*Tobacco.*—Half a ton has been exported to Sydney, return not yet known; the plant grows luxuriantly here.

"*Sugar.*—The natives grow their cane for their own consumption, but there is one regular plantation; the quality is good.

"*Arrowroot, Tapioca, &c.*—A little island trade is done in these articles, but they are not cultivated to any extent.

" Stock.

"*Sheep.*— Upwards of 1000 sheep have been safely landed from Australia this year, making in all 3000 now in Fiji; their importation has been a decided success, and, generally, they are doing well. As the sheep are being introduced by men of capital, it is not improbable this interest will largely increase in a few years.

"*Swine.*—About 5,000.

"*Cattle.*—70 head.

"*Horses.*—13.

"The year 1866.

"With increased capital has come a more careful system of cultivation, the introduction of a better description of food for the labourers, and likewise the assistance of steam power in ginning, cleaning, and pressing the cotton. The Brazilian seed has been superseded by the Sea Island and Egyptian, as these are found to produce more rapidly and more profitably.

"*Cotton.*—The Sea Island being a low growing plant, the crop is readily picked by women and children; the trees are planted 1000 to the acre, occupying each a space of six feet six inches square; each tree produces on an average one pound of clean cotton annually. A native labourer can attend to three acres, and his wages, with the cost of his food, &c., amount to about 6*l.* sterling per annum.

"The year 1867.

* * * * * * * *

" Three years back there were only two cotton gins and one windmill in all Fiji, at the present date there are about thirty gins and five steam-engines.

" For short stapled cottons the saw-gins are preferred, and for the longer, knife-gins.

" In the import of agricultural implements there is also an increase, several ploughs, harrows, and cultivators being now in use, for the working of which, and for breeding purposes, seven horses and thirty-five head of cattle have been imported within the last few months.

* * * * * * * *

" The coming year will no doubt see these islands advance steadily in the path of prosperity. Large sums of money have lately been invested by men possessing the means to enter extensively into agricultural pursuits. A company is in the course of formation for the purpose of cultivating sugar in the Island of Taviuni, the soil of which is peculiar in richness and fertility. From the high opinion competent judges entertain of the sugar-cane grown by the natives, no doubt can be entertained of the success that will attend the undertaking."

Since the above was written the cultivation of the sugar-cane has received considerable impetus, and the present prospects of this industry would fully justify the prediction made by an honourable member of the Lower House not many weeks ago—" that an industry had sprung up which was likely to make Fiji the Mauritius of the Southern Hemisphere."

" * * * In cotton more care is now taken in the selection of seed, in the preparation of the ground and cultivating the plant. The best season for planting cotton is from September to January. The months of July and August are generally dry, enabling the planter to uproot and burn off the weeds upon his land, and prepare it for the general rains of September and October. In dry months the sun is likely to strike through the soil and injure the roots of the young plants, thus producing the disease known as ' sore-shin.' This retards the growth, or causes the death of the tree. If heavy rain falls soon after planting, the seed is very liable to rot in the ground, in many cases owing to unpropitious weather. Infinite trouble must be endured before the planter can obtain a stand of cotton. The plant appears about four days after sowing, and under favourable circumstances grows rapidly.

"Sea Island cotton is generally planted in rows six feet by six feet; but some planters are drilling as in America, the rows being five feet, and the plants thirty inches apart. This variety grows much faster and arrives at maturity sooner than any other. I have observed the first blossoms upon a tree one month after planting, at the end of the second month the blossoms fell and the bolls appeared, at the end of the third month the bolls reached maturity, and the cotton was ready for gathering. The most experienced growers estimate each healthy tree will produce annually five pounds' weight of seed cotton. There are three crops of this variety during the year, the first in January or February, the second in May and June, the third in September and October. The vicissitudes of the seasons however will forward or retard the ripening of the crop by a month. In ginning this cotton loses two-thirds of its gross weight, 300 lbs. of seed cotton producing 100 lbs. of fibre.

"Assuming that each tree would produce on an average three pounds of seed cotton, equal to one pound of clean fibre, at one shilling, and that an acre of land planted six feet by six feet carries 1031 trees, the gross value annually per acre would be 51*l*. 11*s*.

"The demand for Sea Island cotton is limited, but the diminished production of this variety in America, owing to the disorganisation of labour, will probably afford the Fijian planter an opportunity of selling all he can produce at a remunerative figure for some time to come.

"The Kidney and Egyptian cotton is of much larger growth, requiring to be planted twelve feet by twelve feet. It is sown in the same months as the Sea Island. The picking season is in July; a second and lighter crop can be gathered in December.

"The average yield of this cotton is 1,200 lbs. per acre, yielding about 350 lbs. of clean fibre, the value of which in Fiji is about 15*l*. sterling. All varieties of cotton in Fiji are perennial.

"The number of bales leaving Fiji during the present season will be 2500, of which ninety will be Sea Island, thus the remainder, say 2400, will consist of the less valuable varieties, Egyptian, &c., &c.

"A bale of cotton weighs 350 lbs., which, as stated above, is the produce of an acre.

"I estimate the land at present in cultivation by Europeans as follows:—

"Acres in cotton = No. of bales of 350 lbs. . .	2,400
„ „ coffee, corn, beans, yams, and vegetables generally = $\frac{1}{3}$	800
Acres cleared and in course of cultivation . .	1,500
Total in cultivation .	4,700
Estimated area of land held by Europeans .	160,000
Uncultivated	155,300

"The cultivation is carried on by labourers obtained from the neighbouring islands. The implements used are large knives and hoes. Like all Polynesian races, these people prefer sitting to standing whilst at any occupation, therefore they cannot be induced to work with hoes or spades, unless they be perfect toys.

"Nevertheless, a fair amount of work is done, provided they are judiciously managed, well fed, and cared for.

"The expenses in cultivating land at Fiji are the same as stated in the Report of 1866."

"THE YEAR 1868.

"The varieties of cotton grown in Fiji, and mode adopted for its cultivation, together with the weights yielded per acre, have been so fully discussed in former years that preceding reports may be referred to for information.

"During the past year most satisfactory reports have been made by Liverpool and London brokers upon Fijian cotton. For 'Sea Island' cotton shipped in February and March last, sales have been effected from 2s. 6d. to 3s. 11d. per lb., the latter price having been received by Dr. I. M. Brower, proprietor of the island 'Wakaya.'

"There can be no doubt as to the capabilities of these islands for the production of either cotton, coffee, sugar, or tobacco. The greatest difficulty experienced by the planter is the want of sufficient and regular labour to cultivate a large area of ground.

"At present labourers are to some extent introduced from neighbouring groups of islands, but whether it will be possible or permissible to continue their introduction in future years appears doubtful, unless some measures can be adopted for the protection of their rights and persons.

"The quantity of land purchased during the year ending this day by settlers from the aboriginal proprietors is estimated to be 75,000 acres. Natives throughout the group are cultivating cotton to some extent, which with the increased area of land cultivated by Europeans it is hoped will swell the value of next year's exports in a proportionate degree.

"Dated Port Levuka, Ovalau, December 31st, 1868."

"THE YEAR 1869.

"The extent of land planted with cotton is estimated at 5000 acres. Previous to 1868 the crops consisted chiefly of Egyptian seed. This has been abandoned to the natives, and about ninety-five per cent. of the present produce is Sea Island cotton.

"The plantations under cultivation vary in size from 80 to 200 acres. On some of these considerable ravages have been made by the grub, against which no remedy appears to have been discovered. The immunity from hurricanes and floods has enabled the planter to make good the losses he sustained in 1868.

"The cultivation of cotton, as pursued in Fiji, is open to much improvement. There seems to be a great deficiency in practical knowledge, especially in the manner of cleaning and preparing the crop. The use of the saw gin injures the cotton, and lessens its value considerably in the English market. More attention should also be given to the description of cotton best suited to the various localities, and to the time of the year for planting it.

"Horse-labour is being gradually itnroduced. It is supposed that the cultivation of the ground by the plough would nearly double the crop of cotton, and reduce the cost of production by one-half.

"Taking into consideration the spontaneous growth of the cotton plant in Fiji, the imperfect system pursued in its cultivation, and the large tracts of land lying waste over the numerous islands composing the group, it is not too much to say that the movement is yet undeveloped, and that the cotton hitherto shipped is but an indication of the success which will follow upon a proper attention to the capabilities of the soil.

"The productions and resources of Fiji have been described in former reports. It is sufficient therefore to state that these islands, rich and fertile, yield an almost endless variety of vegetable treasures. They abound in edible roots, medicinal plants, scents, and perfumes, and timber of various descriptions; whilst sugar, coffee, and tobacco grow most luxuriantly, and if cultivated would, I think, prove as remunerative as cotton.

"*Land.*—It is difficult to ascertain the area of land owned by Europeans, of whom 90 per cent. are British subjects; but 550,000 acres is certainly not an exaggerated computation.

"The value of land is increasing in proportion to the influx of settlers, and what a few years back could be had at two shillings (2s.) an acre, is now charged from seventeen to twenty shillings. At Levuka, the principal white settlement, the average price is eighteen shillings (18s.) per acre, and the Island of Ovalau may be said to have become the property of Englishmen."

"General Remarks.

"*Immigration.*—The prevalent notion that some civilised government will sooner or later accept the protectorate of these islands is giving great impetus to immigration, and every vessel arriving from Australia and New Zealand brings a batch of new settlers, comprising entire families. With a few exceptions they are all British subjects.

"The natives appear indifferent to the gradual absorption of their land by the white man, and as long as the latter abstains from domineering over them in too marked a manner, there is every probability of this period of transition passing over without a collision of the two races. Should troubles unfortunately supervene, the natives will not be found unprepared. It is a fact, however incredible it may appear, that the evils which have arisen in New Zealand from allowing the aboriginal inhabitants to become possessed of fire-arms and ammunition, have not deterred the settlers in Fiji from pursuing the same suicidal policy, and the evil continues, notwithstanding the protests of the more thinking and less selfish portion of the community."

* * * * * * * *

And in their report, dated Levuka, Fiji, 13th of April, 1874, H. M. Commissioners, in describing the resources of the Islands, say—

"A single sample of ten tons of sugar has been produced and sent to Australia, and two mills are now being erected, three more having been ordered. Every planter is making an experiment of a small acreage of cane, of which there are several indigenous varieties of good quality; and men who have experience of cane-growing in Queensland and in the West Indies have pronounced a very favourable opinion on the quality of the Fijian cane. There can be no doubt whatever that sugar will be the chief industry of the best lands of Viti Levu, Taviuni, and Vanua Levu, while cotton remains the staple produce of the Windward and smaller Islands.

"We have been assured by representatives of good houses in Sydney that they are prepared to advance money to planters for the cultivation of sugar, and to erect crushing-mills immediately if it were known that the government would be taken by Her Majesty. On the other hand, we are assured by many planters that, if the country be not annexed, they will not obtain advances, and will be obliged to leave the Islands.

"Your Lordship will observe that though a large area of land (854,956 acres) is owned by whites, yet only 16,524 acres are under cultivation. This cultivation employs a population of 1500 whites, and therefore we may suppose that if the whole were under cultivation, about 25,000 whites would be employed, and that the labourers, all or nearly all of whom must be imported from other parts, would increase to 200,000 or 250,000."

Although a description of the climate has been already given, the following extracts from an official report by Staff-Surgeon A. B. Messer, dated Fiji, April, 1874, will have a special interest for the colonist:—

"The habits of the people exposing them freely to rain, night-dews, and severe physical work, without the usual results of crippled joints and stiff muscles, as seen in the outdoor working classes of England, is only another proof of the wonderful salubrity of Fiji."

Also—

"The first—viz. sunstroke—would be expected to be common, but although most of the Europeans are in the constant habit of working the whole day in the open air, exposed to a tropical sun, wearing only a straw hat and puggery, or occasionally a pith helmet, yet in no part of the group have I heard of any death from this affection occurring among the planters or others. Headache and slighter forms of insolation of course sometimes happen, but this freedom from the severer attacks is attributable to the purity of the air, combined with the breeze which almost constantly blows, night and day, throughout most of the year over these Islands, keeping the air in motion, and producing evaporation from the surface of the body, and consequent decrease of its temperature."

And again, speaking of the supposed lowering effect of the climate, Dr. Messer says—

"The fact that Englishmen fresh from home are able to work all day exposed to the sun without suffering clearly shows that where there is an object to be gained, men with healthy bodies and minds can successfully contend against this effect of the climate of the Fiji Islands."

Hitherto cotton has been the product to which planters have chiefly turned their attention; no doubt owing to the little difficulty experienced in its cultivation, and the certainty of a quick return. A cotton plantation after the first year should pay its own expenses, and with all working expenses deducted should give a clear profit of at *least* ten pounds per acre. Not being liable to any sudden or injurious changes of temperature, the plants will continue to yield for several years, and without requiring any other attention or labour than keeping them free from weeds and creepers, and pruning them periodically. Sugar however promises to be the future staple product of the Fijian lowlands, while the highlands have been reported on by those most competent to judge, as offering admirable facilities for the cultivation of tea and coffee.

A colonist proceeding to Fiji should not possess less than 500*l*.: with this capital he can purchase some hundreds of acres of valuable land, and still have sufficient to carry on the working of a plantation until it pays its own expenses. Among the settlers already established in Fiji there are many of education, character, means, and enterprise, and in a country of which it may be truly said, "that if you tickle her with a hoe she will smile with a harvest," such qualifications are elements of certain success.

Under other circumstances, even in Fiji, the enterprise

of emigration is undoubtedly hazardous and uncertain; the sole purpose which should determine an emigrant to leave mother country—to forego those associations of home, friends, and relations to all of us so dear—is to procure a settlement in another on far easier and more advantageous terms: under conditions other than these it may be safely laid down that emigration becomes a gamble—a chance fraught with the most doubtful consequences.

Therefore I would say to such of my readers as may perchance have felt tempted by something chronicled in these pages to try his fortunes in these fair islands of the South, unless you can satisfactorily resolve your migratory intentions in the manner above indicated, " Don't go to Fiji."

CHAPTER XV.

ETHNOLOGY.

PERHAPS one of the most interesting questions with which we might at the present moment concern ourselves in ethnology is that relating to the inhabitants of Polynesia—including in the area thus termed, Easter Island as its farthest limit in the east, and excluding Australia and New Guinea, its natural boundary in the west.

Are the people inhabiting the numerous islands dispersed over the ocean within these limits a pure or a mixed race? Whence did they come? Have they any connection with the inhabitants of either of the great continents of Asia or America? All these are questions of the greatest interest, but also unfortunately of the greatest difficulty to solve, for from the fact of the people of this vast Pacific archipelago possessing no written language, and consequently no literature, we find ourselves deprived at the outset of elements of analysis which in an investigation of such a nature are of inappreciable importance. Thus circumstanced, the only mode feasible of further pursuing our inquiry must be, by first establishing certain facts, and thence, proceeding from the known to the unknown, endeavour out of many conjectures to build up a probable theory. The most cursory examination of a map of Eastern Asia, Australia, and the Pacific, will not fail to impress the observer with the fact that the innumerable islands, which in some places absolutely crowd that ocean—while not a solitary rock is to be met with during weeks of sail in the remainder of that wilderness of waters—all trend in a certain direction, and are mostly to be found within certain limits; they also rise, in nearly every instance, almost perpendicularly from the sea, affording no bottom within a very short distance from the shore, except at considerable depths. In short, from their position and general character, we cannot avoid coming to the conclusion that when we are sailing among these countless islands of Polynesia, we are passing over a vast submarine continent, whose mountain tops yet appear above the waters, whilst its plains and valleys remain submerged beneath the waves. But was this always the condition of this continent? We are inclined to think not.

Naturally this submergence must have taken place at a very remote age, but the exact period of its occurrence is impossible even to conjecture.

From whence did the inhabitants of these islands proceed? We are inclined to believe from the Asiatic side, and this in direct opposition to the prevailing notion, which is principally based on the knowledge, that the winds and currents of these oceans almost invariably travel from east to west. We are inclined to hold that in ages long gone by, this Polynesian continent was joined on to the Asiatic continent, and peopled by an Asiatic race,—a people then enjoying a far greater civilisation than that found to exist in Tahiti at the time of Cook's first visit to that island,—and that when these people were overtaken by the great flood or submergence (which we suppose to have taken place), a few were enabled to escape; and having taken refuge on those mountain tops which yet remained above the waters, they became the founders of the Polynesian races of the present day. In the absence of certain indicia, such as monuments and other historical remains, we find ourselves at the outset, in endeavouring to establish this hypothesis, confronted by difficulties of no ordinary nature.

We find also among the people of Polynesia every variety of shade, from the clear fair olive—certainly not darker than the complexion of the inhabitants of Southern Europe—found in the central portions, to the sooty-black of the Fijians, in the west. In the Society Islands we find long, smooth, black glossy hair, which might be the envy of any European belle (and in some islands I am assured that even brown wavy hair is not unfrequently seen), while in the western portion of this archipelago we find the crisp, almost woolly hair of the Papuan, which, associated with his dark colour, would almost prompt the superficial observer to pronounce him to be in every respect alike to the negro of West Africa. I was not however exactly correct, when I said we had *no* ancient monuments in Polynesia to guide us in our researches; at Easter Island, which I have assumed as the extreme eastern limit of the supposed continent, there exist some colossal statues, the origin of which is completely unknown, and whose design, execution, and erection are infinitely beyond the capability of the most advanced among the Polynesians of the present day.

Easter Island has an iron-bound coast, and being rocky, barren, destitute of timber, fresh water, cattle, and other supplies, is but rarely visited; but from what I have been able to gather, these statues which are found near the seashore, on the eastern coast, though of rude workmanship, are neither badly executed, nor are the features of the face ill-formed. They appear originally to have been erected on three platforms of stone, designed perhaps for temples, in the construction of which is displayed a very considerable degree of art. Originally there were four statues to each of these temples or platforms, but at present there is only one temple which is thus intact; of the remaining platforms there is also one on which three of the statues are yet standing, whilst on the others they lie prostrate and dismembered.

They are of different heights and sizes, from fifteen to twenty-seven feet and more, and it must have required no small amount of mechanical knowledge and ingenuity to raise them to their stations on the platforms. They evidently date from a period when Easter Island formed a portion of a continent, inhabited by some higher and more civilised race, which never could have existed on so small and desolate a spot as this. Somewhat similar platforms, of even a higher type of structure, are to be found, I am told, in some of the more secluded valleys of the Marquesas, where successive stages of almost Cyclopean stones are erected one over the other, without cement, in a pyramidical form, their planes facing the four cardinal points.

Structures similar to these are also found elsewhere in Polynesia.

Throughout Polynesia remains are not wanting (in the shape of erect stones, to which a form of worship is rendered by decorating them at stated times with pieces of tapa and daubs of paint) of an ancient Phallic worship, which tends, like several other indications, to show that the Polynesians came originally from Asia, where from a very remote period the Hamite descendants of Adam worshipped the universal Creator under a degraded mythical type, which became more degraded still, the farther it receded from the spot where it originally arose; showing how the sublimest conceptions of religion may be debased and polluted, and are constantly so degraded by man in the present day.

Together with remains of Phallic worship we have ample evidence of Ophidian worship, which also must have been introduced among them, or brought with them from the west. The worship of the serpent seems to have prevailed at some one time or other throughuot the old world, and perhaps even in the new; but though so universally distributed, it is not so easy of explanation as the other. We believe that it is by no means so ancient a type of religious sentiment, and while the other is a degraded form of the worship of the true God, the Creator, the Preserver, the Eternal!—the adoration of the serpent is but the worship of the principle of evil—the worship of Moloch in another form; and we believe that it was selected as the symbol of this worship from the fact of the terror which most people entertain for these reptiles. Moloch was sacrificed to in order to avert his malevolence, and the most horrible offerings were made to propitiate his benevolence, if indeed there were any such quality in him.

The serpent was, and is now, worshipped in Africa exactly on the same grounds, and for the same object; and in Polynesia—in Fiji especially—their gods are made to inhabit the bodies of certain snakes, to whom a degree of reverence is shown.

Another argument in favour of these people being of Asiatic descent may be deducted from the prevalent growth of the bread-fruit-tree throughout the archipelago. This tree, the *Artocarpus incisa* of botanists, could not, like the cocoa-nut, have come from the American Continent, floating on the waves of the South Pacific as they do to the present day, even to the eastern shores of Australia, for on the continent of the ' New World ' it is nowhere to be found. It is true that the *Artocarpus incisa* is found only in Polynesia, and nowhere else, but its near, very near relative and congener, the *Artocarpus integrifolia*, is found in South Eastern Asia in abundant quantities. There are no currents which could have brought this fruit from the 'Old World' to Polynesia, and even if such currents did exist, the fruit would soon perish by immersion in sea-water, being thus unlike the cocoa-nut, which will float for months on the ocean without injury. But how are we to account for such different varieties and such opposite characteristics being found in one race ; considerable beauty and gentleness, combined with a comparative degree of civilisation, as in Tahiti, on the one hand, and extreme ugliness and ferocity, associated with barbarism, as met with in the western limits of this region on the other?

I believe that in Tahiti and the neighbouring islands, notably the Marquesas, we have as nearly as possible the pure descendants of that ancient people who once inhabited this now submerged continent of the Pacific.

The emigration by which it was peopled was probably either Hamitic, and subsequent to the dispersion of the sons of Noah in Shinar, or *possibly* may be due to a continued progression eastward of that still more ancient and antediluvian dispersion when — as we are informed in Genesis — Cain fled from the tents of Adam, and plunging eastward into the wilderness, allied himself with the

P

pre-Adamite savages which inhabited those regions, and founded *a nation.*

Whether descended from Ham or Cain, I would claim for the Polynesians an Adamic descent, and thus account for their capability for still greater progress, and their marked superiority over the savages of Australia and New Guinea.

As we proceed westward the characteristic features of the pure Polynesian disappear by degrees, until finally in the Papuan they become extinct. This I attribute to a gradually increasing admixture of the savage uncivilisable pre-Adamite Australian blood. The aboriginal Australian is perhaps the lowest type of any human being, as he is certainly the ugliest and most degraded.

Notwithstanding the existence however of these decidedly objectionable characteristics in the western limits, we find in the hybrid Fijians—for I hold that they are the result of an admixture of the Australian and Polynesian races,—a people even perhaps surpassing in quality the preferable of the two originals from which it has sprung, and possessing a considerable adaptability for improvement. The Tahitian has acquired vigour of mind and of body, while the Australian in a considerable degree has parted with his ugliness and ferocity, and thus in the Fijian we find a quasi-new species—certainly a new variety, which I trust may be rescued both from the debasement of savagedom and the equally great dangers of civilisation.

That judicious hybridisation and selection has constantly produced breeds superior to the original stocks (whether experimented on by nature herself in her regular course, or artificially by man), is a fact well known to naturalists and to physiologists. It would indeed be difficult to find a better illustration of this fact than we possess in our own Anglo-Saxon, or rather Celto-Teutonic race; a race strictly hybrid, combining the energy, courage, and iron will of the Teuton, with the genius and the civilisability of the more elegant and brilliant Celt—in short a people unequalled for greatness and excellence of qualities, the leaders of civilisation in morals and in the arts.

But when did this supposed submergence take place, and when were these remnants of its inhabitants cut off from communication with the ancient world? As I have already said, this must have happened at a very remote age, and inasmuch as up to the present time we are wholly without any data, which in this respect would warrant definite conclusions, it becomes quite impossible to assign even an approximate date to this event.

Thus we must be satisfied to wait until the geology of Eastern Asia, and of that vast archipelago extending from its shores to the South Pacific, is better known and more accurately decyphered, and especially until a more perfect knowledge of the terrestrial shells of those countries, both recent and fossil, is fully obtained.

Negatively, we know that when Sanskrit was the language of a large portion of Southern Asia, the inhabitants of that part of the world were well acquainted with the art of making an intoxicating drink from the sap of the stem of the cocoa-nut palm (*Cocos nucifera*) called 'tade,' of which 'toddy' is the Anglo-Indian corruption. Now *nowhere* throughout Polynesia, though palms of many kinds are abundant, and although the Polynesians are inordinately fond of intoxicating drinks, is there any knowledge of the art of manufacturing toddy. A nation so fond of fermented liquor as to endure drinking 'kava' rather than be deprived of every stimulant, would never have lost the art (had they ever been acquainted with it) of making an intoxicating drink out of the most abundant of all Polynesian plants. This fact I think shows that, at any rate, the ancestors of these Polynesians had separated themselves from their Asiatic relatives, before the art of making toddy had been acquired by them.

We also are aware of the fact that the Sanskrit word *tade* is found in some of the most ancient manuscripts of that very ancient language, which had ceased to be spoken nearly 500 years before Christ, which, coupled with what has been already stated, would tend to show that whatever the exact period of the peopling of this continent may have been, at least 3000 years must have elapsed since they detached themselves from their parent Asiatic stock.

CHAPTER XVI.

FAUNA.

THE only animals on these islands known to the early navigators, appear to have been those which were domesticated among the aborigines, viz., the dog, the pig, the fowl, and the duck; and considering the facilities afforded of late years for a thorough zoological examination of the group, our present knowledge of the fauna of Fiji cannot be said to be much more accurate or complete. The mammals of these islands cannot be termed numerous: they are the rat, five species of bats, of which two have tails, and three have not, and four cetaceous animals, viz., two kinds of porpoise and whale.

Birds, on the contrary, are very well represented, and among the various different species may be enumerated: wild duck, teal, pigeons, bitterns, hawks, owls, and various kinds of paroquets.

The natives distinguish the wild duck—which are found in considerable numbers on all the rivers—into two kinds, viz., the Nga ndamu (red), and Nga loa (black). The former is the rarer species of the two, and difficult to get at, but the latter are not so wild, and afford good sport.

The scarlet plumage of a beautiful species of paroquet (*Coriphilus solitarius*), found in the island of Taviuni, was formerly a source of irresistible attraction to the traders from the Friendly Islands who visited Fiji; and so much were these paroquets coveted, and in request, that it was not an uncommon occurrence for the Tongan to exchange, *pro tempore*, even the charms of his women in order to obtain possession of these pretty birds.

There is also a goodly display of fish, both in species and quantity, many of which are very excellent eating. Of the twenty-three different kinds mentioned by Dr. Macdonald, there are eleven different sorts which are peculiar to the fresh water, amongst which there is a species of shark (nggio), which infests some parts of the River Rewa to an unpleasant extent.

"These sharks are said never to attack the Mbau people when they enter the river; so that it was not unusual in former times to hear those favoured individuals exclaim, '*Mai Kumbuna*,'—I am from Kumbuna,—one of the names of Mbau." There are twelve other species of fish known, which are found in fresh water, but are said also to exist in the sea. Many of these attain considerable sizes; and one, of a species known by the natives as wailangi—caught at Navuso,—is said to have measured as much as five feet in length and three feet in girth.

The salt water sharks, of which nine species are known, are collectively termed 'qio,' and are much dreaded by the natives.

The Fijians have the following curious tradition about a species of sole called 'davilai':—*

"Mr. Davilai used to be the leader of the songs amongst the fishes, and one day, when all his band were together, and he was requested to commence the strain, he obstinately refused to comply. Enraged at such behaviour, the other fishes trod him under foot till he became flat; and hence when a person refuses to sing a song, the proverb is, 'Oh, here is Mr. Davilai.'"

* *Vide* Seemann.

FAUNA. 215

There is a large variety of shells, many of which are peculiar to Fiji. The orange cowry (*Cypræa Aurantium*) is remarkable amongst these, and is much prized for ornamental purposes by the natives. Physæ and cyrenæ abound in the fresh water streams and pools, and occasionally attain a considerable size. There is also a good supply of oysters, of which there are several kinds, and there appears good prospect of the establishment of successful pearl fisheries in the adjacent seas.

Invertebrates.—These, with the exception of numerous varieties of sea-slugs, principally represented by bêche-de-mer, are not different from the invertebrates usually found in these latitudes.

There are three kinds of turtle, including the green turtle and that which yields the shell, and they are collectively termed by the natives 'vonu.'

When caught they are kept, until required for use, in turtle-ponds, enclosed by stone or wooden fences.

Here is an interesting description of the native manner of fishing for them:—

"For this work nets are used made of sinnet, and very inferior ones of *vau*. They should not be less than sixty yards long; the best are two hundred. Sixteen meshes, each seven or eight inches square, give a depth of about ten feet.

"The floats are of light wood, about two feet long, and five feet apart; pebbles or large trochus shells are used to weight the lower edge. This net is carried out on a canoe into deep water, and let down just outside the reef; both ends are next brought close to the reef, or, should there be water enough, a little way upon it; thus there is formed a semicircular fence, which intercepts the turtle on its way back from feeding. If the animal turns from the net, it is frightened back by the fishermen, who shout, strike the water with poles, and stamp furiously on the deck of the canoe, until their prey becomes entangled by its attempts to pass through the net.

"A plan not generally known is practised at night by some of the Malakis. The net is then said to be nursed; that is, several persons, stationed at intervals along the net, which is fully stretched out, hold it gathered up in their arms. The approach of the turtle is then listened for, and the man towards whom it comes drops the net, and the animal is secured. But the most difficult part of the business—that of getting actual possession—yet remains. The men have to dive and seize their captive in an element where he is more at home than they. The struggle is sometimes violent, and the turtle, if large, requires the exertions of four or five men. The first diver aims to secure the extremity of the fore-fin, it being thought that by depressing the fore-part of its body the turtle is made more eager to ascend: to lay hold of the body-joint of the fin would endanger a man's hand. If their captive is very troublesome, the men try to insert a finger and thumb in the sockets of the eyes, so as to insure a firmer hold. Finding resistance vain, the creature moves upward, and his enemies rise too, glad enough to leave the unnatural element which has been the scene of the conflict. On their appearance above water the men on the canoe help to drag the prize on board, where it is turned on its back, its flat buckler preventing its regaining its natural position. Loud blasts on the conch-shell announce the triumph of the fishermen."*

Crustacea.—These are plentiful, and include lobsters, crabs, shrimps, prawns, &c. In some of the smaller islands a large species of land-crab is found, called 'ugavule,' which, being strong and fierce, should be avoided. They climb the most lofty palms in search of cocoa-nuts, from which they succeed in extracting the flesh in a remarkably expeditious manner. But the natives also relish *their* flesh, and not much caring to gratify their desires by disagreeable encounters on *terra firma*, they take a watchful advantage of the nutting tendencies of the 'ugavule,' and encompass his destruction when up a tree; this is accomplished by securely binding a bundle of grass round the stem of the palm, about half way up: the 'ugavule' naturally, true to its family instincts, comes down crab-fashion, and consequently not being in a position to see much for itself, fondly imagines on

* *Vide* Calvert's 'Fiji and the Fijians.'

reaching this obstacle that it is at the bottom of the tree, and letting go its hold, falls forty or fifty feet instead. Thus stunned, a victim to its simple tastes, it becomes an easy capture.

Reptilia.—There are comparatively few species of serpents in Fiji; the 'ngata yasi' is the largest with which we are acquainted, and that never exceeds six feet in length. There is a snake called 'mbolo' of a bluish black colour, which if seen by warriors before battle, or should it cross their path, is considered an evil omen and a presager of misfortune.

The *Coluberidæ* species and some others inhabit trees, from which they may be seen dropping occasionally.

There is a large lizard (the *Chloroscartes fasciatus*) which also inhabits trees; its body is of a beautiful green colour, and is about twenty-four inches in length. There are four other species of this tribe, amongst which is found the chameleon.

The insect tribe is well represented by a long list of butterflies, beetles, fire-flies, centipedes, scorpions, mosquitoes, spiders, cockroaches, flies, fleas, &c. Amongst the irritants, the mosquitoes and the flies are the most annoying; the latter particularly swarm in myriads, and during meal-times are an intolerable nuisance.

Horses were first introduced in the year 1851, and appear to have been the cause of as great excitement and terror to the natives, as those brought to Mexico by Cortes were to the inhabitants of that country in 1518. But even yet greater appears to have been their dismay when they saw these strange animals surmounted by human forms; trees, house-tops, anything seeming to offer protection was eagerly sought as a refuge from these 'papalangi' monsters.

Dr. Brower, the late American Consul, was the first to introduce sheep, which are stated to do well, although it has been supposed that the climate is too warm for them.

Cattle, goats, rabbits, cats, &c., have also been imported by the white settlers, and seem to thrive well. Civilised turkeys, fowls, &c., have also been introduced, the latter being a very decided improvement on the native breeds, which are not only diminutive to a degree, but have become perfectly wild in many of the districts.

The domesticated porker of the aborigines has likewise numerously developed into the fierce Fijian jungle-boar, and it yet remains to be proved what sport he may not furnish to "saddle, spur, and spear."

CHAPTER XVII.

HISTORICAL NOTICE.

FIJI was discovered in the year 1643 by the celebrated Dutch navigator Abel Janson Tasman, who conferred upon it the name of Prince William's Islands. Amongst other early navigators who afterwards verified this now important addition to geography, may be mentioned Captain Cook, Captain Bligh, of the ill-fated ship *Bounty*, and Captain Wilson, of the ship *Duff*, who nearly managed to lose his vessel and his life on the reef of Taviuni.

These latter visits however, unfortunately, in nowise helped to augment our previous information, which was practically nil, and it was not until nearly two centuries after Tasman's discovery, that accurate knowledge concerning the group began to accumulate. Captain Sir Edward Belcher explored Fiji in 1840, and the Islands were also visited about this time by the United States Exploring Expedition commanded by Commodore Wilkes. Otherwise, since our first acquaintance with the archipelago, its history may be summed up as being a series of intertribal strivings for supremacy, interlarded with occasional petty foreign wars, principally with their neighbours the Tongans, and a devotion to agricultural pursuits sufficient for the few exigencies of an existence, more bountifully provided for by nature than perhaps in any other part of the globe. Prior to 1857 Fiji had been included in the consular district of Tahiti, Samoa, Tonga, and Fiji, with the intermediate islands, and had been presided over by the Rev. Mr. Pritchard, who was appointed consul in 1825 by His Majesty George IV. Tahiti was the head-quarters of the consulate until 1845, when, in consequence of misunderstandings with the authorities of the French Government, which had assumed the protectorate of this island, they were removed to Samoa, and there continued until Mr. William T. Pritchard's appointment as Her Britannic Majesty's Resident Consul at Fiji, 28th September, 1857.

At this time the bad repute into which the natives had fallen through their abominable practice of cannibalism, their frequent outrages on the whites, and constant intertribal wars, had deterred visits of traders, and reduced the prospects of the Islands to the lowest ebb. The difficulties with which our Consul had to contend on his arrival were not few. The site of the now flourishing town of Levuka, was at that time a Wesleyan mission station of the most primitive description; the only habitation in the place approaching in resemblance to a house, being a log-hut belonging to and occupied by the missionary in charge. The remainder of the inhabitants, aborigines and whites —of which latter there were about thirty—existed indiscriminately in native huts. As to means of upholding consular authority, there appears to have been absolutely none; and ruffianism, social disturbance, and club-law were the order of the day.

From this period dates the rapid development of the material prosperity and welfare of Fiji.

Notwithstanding the deteriorating influence of wanton barbarism, and the repeated failures (owing to the indifference of the people and the faithlessness of the chiefs) to introduce a civilised form of government, the prospects of industry and commerce have continued to surpass the most sanguine expectations. The greatest difficulty with which settlers had to contend in the establishment of a systematic form of administration, appears to have been due to the absence of a generally acknowledged 'principal' chief.' Colonel Smythe reported in 1860 that there were not less than forty independent tribes, of which however twelve only exercised any influence in the government of the group. The names of these are Mbau, Mbena, Narua, Nadroga, Vudd, Mba, Rakeraki, Vura, Mbua, Mucuata, Cakadrove, and Lakemba. It is true that Thakombau, or Cakobau, the Chief of Mbau, had long arrogated to himself the style of 'Tui Viti,' or King of Fiji, but it is clear that beyond being the most influential chief in the group he had no substantially valid claim to the title. At the date of the report on the cession of Fiji, 1874, by Commodore Goodenough and Mr. Consul Layard, the virtual sovereignty of Thakombau was limited to a total area of less than one half of Viti Levu, or a third of the entire group. Thakombau has, however, without doubt been duly recognised and acknowledged, by different commanders of English, French, and American vessels of war as King of Fiji, and the French and American Governments have treaties with him as such. His dignity and influence have been further augmented, from the generally felt necessity of upholding his authority in the interests of order, and the welfare of the community. Much difference of opinion, however, having prevailed regarding this supremacy, I quote the following extract* as bearing directly on the question :—

"Cakobau calls himself 'Tui Viti,' or King of Fiji, and has a perfect right to it. True, Fiji is divided into a number of petty states, yet all of them acknowledge vassalage to Bau, by paying either a direct tribute to it, or being tributary to the state so circumstanced. It is highly probable however that at one time all Fijians were under one head, and formed perhaps a more compact nation than they do at present. Of course I am aware the title 'Tui Viti' has been revived only lately, owing, it is stated, to a letter which General Miller, formerly Her Britannic Majesty's Consul-General at the Hawaiian or Sandwich Islands, addressed to 'Tui Viti,' and which Cakobau, as the most powerful chief of the leading state, thought it right to open; but the title 'Tui Viti' occurs in many ancient legends current in various groups of Polynesia, and could scarcely have originated with such close neighbours, who would rather be apt to detract than to magnify the power of a foreign nation already far above them in the exercise of various useful arts and manufactures.

"Old traditions further state the Fijians to have been an unwarlike people, until they had established a more intimate and frequent intercourse with the light-coloured races of the eastern groups, when sanguinary intertribal quarrels became almost their normal condition. These traditions would be favourable to the existence of a powerful monarchy in Fiji, such as legendary evidence represents it as being at one time, and also its ultimate extinction and remoulding by the growing power of petty chiefs skilful in new practices of war acquired whilst abroad. The hypothesis advanced derives additional strength from the fact of all Fijians, though scattered over a group of more than two hundred different islands, speaking one language, having a powerfully developed sense of nationality, and feeling as one people. No ancient Roman could have pronounced the words '*Civis Romanus sum*' with greater pride or dignity than a modern Fijian calls himself a '*Kai Viti*,' a Fijian. We can scarcely conceive these sentiments to have taken hold of the popular mind with such force if the people had always been divided into petty states, as at present.

"Away from the capital and Cakobau, some of the Fijian kinglets talk very boastfully of their total independence, and wish you to believe the suzerainty of Bau merely applies to certain inferior chieftains; whilst the social supremacy is seldom disputed, and the court dialect is

* Seemann's 'Mission to Viti.' p. 74. *et seq.*

understood by all the chiefs, even those living in the remotest parts of the group, and it has therefore very properly been adopted by the Wesleyan missionaries in their translation of the Bible."

But in order clearly to understand Thakombau's claim to the title of Tui Viti, a short *résumé* of Fijian history will be necessary.

The first authentic knowledge which we possess on this subject dates from the commencement of this century, when of the seven principal districts composing the group, i.e., Mbau, Rewa, Mucuata, Somo Somo, Naitasiri, Mbua, and Verata, the latter was in the ascendant. This town, which was then considered the principal city of the Fijis, was situated on the mainland, Viti Levu, about eight miles from Mbau, which was one of its tributaries, as was also Rewa. But in the year 1808 the brig *Eliza*, wrecked off the reef of Nairai, introduced powder and shot, a new element in Fijian schemes of supremacy and government, which hitherto had not entered into their calculations. The crew of the vessel who were saved joined the Mbau people, then ruled over by Na-Ulivou, and, under the leadership of Charley Savage, made such good use of their time and their muskets, that, in conjunction with the people of Mbau, they soon succeeded in completely subduing Verata and its dependencies. From this time the supremacy of Mbau was assured.

Na-Ulivou, who succeeded his father Mbanuvi, was an energetic and brave chief, and was distinguished by the title of Na-vu-ni-valu ('The Root of War'), which has since been continued to his successors.

In the early part of his reign a conspiracy was entered into against him, but it was discovered, and the rebels were expelled from Mbau. They again rallied, and collected a large fleet of canoes, and made other preparations for a hostile expedition against the capital, but they were again pursued, and being met at sea, they were completely destroyed. Na-Ulivou's authority was now firmly established, and until his decease, in 1829, he reigned in peace.

He was succeeded by his brother Tanoa, whose turbulent reign of twenty-three years was marked by constant disturbance and rebellion.

Within four years indeed from his accession to his title and dignities, through conspiracy and intrigue, he found himself almost divested of regal power, and was obliged to flee from his capital for his life. After his expulsion by the rebels his brother Komaino-Karina Kula was installed as king, and reigned for five years. During this period Tanoa, who had sought refuge at Somo Somo, the capital of Tavinni, carried on with the aid of the chief of that place, and other faithful allies, an intermittent warfare with the rebels. Latterly he established himself at Rewa, where he was so successful in his intrigues, that within a short time he had gained over all the enemies' allies, and even many of the chiefs of Mbau. In 1837 affairs were considered sufficiently ripe for action, and accordingly a preconcerted attack was made on Mbau with such success that Tanoa found himself re-established on his throne after an exile of five years.

"He who is good is happy!"

We are told that poor Tanoa was not good, and therefore we must not be surprised to learn that the remaining years of his reign were not happy, but embittered by domestic trouble and regal anxieties. He died on the 8th December, 1852, at a good old age, a heathen and a cannibal.

His son Thakombau, who had been virtually supreme for some years, now succeeded to the title of Vunivalu, and was formally acknowledged 'Tui Viti,' by the other chiefs.

Thakombau's inheritance was by no means a sinecure, and very speedily did he discover that "uneasy lies the head that wears a crown." In the competition for imperial supremacy, he soon found a dangerous rival in Maafu the Tongan, so much so that were it not for the judicious influence exercised from time to time by the resident Consuls, backed up by ships of war, there can be no doubt that ere now he would have been paramount in Fiji. This Chief first made his appearance in these islands in 1847, having been exiled from his native country, a step which his royal relative, King George of Tonga, with a keen appreciation of Maafu's dangerously ambitious proclivities, wisely concluded to be most necessary.

Prior to this date the history of the relations of the Tongans with the Fijians had been of an essentially pacific character. Inhabiting three groups of islands some 250 miles south-east of Fiji, they are justly styled the flower of the Polynesian race. Tall athletic men, of a light-brown complexion and intelligent features, they far surpass the Fijians in their good looks. From the beginning of this century their intercourse with the Fijians has gradually become more frequent. When visited by Wilkes in 1840, they then looked up to the Fiji islanders as being more polished, a fact which was not only noticed from their conversation, but also evidenced in the deference they paid to the opinions of such of their countrymen as had visited the group, as well as by their adoption of Fijian manners and customs.

When Cook visited Tonga, little was known of the

Fijis; but thirty years afterwards Mariner tells us that intercourse had become much more frequent. Tongan intercourse with Fiji, however, dates far back, and no doubt originated by their canoes being drifted by the prevailing easterly winds on the shores of Kandavu, Lakemba, and the other islands of the Windward group. The story of it is told in the legend of the Princess Vilivilitabua, and in the Vasu Ki Lagi, and is also mentioned in other Fijian legends. From the Fijians they first obtained their canoes, and learned the art of sailing and navigating them; and lacking suitable timber in their own islands for building purposes, they were also on this account obliged to resort to Fiji. Many of the traders thus visiting Fiji established themselves permanently in Lakemba and in other of the eastern islands, settlements which in course of time developed into small colonies. Being of ready device and daring, their assistance was eagerly sought after by contending Fijian chiefs, who rewarded their services by grants of land, supplies, and other various privileges.

Maafu did not fail to avail himself of this state of affairs, and to such good purpose that the native chiefs soon learned that a victory gained with the aid of the Tongan chief and his followers, was indeed little preferable to defeat, for they invariably found themselves heavily indebted to their mercenary ally, and completely at his mercy.

The first exploit of this unscrupulously ambitious savage took place at Lomo Lomo, where, having espoused the cause of the weaker of two Fijian chiefs then at war, the other side was speedily defeated, and Maafu made himself master of the whole of the grouplet of Vanua Balavu. Having thus obtained a solid footing, his rise was now rapid, and one or two successes of a similar nature soon induced him to form the conception of subduing the entire group. With this object he set about building a schooner of thirty-five tons, and making other preparations for immediate hostilities, when the unexpected arrival of Her Britannic Majesty's Consul, in the month of September, 1858, who had come to take up his permanent residence in the group, temporarily checked his schemes of conquest and violence.

Within a short time, however, fortune again favoured his crafty designs, and the outbreak of hostilities between Ritova and Mbete, rival chiefs of the Macuata coast of Vanua Levu, gave him an opportunity of insinuating his dangerous interference. Friendly messages were despatched to Mbete and his ally, Tui Mbua, a chief of importance on the south-western coast of Vanua Levu, which resulted in a triple alliance; a combination which could not but excite grave apprehensions at Mbau. Operations now commenced, and not only was the entire province of Macuata conquered, but Solevu, a little district on the southern side of Vanua Levu, which acknowledged a sort of vassalage to Mbau, was likewise invaded, and succumbed to the combined forces.

The victorious chief next proceeded to dispose of the conquered territories, the distribution being conducted in such a manner, that the claims of Mbau on Solevu were altogether ignored; those chiefs only being favoured who unconditionally agreed to pay a stipulated tribute to Maafu. Maafu's vaulting ambition, thus whetted by victory, did not rest, and another successful expedition was despatched against the island of Mbega (also subject to Mbau), the inhabitants of which surrendered at discretion. At this critical moment for Mbau, while its supremacy was shattered and undermined and its very existence trembled in the balance, it unexpectedly found a "ray of hope, a crumb of comfort," in the opportune return of Mr. Pritchard from England, whither he had gone with the proffered cession of the Islands by Thakombau.

Soon after his arrival a meeting of the chiefs took place, and they availed themselves of the opportunity to request Her Britannic Majesty's Consul's assistance in checking Maafu's designs.*

Mr. Pritchard accordingly, backed up by Her Majesty's ship *Elk*, obtained Maafu's signature to the following instrument in the presence of all the chiefs assembled:

"Know all men by these presents:

"1. That I, Maafu, a chief of and in Tonga, do hereby expressly and definitely state that I am in Fiji by the orders of George, King of Tonga, as his representative, and that I am here solely to manage and control the Tonguese in Fiji. 2. That I have, hold, exercise, and enjoy no position nor claim as a chief of or in Fiji. 3. That all Tonguese claims in or to Fiji are hereby renounced. 4. That no Tonguese in Fiji shall exact or demand anything whatever from any Fijian under any circumstances whatever, but they shall enjoy the privileges and rights accorded to other nations in Fiji. 5. That the lands and districts of Fiji which have been offered by various chiefs to me are not accepted and are not mine, nor are they Tonguese but wholly and solely Fijian. 6. That the cession of Fiji to England is hereby acknowledged.

"In witness whereof I have hereto set my name, this fourteenth day of December, 1859.

"MAAFU."

"We hereby certify that the foregoing Chief Maafu signed the above document in our presence this 14th day of December, 1859.

"(Signed)   WILLIAM T. PRITCHARD, Consul.
"(Signed)   H. CAMPION,
            "Commander R.N., H.M.S. *Elk*.

* Founded on the supposition that Fiji was already ceded to Her Majesty the Queen, and that the foreigner, Maafu, was in fact intriguing against her authority.

"We hereby certify that we translated the foregoing document to Maafu, a chief of Tonga, who has signed, and that he thoroughly understands its meaning.

"(Signed) W. COLLIS,
   "Wesleyan Training Master.
"(Signed) E. P. MARTIN,
   "Wesleyan Mission Printer."

His ambition thus curbed but not stamped out, Maafu exhibited little inclination to return to Tonga; but enjoined discretion on the part of his followers, long accustomed to regard Fiji in no other light save a fair field for lust and plunder; for he had still a hope that England would reject the cession, and that the triumph of Tongan arms might yet become a reality. Ritova, since his loss of power, had repeatedly represented his case to Her Britannic Majesty's Consul, showing how treacherously he had been deprived of his estates by Maafu, and requesting permission, with the aid of friendly chiefs, to reinstate himself by force of arms.

The proposition could not of course be acceded to, but the Consul having carefully gone into Ritova's case, in consultation with the chiefs of Vanua Levu (having due regard to the circumstance, that by removing all right of interference in Fijian affairs, Maafu's distribution of territory had become, *ipso facto*, null and void), he justly came to the conclusion that Mbete, the usurper, should be deposed, and that Ritova should be restored to his lawful rights and patrimonial inheritance.

This Mr. Pritchard was happily enabled to accomplish pacifically, and under the benign rule of its old chief, Macuata, this fairest province of Fiji, again began to revive. This turn of affairs was hardly pleasing to the Tongan leader, who once more had resort to intrigue and sedition, and troubles recommenced.

At this juncture, Commodore Seymour, Her Majesty's Ship *Pelorus*, fortunately arrived at Fiji, and used his influence to such purpose, that the pending troubles were soon satisfactorily disposed of. The good results of this timely visit, which have endured to the present day, and have proved of much material benefit to Fiji, are fully stated in the following extracts from official correspondence :—

'*Pelorus*,' *Auckland, September* 2, 1861.

"Sir,—I HAVE the honour to report, for the information of my Lords Commissioners of the Admiralty, that Her Majesty's ship under my command sailed from Coromandel Harbour, east coast of New Zealand, on the 8th July, and arrived at Levuka Harbour, island of Ovalu, Fiji group, on the 15th, after a favourable passage made under sail.

"2. I was glad to find that affairs in the Fiji group generally were progressing satisfactorily, and that the only complaints laid before me by British residents at Levuka were of a nature which it was more the province of an attorney to settle than for a naval officer to interfere in. * * * *

"3. Having been informed by Mr. Pritchard that the trade in 'bêche-de-mer' and sandalwood on the north-west coast of Vanua Levu was entirely stopped in consequence of a war which was being carried on there between two rival chiefs, one of whom was supported by a body of Tongans, whose usual residence is on Lakemba, one of the Windward Islands, I decided on endeavouring to put a stop to a state of affairs so prejudicial to British interests; and, in order that my measures should be backed by the highest native authority in Fiji, I requested Mr. Pritchard to propose to Thakombau, King of Mbau, and Maafu, the principal chief of the Tongans resident in Fiji, to accompany me to the Mathuata district in the *Pelorus*.

"4. This, after a little diplomatic shuffling, they consented to do; and having received them, Mr. Pritchard, Her Britannic Majesty's Consul, and the Consulate Interpreter on board, we left Levuka on the morning of the 18th, entering the great reef which encircles Vanua Levu by a pass a little to the northward of the Nandi passage, after which our course lay through a very intricate channel formed by sunken reefs and patches of which no regular survey exists, but through which we were piloted in the most able manner by one of the English residents at Ovalau, a person named Christopher Carr, the owner of a small 'bêche-de-mer' trader. Under his direction we reached an anchorage off Levuta about 20 miles from our destination, Mathuata, that evening, and the following morning, having weighed as soon as the sun was sufficiently high to enable us to distinguish the shoals, we anchored in Maduri Harbour, Mathuata Bay, about 1,500 yards from where some houses were visible on the beach, at 9.45 A.M.

"5. On sending on shore to ascertain the state of affairs, we found, as I had anticipated would be the case, that the combined force of Tongans and Fijians had driven their opponents off the main land, and that the latter had taken refuge on Kea Island, about 10 miles from our anchorage. Since their expulsion their enemies had committed great havoc amongst their plantations, had destroyed nearly all the large canoes for which this district was formerly famous, and almost daily put one or more persons to death whose only crime was being related to the vanquished party. In these outrages the Tongans were the most prominent actors, and I may here state my opinion that, in the event of Her Majesty's Government accepting the protectorate of the Fijis, it will be necessary, from the very first, to put a stop to the raids which the Tongans have for the last five years been in the habit of carrying into the various islands lying to the west of Lakemba.

"6. On the morning of the 20th I sent over to the Island of Kea for Ritova, the chief of the tribe which had been driven out of Mathuata, and in the afternoon he came on board in a cutter of the *Pelorus*, followed by 15 canoes filled with his retainers. After he had had an hour's conversation with Thakombau and Maafu, we made a preconcerted signal, on seeing which Wainiongolo, chief of the Tongans in Mathuata, but subject to Maafu, and two Fijian chiefs, came on board, and after they and their opponents had discussed matters for an hour, I told them, through the Consular Interpreter, that we had no wish to injure or interfere with either the Fijians or Tongans in any way, but that, owing to the senseless quarrels of the former, fomented by the latter, the interests of the white traders in Fiji were compromised, and that I was determined on putting a stop to a state of affairs which was equally prejudicial to their own and to British interests. I should therefore leave them to settle by what means they could arrange matters amongst themselves, and any advice I could give them was at their service. My observations were listened to with great attention by both parties of Fijians, but were evidently unsatisfactory to the Tongan chief, who, throughout the entire business, was less manageable than either his associates or his enemies.

"7. The discussion, which terminated at sunset, was renewed the next day, when the following terms were agreed to by the chiefs of Fiji and Tonga present, being those which, with Mr. Pritchard's concurrence, I had decided from the first on seeing carried out:

"1st. To forget all past grievances and causes of quarrel.

"2nd. To commence from this date an era of peace and friendship.

"3rd. To receive and protect the teachers of the Christian religion.

"4th. To encourage trade and commerce throughout the Mathuata territories and to protect all legitimate traders and settlers.

"5th. To dissolve all political connexion and to confine themselves to legitimate and friendly intercourse with the Tongans.

"1st. That Maniongolo shall within 14 hours retire for ever from the Mathuata territories, and shall not again appear within the line of country from Natewa Bay on the one side, to Bua Bay on the other.

"2nd. That no Tongans shall visit the Mathuata territories or appear within the above-named limits for 12 months from this date.

"3rd. That Tongans in the service of the Wesleyan or other missions are exempted from the above restrictions.

"4th. That if any of the above articles are infringed, Maafu agrees that Maniongolo shall be sent from Fiji to his native country.

"The three last articles were inserted in the treaty at my recommendation, as I foresaw that, if the Tongans were allowed to remain on Vanua Levu, any good effect which might otherwise result from our visit would be completely done away with, and in compliance with them, at dawn on the morning of the 22nd of July, the two large double canoes, in which Mainiongolo and his followers had come to Mathuata, were launched, and by 8 A.M. were under weigh with a strong and fair wind for Lakemba; a more picturesque scene than their departure, as they crossed the *Pelorus*'s bow, beating their drums and cheering most lustily, I have seldom witnessed. In the course of the same day Thakombau and Maafu quitted the ship, and sailed for Levuka in Thakombau's large canoe, and in the afternoon I landed at Mathuata, accompanied by Ritova, and saw him and many of his people re-established in their former habitations.

"8. The Fijians in this district are still heathens, but at their earnest desire Mr. Calvert of the mission of Levuka, had promised to send some native teachers among them, and they were anxiously awaiting their arrival. As far as I could learn, there was a general feeling throughout the island in favour of their being taken under the protection of Great Britain, but though often asked, I studiously abstained from giving an opinion on the subject. There is no doubt that cotton of superior quality can be grown on the islands, but it is out of the question to expect native labour, and consequently we must look to the same source that supplies Demerara to furnish the requisite colonists for Fiji, should their protectorate be accepted by Great Britain.

"9. Having thus seen tranquillity re-established in Vanua Levu, I quitted Mathuata on the morning of the 23rd July, having Ritova and two of his retainers on board, they being desirous of seeing the working of the engines; and on getting clear of the Mali passage we discharged them and Mr. Pritchard to the latter's schooner, after which we made sail, by noon were clear of Kea Island, and steering a course for Aneiteum.

"10. I cannot conclude this letter without expressing the obligations I am under to Mr. Pritchard, whose manner with the native chiefs (being neither too deferential nor the reverse) seemed to me to be exactly what it should be. He speaks the language and is evidently liked by all parties of Fijians, and without his ready assistance and the presence of Thakombau and Maafu, it would have been impossible to have arrived at so speedy a settlement of affairs in the north-west of Fiji as our visit effected.

"I have, &c.,
"(Signed)   J. BEAUCHAMP SEYMOUR,
"Commodore."

COPY OF A LETTER FROM JAMES MURRAY, ESQ., TO SIR FREDERIC ROGERS, BART.

"*Foreign Office, December 31st,* 1861.

"SIR,—With reference to your letter of the 16th instant, I am directed by Earl Russell to request that you will state to the Duke of Newcastle that his Lordship has learnt with satisfaction the steps taken by Commodore Seymour for terminating the wars which have been raging between the Tongans and the Fijians.

"I have, &c.,
"(Signed)   JAMES MURRAY.
"*Sir F. Rogers, Bart.*
"*&c.   &c.*"

"The desire of power in excess caused the angels to fall," but not Maafu. Not even this signal discomfiture could make him forsake the land of his adoption, and he is at present the acknowledged chief of the Windward group of islands, and displays considerable ability in governing his people. He has forsaken his old ways and, although a foreigner, he is liked and respected by both natives and whites in his own district; and this, notwithstanding the constant efforts to get rid of him made by the Fijian chiefs, who are yet jealous of his position and influence in their country. But Maafu was not the only chief with whom Thakombau had to contend in the fierce struggle for supremacy. From the year 1843 Mbau had been engaged in constant hostilities with the neighbouring state of Rewa, the history of which is thus related by Thokanauto (otherwise known as Mr. Philips) to Commodore Wilkes:

"By the aid of the whites Tambiavalu, father of Kania, was established as king upon the dethronement of the reigning family, of whom Vunivalu, the governor, is a descendant. Rewa at this time was of little consequence, comprising only the small town of Ndraketi, from which the king now derives his title. Tambiavalu governed with great firmness and wisdom. During his reign all criminals met with exemplary punishment. According to the Fiji custom he had many wives, the chief among whom was a descendant of the family of Mbatitombe, who reigned at Ambau before Bamiva, the father of Tanoa, succeeded in gaining the kingdom. Although considered the queen, and holding the title of Ramdini-Ndraketi, she was not the highest in rank. There was also among the wives of Tambiavalu a sister of Tanoa named Salaiwai, who was younger, and in consequence had not the station to which her rank entitled her. Philips gives Tambiavalu the credit of having had a hundred children by his numerous wives and concubines, a statement of which those best acquainted with Fiji history do not doubt the correctness.

"Of this large progeny the children of the above two mentioned females are alone entitled to any rank. By the queen Ramdini-Ndraketi, he had four sons, named Mandonovi, Kania, Valivuaka, Ngaraningion. By Salaiwai, he had only two, Seru and Thokanauto (Mr. Philips). Of the six, Kania, Ngaraningion, and Thokanauto are still living. Tambiavalu had a long and prosperous reign, and under him Rewa assumed a rank among the chief cities of the Feejees, having acquired much territory and among the rest the island of Katnavu. His eldest son, Koraitamano, was the child of a Katnavu woman of rank; he was in consequence a vasu of the most important possessions of Rewa, and had many connections and friends throughout the country; he had so ingratiated himself with the chiefs and people that he could have made himself king on the death of his father.

"Ramdini-Ndraketi, the queen, who is represented as a most artful as well as unscrupulous woman, was fearful that his popularity might become disadvantageous to her children, and she determined to have him removed. She managed to instil into the king's mind suspicions that Koraitamano intended to seize upon the succession, which determined him to put his son to death. Koraitamano received a hint of his intentions, and was able to evade every attempt. On some occasions he was obliged to flee to distant places, once to Ra, the western end of Viti Levu and another time to Mbenga, where he remained until a kind of reconciliation took place, when he was induced to return. He had not been long in Rewa before the queen recommenced her machinations for his destruction, and his father also resumed his designs against him. Koraitamano was doubtful whether again to resort to flight or remain, when some chiefs who were hostile to the king represented to the young chief that the only method to secure his own safety effectually was to put his father to death, assuring him they would stand by him in the struggle. By their persuasions he was induced to accede to their designs. At night he set fire to a canoe house and, coming into his father's dwelling, he approached the place where he was sleeping, and cried out: "Do you lie here asleep, when your city is burning!" Tambiavalu immediately started up and ran out; Koraitamano following closely after him, watched an occasion, struck him with his club on the back of his head, and killed him on the spot, after which he retired to his own house, trusting to the promises of his friends and adherents that they would protect and defend him. But the queen was more than an equal for his cunning, and her hatred caused her to go the greatest lengths in wreaking her vengeance upon him. She had the body brought to the house, where, observing that the external injury to the head was slight, she conceived the singular plan of making the deed of the assassin and his friends recoil upon their own heads. She therefore at once raised a cry that the body showed signs of life, and that her husband was not dead. She then had the body conveyed to the farther end of his house, under the plea that he required to be removed from the noise, and no one suffered to approach the body but herself and a Tonga woman who was her confidante. She soon spread the report that the king had recovered his senses but was very weak, and called upon several chiefs in the king's name, saying that he required the instant death of Koraitamano. The chiefs convened a meeting to consider the course that ought to be pursued, but could come to no decision in consequence of the general opinion that the conduct of Koraitamano was justifiable, although, on the other hand, they feared the wrath of the king in case he should recover, particularly those who had advised and wished to uphold Koraitamano.

"The queen becoming aware of their hesitation, on the following morning took some whales' teeth and other valuables, and presented them herself to the chiefs, saying they were sent by the king to purchase the death of his son. Fearing to hold out any longer, they went to Koraitamano and announced to him the fatal mandate, and he was immediately killed. They then proceeded to the king's house to report that the deed was done, and on approaching the couch of the king, the putrescent odour which proceeded from the corpse at once disclosed to them the deception that had been practised.

"It was, however, too late to mend the matter, and Mandonovi, the eldest son of the queen, now succeeded his father without opposition. One of the first acts of Mandonovi was to build a mbure over the spot where his father was murdered.

"This succession deprived Seru and Thokauauto (Philips) of their right to the throne, and of course excited their hostility to the reigning chief, who was by no means so popular as his father, and did not govern to the satisfaction of his subjects. Seru, who was the eldest of the two malcontents, was a very tall and remarkably handsome man, and had great influence among the people, which excited the jealousy of the king. Such was his strength that it was said he could knock down a full-grown hog by a blow on the forehead, and would break a cocoa-nut by striking it on his elbow.

"Mutual words of defiance had passed between the two brothers, and they were living in daily expectation of some encounter that would bring on serious disturbances.

"During the height of this feeling they met on the road, where the scene that was enacted was quite remarkable, and the narration of it by Philips equally so.

"Seru had one of those short missile clubs (ula) in his girdle, which Feejee men usually wear stuck in behind. As Mandonovi approached, Seru placed his back against the fence without any design. The king had three shaddocks (molitive) in his hand, of which, as he came up to Seru, he held one up and called out in sport that he 'meant to throw it at him.' The thought then came into Seru's mind that, if the king threw and hit him, he would let him pass, but that if he missed, he would take the opportunity to put him to death.

"He therefore replied to his brother, in the same jocose manner, 'Throw, but if you miss, then I'll try.' The king threw, but missed. He then drew nearer, and holding up another of the shaddocks, cried out, 'This time I will hit you.' To which Seru replied, 'Take care; if you miss, then I'll try.' The king threw again, but Seru by a quick movement, avoided the missile. Mandonovi, then advanced to within two or three yards of Seru saying, 'This time I think I shall hit you,' Seru made himself ready to avoid it and, with his hands behind him, said, 'If you miss then I take my turn.' The king threw the third time and missed, for Seru stooped, and the missile passed over his shoulder. Seru then drew himself up, flourished his club in the air, and exclaimed in tones of exulting mockery, "Aha, I think you did not see this!" With that he hurled his weapon with so deadly an aim, that it crushed the skull of the king and killed him on the spot.

"As soon as the event became known, the queen with her other sons fled to Ambau, leaving the supreme power in the hands of Seru, who, however, did not take the title of Ndraketi, but adopted that of Tui Sawan, after the chief town of Mbenga, on which he had made war and captured, and by which title he was thenceforth known.

"He was not, however, long left to enjoy his authority. The exiled family made several unsuccessful attempts to destroy him, and at last induced Vendovi, by a large bribe, to undertake his destruction.

"Vendovi managed to get to Rewa unobserved, and looking in at the door of Thokanauto's house, saw Tui Sawan lying on his mat eating. He immediately levelled his musket and shot him, four balls passed through his breast, but such was the strength of his constitution that he survived for eight days. This occurred in the year 1827. When it became known at Ambau that this fratricide had been committed, the queen and her sons returned to Rewa, and Kania assumed the direction of the government to the exclusion of Thokanauto."

In 1846 the fortunes of the Rewa people received a serious blow in the death of their Vasu Raivalita (whose mother was sister to Kania, King of Rewa), who had engaged to kill his brother Thakombau on the condition that Rewa should become tributary to Mbau on his assuming the reins of government.

Thakombau received timely warning of this treachery, and Riavalita was put to death.

Soon after this occurrence the Mbau people attacked Rewa, whose inhabitants were defeated with great slaughter, and Thokanauto, or Philips (who was *Vasu Taukei* to Mbau, and had previously rendered considerable assistance to Tanoa), was named king. Mr. Philips, however, was soon overthrown by his brother Ratu Nggara, who, notwithstanding that his capital was again attacked by the Mbau people in 1847 and completely destroyed, became firmly established as chief of Rewa.

Mr. Philips soon afterwards died at Nukui and was buried at Mbau. Meanwhile the tide of fortune had turned against Thakombau, whose resources became exhausted, and in 1854 Ratu Nggara boldly declared it his fixed purpose to eat the Mbauan chief. However, in the following year, in the midst of warlike preparations, this much dreaded warrior sickened and died.

Peace was now made for a short time. But Mara, the reputed brother of Thakombau, and *Vasu* to Lakemba, soon assumed the conduct of a new war, which he threatened would be one of extermination, for he calculated on the allegiance of the island of Ovalau and the white residents there. He also hoped to be successful in gaining over the powerful tribe of Lasikaus or fisherman at Mbau, while he retained all those towns which had revolted from Thakombau's authority. At this crisis, whilst struggling for life, sorely pressed by his enemies and revolutionary violence, King George of Tonga arrived in Fiji with thirty canoes on a visit to Thakombau. Fortunately for

him a canoe which King George had sent to Ovalau, with
letters to the French priests there, was fired on by the
natives, an insult which he was bound to resent, and,
malgré lui, he became involved in the war that was raging.
To such good purpose did he become engaged that, before
saying good-bye to Fiji and Thakombau, he had relieved
him of most of his difficulties and his enemies. Seventy
of the rebel towns again acknowledged the supremacy of
Mbau, whilst Thakombau, in order further to confirm the
peace now established and cement their allegiance, wisely
exercised with effect his kingly prerogative of clemency,
but hitherto little known in Fiji, and extended it to all
who had taken part in the rebellion.

Although King George took part in these hostilities
almost entirely on his own account, and although his
services were amply acknowledged by Thakombau, who
made him many handsome presents before his departure
from Fiji, we are told that this Christian monarch, and
missionary pet, did not hesitate in 1858 to prefer a claim
for 12,000*l.* on Thakombau, as a subsidy for victorious
war and losses of valuable men. This startling demand
formally made, and the enmity that arose between the
two powers, was a new difficulty and a great calamity in
itself; but its greater evil was that those chiefs in Fiji who
were slightly in subjection to Thakombau were thereby
encouraged to be bold, defiant, and rebellious; and the
malcontents courted the Tongans, to whom they clung.

But the heaviest and most difficult of all Thakombau's
many grievous troubles has been the indemnity claimed
from him by the United States Government. The
amount of this demand was first adjudged by Captain
Boutwell of the United States Navy, to be $30,000, i.e.,
6000*l.*, but was afterwards increased to $45,000, or 9000*l.*,

because of certain alleged difficulties thrown in the way by the English missionaries, this so-called interference being merely an attempt to obtain a fair investigation, and not, as has been suggested, to screen the guilty parties. Her Majesty's Commisioner, who reported in 1861 on the then proffered cession of the island, said :

> "From all I can learn, one third of the sum demanded by the United States Government would be amply sufficient, both as compensation for the loss of property, and as a fine."

This opinion is also further confirmed by Her Majesty's Commissioners in Paragraph 49 of their Report, dated, Levuka, Fiji, 13th April, 1874, in which they say :

> "We have nothing to add to the statements previously made to Her Majesty's Government, and published in England, on the subject of the claim of the United States against King Cakobau—a claim which was unfairly made and unfairly pressed, and which has led to speculations of a questionable character."

And, in *Blackwood's Magazine* for July, 1869, the injustice of the claim is again strongly urged. The various circumstances connected with the origin of this demand are fully treated in the following extract, quoted from Parliamentary Return, dated May 1862, "Correspondence relative to the Fiji Islands " :—

Extracts from a letter by Captain THOMAS C. DUNN, of the barque *Dragon*, Salem. (From the *New York Herald* of November 9, 1856.)

To the Editor of the New York Herald.

"*Salem, November 2nd,* 1856.

"Having lately returned from a trading voyage to the Fiji Islands, my attention has been called to a communication, published in the columns of the *Herald* of the 16th February last, purporting to have been written at those Islands, and signed 'David Stuart,' giving a long list of massacres and crimes committed by the natives against the whites residing there: and also charging the English Wesleyan missionaries with being accessory to and instigating many of the atrocities so minutely detailed. Feeling assured that such a communication would never have found admission to the columns of your paper had you been aware of the errors it contained, I take this the earliest opportunity afforded me of replying to it, and of vindicating the character of a body of noble-minded and self-denying men.

* * * * * * * *

"I will now proceed to remark upon the style of investigation pursued by Commander Boutwell, in his recent examination of the claims of American citizens against the native chiefs, and which is so much lauded by your correspondent. Before doing this it will be necessary to state some particulars regarding the affairs at the islands. For some time previous to Commander Boutwell's arrival there had been, as your correspondent states, a sort of civil war existing between the several chiefs of Fiji; but as the American public are probably very little interested in the contests of savages, I will confine myself to the recital of events in which the foreign white residents were concerned.

"In 1849 the whites, to the number of about fifty, resided at the town of Levuka, upon the island of Ovalau, the Chief of which, Tui Levuka, was upon friendly terms with Thakombau, one of the principal chiefs engaged in the war. Though not actually subject to Thakombau, Tui Levuka frequently assisted him in his wars, and was considered throughout the Islands as being one of his party. The whites also very generally espoused the cause of Thakombau in opinion, although none of them took any active part in the war. The American Consul, John B. Williams, Esq., resided upon a small island, called Nukulau, which, I believe, he had purchased from Ngarrengeo, a chief of Rewa, who was the principal chief opposed to Thakombau. Upon the 4th of July, 1849, while he was celebrating the day by firing cannon, the house of the Consul accidentally took fire, and was burned to the ground. During the progress of the fire a crowd of natives collected, and indulged their thievish propensities by seizing and carrying off whatever they could lay their hands upon. In such a case it was of course impossible to say how much was stolen and how much destroyed by the fire. But as the natives were pretty expert in saving articles where there was such a prospect of their securing them for their own use, it is probable that a good deal was stolen. Soon after, in 1851, the United States ship *St. Mary's*, Captain Magruder, visiting the

R

Islands, Mr. Williams applied to that officer for compensation to be required of the chiefs, and handed in a schedule of goods stolen, amounting to 5001 dollars 38 cents (it seems singular that he could know the exact articles stolen, so as to charge such an exact account, even to the thirty-eight cents), the truth of which, that officer not being able (as his time was limited) to satisfy himself concerning its accuracy, left in the hands of the Rev. Mr. Calvert, one of the missionaries, and Mr. David Whippy, United States Vice-commercial Agent, requesting them to examine Mr. Williams's claim, and also several other small claims preferred by Mr. Williams against native chiefs on behalf of American citizens; to arbitrate upon the same, and to report to the commander of the next United States ship-of-war which should visit Fiji, and to the Secretary of State at Washington. Mr. Calvert accordingly wrote to Commander Boutwell, upon his arrival at Fiji, upon the subject. But as his report did not at all agree with the notions of Mr. Consul Williams, being rather unfavourable to the justice of his claim, he was very coolly informed by that gentleman that,—

"'It was considered a piece of presumption for him to interfere in matters concerning American citizens or their interests, as he (Mr. Williams) and Commander Boutwell were fully competent to settle all such affairs without any of his assistance.'

"In 1853 a boat belonging to some of the white residents of Levuka was taken and robbed by the natives of a place called Malaki. The three men composing her crew escaped in their dingy (a small boat), came to Levuka, and reported the outrage. The whites, exasperated at the story, determined to punish the offenders. They accordingly organised an expedition, and, accompanied by the chief of the town where they resided, with a number of his native warriors, went to the place, which they captured and burned; and the native force which accompanied them killed a number of the people of the town, although no resistance was made. That the whites did right in this affair is unquestioned, as it was requisite for them to show the natives that they would not allow any of their number to be robbed with impunity. The people of the destroyed town were subject to the Chief of an island called Viwa. They carried complaint to him of the destruction of their town by the whites; and it is asserted by the whites that he, the Viwa Chief, applied to Thakombau for permission to avenge himself by destroying Levuka. Although Thakombau positively denies all knowledge of the matter, rumours of the meditated burning of their town coming to the ears of the whites, they organised and kept a regular night-watch to guard against treachery. Notwithstanding this precaution, the town was fired in the night, and most of it reduced to ashes. As there was a native teacher belonging to Viwa living in the town at the time, the exasperated whites at once fixed upon him as the incendiary, for no other reason, so far as I have been able to ascertain, than that, being a native of Viwa, he must have been ordered by his chief to set fire to the town. Although at no subsequent investigation could any reliable proof be adduced to fix the fact upon him, the impression becoming general among the whites that Thakombau had authorized the destruction of their town, the Chief, Tui Levuka, declared against him, and was joined by all the whites. They immediately constructed a few temporary dwellings, around which they built a fence, which they fortified with several pieces of cannon against any anticipated attack of Thakombau. But he never went near them, although your correspondent states that several ineffectual attempts were made to carry the town. He sent several peaceful messages, assuring them that he had nothing to do with the burning of their town, that he was very sorry for the occurrence, and that he would do all in his power to discover and punish the perpetrators of the outrage. All this I state as facts. Having had considerable property in the hands of an agent living in the town, which was all destroyed by the fire, I have taken considerable pains to investigate the matter with a view of demanding indemnity, if the destruction could be traced to any responsible party. But it is still shrouded in mystery; the native teacher and the Viwa chief, who were charged with the act, having been killed a few days after by the mountain tribes of Ovalau.

"It was right that Commander Boutwell should have endeavoured to examine into the matter, as considerable American property had been destroyed; but he should have done so in an impartial spirit, according to the instructions of Commodore Mervine, Commander-in-Chief of the Pacific squadron, by whom he was despatched upon this business. I quote from those instructions:—'You will not take it for granted that all the allegations against the supposed offenders are true, simply because claimants have filed their reports at the State Department. In prosecuting the important duty intrusted to your management and discretion, sound policy dictates that a close and thorough examination, upon the strictest principles of justice, should be made into every case presented for adjustment.'

"To show how far these wise and equitable instructions of Commodore Mervine were carried out by Commander Boutwell, I will here insert some of the correspondence which passed between him and the native chiefs upon the subject. The first is a letter from Commander Boutwell, dated a few days after his arrival at the Islands, and addressed to Thakombau. I give it entire.

"'To THAKOMBAU TUI VITI, OR THE PRESIDING CHIEF IN HIS ABSENCE.

"'I have been directed by the Government of the United States to visit the Fiji Islands in the United States ship *John Adams*, for the purpose of inquiring into and redressing the wrongs which American citizens have received at your hands. The great chief who has charged me with this mission presides over a country whose resources are inexhaustible, and whose power to punish her enemies are beyond the comprehension of those who have never visited her empire. It is charged against you that you have caused American property to a very large amount, and valued at many thousands of dollars, to be taken from the island of Nukulau and other places, and appropriated to your own purpose and to that of your friends. You have treated the persons who came here in ships bearing the same flag that you now see floating over the *John Adams* in a manner that will not be submitted to by the Government of the United States of America. You are therefore required to restore that, or its value, with interest, to ask pardon of my nation, and to promise to respect its flag for the future.

"'E. B. BOUTWELL,
"'Commanding U. S. Ship *John Adams*.'

"The following day, and before any answer to the above had been received, another letter in the following style was sent, accompanied with the appended agreement for the Chiefs of Bau to sign.

"'*United States Ship John Adams, Levuka,*
"'*Oralau, Sept. 27th, 1855.*

"I, Commander Boutwell, do, on behalf of the Government of the United States of America, demand of the Chief of Bau thirty thousand dollars, or that amount to be paid in fish, cocoa-nut oil, gum, pigs, and yams, within twelve months from this date; the money or its equivalent to be paid into the hands of John B. Williams, Esq., United States commercial agent at the Fiji Islands, and to be distributed in the following manner :—15,000 dollars to John B. Williams, Esq., for the loss of property on the island of Nukulau; 3,000 dollars to James H. Williams, Esq., for the loss of property on the island of

Namuka; 4000 dollars to Messrs. Chamberlain and Co. of Salem, for the loss of property at the burning of Levuka; 4000 dollars to Mr. Whippy, United States Vice-Consul at Levuka, for the loss of his property at Ovalau; 1500 dollars to Shattuck and M'Comber, each as compensation for the loss of their property, and for being clubbed by the natives of Namuka at the time they robbed Mr. Williams, of Sydney; and 1000 dollars for the robbery of the barque *Elizabeth*, at Totonga.

"'As I have many claims on these and other islands to settle, and my time being limited, I must urge the authorities of Bau to act speedily, and not compel me to go after the so-called Tui Viti, or approach nearer Bau, as my powder is quick and my balls are round.

"'E. B. BOUTWELL, Commander.'

"Appended to this was the following document:—

"'Bau, Sept. 28th, 1855.

"'We, the undersigned, Chiefs of Bau, admit the justice of John B. Williams' claim, as also that of the other American citizens, and promise on our part to pay the amount demanded by Commander Boutwell within twelve months from this date.'

"Thakombau, the principal chief of Bau, being absent from his town at the time the above letters were received, Yagodamu, the second chief, replied to the demand of Commander Boutwell by the following humble remonstrance against the unjust proceeding.

"'To E. B. BOUTWELL, ESQ., COMMANDING U. S. SHIP *John Adams*.

"'Bau, Sept. 29th, 1855.

"'SIR,—I beg most respectfully to inform you that the claim now made on us by John B. Williams, Esq., is unjust: first, because we were not accessories in any degree whatever to the seizure of the property belonging to J. B. Williams, James H. Williams, and Messrs. Shattuck and M'Comber; secondly, because the place where these outrages were committed, the islands of Nukulau and Namuka, were not included in our dominions at the time, neither are they now. In proof of this we refer to the statements of Commodore Wilkes, of the United States Exploring Expedition, in 1840, and of every commander in the naval and merchant service who have visited these parts. We refer to the record of the inquiry lately instituted on board H. B. M. Ship *Herald*, at which Mr. Whippy, United States Vice-Consul at Levuka, Ovalau, was present. We refer to those American citizens at

Ovalau who are acquainted with the subject. Lastly, we refer to the claims which John B. Williams himself made on Phillips, the late Chief of Rewa, and which that Chief admitted, and engaged to discharge. With reference to the claim of Messrs. Chamberlain and Co., we can only inform you that the burning of Levuka is still involved in mystery. We maintain that we were not accessories, and would again most respectfully refer to the evidence given on the subject by the whites on board the *Herald*.

"'I am, &c.,
"'(Signed by a mark)   YAGODAMU.
"'On behalf of himself and the other chiefs now present in Bau.'

"To this letter of Yagodamu, Commander Boutwell, who had been instructed by his Commander-in-Chief to 'institute a close and thorough inquiry, upon the strictest principles of justice, into every case presented for his adjustment,' replies in the following unique specimen of quarter-deck judgment :—

"'*United States Ship John Adams,*
"'*Levuka, Ovalau, Oct.* 2*nd,* 1855.

"'When I made the demand on the chiefs of Bau for indemnity, I expected an acknowledgment of your indebtedness and willingness to pay, and not a letter of explanation. My officer had no authority from me to enter into any agreement with you or the head of your nation. I am satisfied of the guilt of Tui Viti, as the Chief of Bau. I know that his influence prevented Philips from paying Mr. Williams for his losses on Nukulau. I know that a whale's tooth was sent to Suva, from Bau, with orders to club Shattuck and M'Comber. I know that the Viwa people robbed Americans at Levuka, and that Bau sanctioned it; and I am satisfied in my own mind that the native teacher set fire to the town of Levuka, and that Tui Viti sanctioned it. The chief, Tui Levuka, states that the Bau people robbed the whale-ship *Elizabeth* at Ovalau. Mr. Williams and Mr. Whippy both testify to the same fact. I am well aware that there are other chiefs and their people guilty of having injured Americans; I will in time call them to account, but at present I am in pursuit of Bau or her principal chief. I have to request that you will write me no more letters, but forthwith pay the money, or give me ample security that it will be paid in twelve months. The brave never threaten, nor do the virtuous boast of their chastity. I therefore do not tell you of the consequences of a non-compliance with these requirements. I would however remind your teachers of ethics that the golden rule is too often forgotten, and that the eleventh commandment has, by general consent, become binding on all those who keep the other ten.

"'I am, &c.,
"'E. B. BOUTWELL,
"'Commander.
"'To Yagodamu, Chief.'

"From the above letter may be seen the manner in which Commander Boutwell commenced to carry out the instructions of Commodore Mervine, in which he is ordered 'not to take for granted that all the allegations against the supposed offenders are true,' but to 'make full inquiry, upon the strictest principles of justice, into every case presented to him for adjustment.' He arrives at the Islands, and is immediately waited upon by Mr. John B. Williams, United States Commercial Agent, one of the principal claimants for indemnity, and by several others, who also have claims upon the chiefs. These persons tell their own story. (And your correspondent David Stuart, in his letter, gives us a pretty good idea what kind of a story that was.) Commander Boutwell, without inquiring into the truth of the charges from any but the avowed enemies of the Bau chiefs, immediately becomes 'assured in his own mind of the guilt of Thakombau,' and without giving him any opportunity of defending himself, demands compensation to the amount of thirty thousand dollars—fifteen thousand of which is awarded 'to John B. Williams, Esq., for the loss of property on the island of Nukulau,' when the original claim, as presented to Captain Magruder, two years after the fire, was only five thousand. The poor chiefs, not feeling quite so assured of their guilt, ventured to remonstrate against this summary proceeding, and to ask to be allowed opportunity to endeavour to justify themselves. But the gallant commander did not want any letters of explanation, but an 'acknowledgment of their indebtedness and willingness to pay;' and though the 'brave never threaten,' yet he just intimates that his 'balls are round, and his powder quick.' He then goes on to say, 'I know,' 'I know,' 'I know,' this, that, and the other: and 'I therefore request that you will write me no more letters, but forthwith pay the money, or give me ample security that it will be paid in twelve months.' In their extremity, the chiefs applied to the Wesleyan missionaries to write to Commander Boutwell on their behalf, which they did, but were politely informed by that gentleman that he could settle the matter without any of their assistance. At this juncture another

American ship-of-war, the *St. Mary's*, Commander Bailey, arrived at Ovalau, to whom Mr. Calvert, the chairman of the Wesleyan Mission, addressed the following letter :—

"'*Viwa, Fiji, October 9th*, 1855.

"'Sir,—I hail with great pleasure your arrival in Fiji, which I deem most opportune, as intricate affairs are now pending between Bau and J. B. Williams, Esq., United States Commercial Agent. Having been requested by G. A. Magruder, Esq., of the United States Navy, to arbitrate, in connection with Mr. Whippy, respecting claims said to be due to J. B. Williams, Esq., and also respecting the barque *Elizabeth*, and after with reluctance (after objecting to do it) undertaking to do what I could in the complicated affairs, I thought it right to report what had been done in the matter to E. B. Boutwell, Esq., Commanding United States Ship *John Adams*.

"'To my letter I have received two replies: one from Mr. Williams, who complains that my interference is uncalled for, &c.

"'A copy of my letter to Commander Boutwell, with the replies thereto, I enclose, begging you will peruse and consider the same, as I think it unfair that I should be represented to your Government as 'presumptuous,' after I had been requested to do what I have done by a naval officer in the United States service. Herewith I beg to inclose to you a copy of a letter addressed to the Honourable Secretary of State, United States of America, respecting a levy which Mr. Whippy and I, after due deliberation, in virtue of Commander Magruder's request, conjointly made, as being the only claim we could fairly make out for depredations on the property of the *Elizabeth*.

"'I forward this by the Rev. Joseph Waterhouse, who has had the honour to be the first missionary at Bau, and who has been the means of bringing about a great change on that island. He was at Levuka at the time it was burnt; with reference to which I am shocked to find Commander Boutwell writes,—"I am well assured in my own mind that the native teacher set fire to the town." This is indeed a most grave implication, and which I hope Mr. Waterhouse will have the opportunity of proving is without foundation.

"'Hoping that these matters may now at length be fully investigated and properly settled, so that Fiji, after its wars, heathenism and cannibalism, may begin afresh, on better principles, and become enlightened, honourable, and religious,

"'I am, &c.,

"'*To Commander Bailey*,
"'*United States Ship St. Mary's*.'"

"'James Calvert.

"A letter was also addressed by John B. Williams, Esq., to Commander Bailey, in the following style :—

"'To COMMANDER BAILEY, *commanding United States Ship*
"'*St. Mary's.*

"'*United States Ship John Adams, October 6th,* 1855.
"'SIR,—The United States Ship *John Adams,* Commander E. B. Boutwell, having arrived some weeks previous to yourself, and having made himself acquainted with the subjects of complaints of American citizens, and having made his demands on Bau and other places for indemnity, it may be safe to leave the affair in his hands, as they are now in a fair train for settlement. And in my opinion, any change in the demands or requirements made on them (the natives) by the commander of the *John Adams* might be injurious to American citizens.
"'I have, &c.,
"'JOHN B. WILLIAMS,
"'U. S. Commercial Agent.'

"Commander Boutwell, hearing that Mr. Calvert had written to Commander Bailey, and that the latter gentleman was displeased with his (Commander Boutwell's) summary mode of procedure, wrote to Commander Bailey, requesting him to remain in Fiji and settle the affair himself; to which Commander Bailey replied, that as he (Commander Boutwell) appeared to be pursuing a course involving a deviation from his instructions, he should have felt compelled to remain and settle it himself, were it not that Mr. Williams, the principal claimant, and also, as United States Commercial Agent, representative of the other American claimants, had expressed a decided preference for his (Boutwell's) adjustment. He therefore left it in his hands, with a caution as to his deviating in the slightest degree from his original instructions, and an express order 'to afford the accused every opportunity upon all formal occasions to appear in person, as well as by respectable counsel, without regard to their nation or religion.' This order from Bailey, Boutwell, as junior, was bound to obey, but he chose to obey it after his own fashion. He sent a notice to Thakombau to appear on board his ship upon a certain day, to answer the charges preferred against him. He also notified the Rev. Joseph Waterhouse that he would be permitted to act as counsel for the accused, and appointed a board of arbitration, consisting of two of his own officers, who had already made up their minds to decide upon the matter. On the day appointed, Mr. Waterhouse, with Thakombau, repaired on board, and was permitted to speak in his behalf; but he was treated with insult and contempt, and was not permitted to call in any witnesses as evidence against the allegations of John B. Williams. The board of arbitration therefore decided that all the claims were just, and Commander Boutwell added on fifteen thousand dollars more, on account, as he informed Mr. Waterhouse, "of the interference of Commander Bailey and the representations of the Rev. Mr. Calvert." The award now stood thus: 'To John B. Williams, Esq., 18,331 dollars; Chamberlain and Co., 7300 dollars; David Whippy, 6000 dollars; owners of barque *Elizabeth*, 1,000 dollars; owners of brig *Tim Pickering*, 2800 dollars; Thomas Ryder, 1500 dollars; Wilkinson, Brothers, and Co., Sydney, 4000 dollars; Messrs. Shattuck and M'Comber, 2,600 dollars.

"Here, then, is the final decision of Commander Boutwell. The claim of John B. Williams, originally 5,000 dollars, has, through this beautiful system of investigation, grown to 18,331 dollars, upon what grounds we are not informed. Having arrived at this satisfactory conclusion, a paper was drawn up, which was called a treaty, and which Thakombau was compelled to sign—by which he agreed to discharge the sum in two years—under the heaviest threats if he refused to comply; and the 'promise, on the arrival of a ship of war belonging to the American nation, to resign the government of Bau, and to go voluntarily on board that ship, and submit to any punishment which it might be the pleasure of the Commander to inflict.' This was the prompt justice which your correspondent so much lauds. He says—'Omnipotence had heard our prayers, and Commander Boutwell was the chosen one to give us aid.' In my opinion David Stuart would be the one most largely benefited if the award of Commander Boutwell should be enforced by the American Government; but I cannot believe it will be. Our Government has always been just in its dealings with the Polynesian communities; and the partial, harsh, and unjust proceedings related above will, I am persuaded, undergo a severe scrutiny at Washington. That there were claims which it was Commander Boutwell's duty to examine and enforce was undoubted. The loss of 7000 dollars of Messrs. Chamberlain and Co., of Salem, was real; it was property left by me in the hands of an agent at Levuka, on their account, which was all destroyed by the fire. Other Americans residing at the place lost their all. It is not at present clear by what chief's orders the place was fired. This was a question for Commander Boutwell to inquire into; but it would seem that Mr. John B. Williams took advantage of these real and just claims to introduce his original claim of 5000 dollars, now, by some species of mercantile legerdemain, increased to 18,000 dollars; and crushing all fair inquiry, by endeavouring to blacken the characters of the Wesleyan missionaries, whose truthful testimony he feared might defeat his deep-laid plans to get Commander Boutwell to enforce the whole amount against Thakombau, who for some years has been the object of his special enmity. That Commander Boutwell listened to his tales, and imbibed that prejudice they would so naturally engender, is but too evident from his subsequent proceedings.

"Immediately upon returning to Bau from the *John Adams*, where he had been compelled to sign the so-called treaty, acknowledging the justice of the claims, and promising to pay the 45,000 dollars in two years, Thakombau addressed the following protest to the United States Consul at Sydney, New South Wales, requesting it might be forwarded to the Government of the United States.

"'*Bau, Fiji, October 29th,* 1855.

"'I, Thakombau, the Vunivalu of Bau, Fiji, do humbly make known my protest against the oppressive conduct of Captain Boutwell. I do hereby declare and make known to you, Sir, the United States Consul nearest Fiji, that I did not sign the treaty with Captain Boutwell of my own accord, but under the greatest fear. He threatened to take me away to America, and stamped on the floor right in my face, because I objected to give my signature, and then I was afraid, and signed it. I make known that I now protest against that treaty, and declare it to be unrighteous, tyrannical, unwarrantable, and unworthy of the Government of America. It is not my deed.

"'I also make known, Sir, that he told another chief that he would hang me; but there is nothing for which he should hang me. I besought him to investigate the charges made against me by the whites of Ovalau, but he refused.

"'I beseech you, Sir, to inform the Government of the United States of America of these transactions. I am continually in fear lest this Captain kill me, whilst I am innocent. I had hoped that my profession of Christianity would have prevented such arbitrary conduct. I cannot believe that it will be sustained by the American authorities.

"'(Signed by a mark)   THAKOMBAU.

"'Witnesses—William Moore and Joseph Waterhouse, Wesleyan missionaries.'

"Copies of the above protest, duly authenticated, have been forwarded by the United States Consul at Sydney to the authorities at Washington, and also to the Commander-in-Chief of the Pacific squadron. There is therefore no doubt that the affair will undergo a more thorough and just investigation by the orders of the American Government.

" I have here given a true account of the proceedings of Commander Boutwell in relation to these affairs, taken from authenticated copies of all the correspondence that passed upon the subject, now in my possession. Your readers no doubt will be surprised, upon referring to the *Herald* of the 16th of February last, to find your correspondent, David Stuart, so highly applauding Commander Boutwell. He says, speaking of the action of preceding commanders, 'This course has however been changed by Commander Boutwell; and the truly republican conduct of that officer, and his praiseworthy resistance of all attempts to induce him to abandon his countrymen to the power of the English missionaries has, it is well known here, incurred the manifest displeasure of the missionaries; but he has the consolation of knowing that he left us with the united and heartfelt thanks of our young islandic republic; and after the tedious and unpleasant task he has accomplished, he will return to a country and a people whose motto is "Liberty and Justice," and whose approbation will in this instance be no less deserving than just.' It is to be hoped that the Government of the 'people whose motto is "Liberty and Justice,"' will visit upon Commander Boutwell that censure and displeasure which his unjust and oppressive proceedings are so justly calculated to inspire.

" Hoping that you will not fail to give the above an early insertion in your paper,

" I am, Sir, yours, &c.,

" THOMAS C. DUNN."

COPY OF A LETTER FROM CAPTAIN MAGRUDER.

" *United States Frigate* ' *Congress*,'
" *Gibraltar, July* 24*th*, 1856.

" MY DEAR SIR,—Your letter, dated at Sydney in January last, and directed to me at Washington City, has just reached me at this place. I have been attached to this squadron, as captain of the fleet, for a year past, which accounts for the delay in its receipt. I heartily congratulate you and your fellow-labourers in the success of your efforts among the Fijis. I thought I saw indications of a favourable change when I had the pleasure to see you there; but the magnitude of the work you have described as accomplished I was by no means prepared for. I heartily wish you continued success. It is a work over which the Christian and philanthropist may rejoice with thanksgiving to the Most High.

"I am sorry to hear of further difficulties between our agent Mr. Williams and the Chief of Mbau, and especially that it has resulted in the punishment of innocent people. I do not know what has happened since I investigated the claims of Mr. Williams against the Chief, but I well remember that I considered some of the claims preferred unjust, and thought Mr. Williams in the wrong, and so reported to the Government. My official letter is on record on the files of the Navy Department. It was dated, 'U. S. S. *St. Mary's*, Valparaiso, Sept. 28th, 1851,' and was addressed to Commodore Ch. S. M'Cauley, commanding Pacific squadron. In the letter I stated that ' I was sorry to find a bad state of feeling existing between our agent and the King. They had had business transactions together, in some of which I thought Mr. Williams in the wrong, and that it was unfortunate for our commercial interests that this state of things should exist.'

"I did not state, in the report above referred to, the particulars of my investigation of the claim of Mr. Williams; but I well remember that in the inventory of articles said to have been stolen by the natives and not returned, charges were made in some instances for articles which it was ascertained afterwards had been received by Mr. Williams.

"If it is necessary to refer to my letter in any investigation before the Department it can be easily done. Were I at home I would cheerfully aid you in having the matter fully investigated, and justice done to any parties who may have been injured.

"I am, my dear Sir, very truly yours,
"G. A. MAGRUDER.

" *Rev. James Calvert,*
" *Wesleyan Mission House, London.*"

At length, in the latter part of the year 1869, the attention of the American Government having been called to the magazine article already mentioned, Captain Truxton was deputed to Fiji, duly " authorized to investigate and settle all unadjusted claims, either of long standing or more recent date," and Thakombau was promised that "himself and his witnesses should receive a calm and patient hearing, and be treated with the courtesy and respect belonging to his high office and Christian profession; and he was assured that the Government would then, and at all times, treat himself and his subjects with all possible fairness and consideration."

Captain Truxton, acting under these fair and ample instructions, arrived in Fiji in the month of October of the same year, and immediately formed a Court of Inquiry or Arbitration, for investigating the various claims and awards. This was constituted of two officers of the United States Ship *Jamestown*, and two American residents, one of whom was a heavy claimant in Fiji, with Captain Truxton as president.

Firstly, the Court found an "unaccountable difference between the registered and allowed claims of Mr. Williams," late American Consul : " A total of $7,199 and 67 cents is all the amount of his claim sustained by tradition, or on the records of the consulate, and yet he stands on the list of awards as entitled to $19,365. There is no possible way of accounting for this great and strange discrepancy," i.e., $12,165. Secondly, the Court having proceeded to "most strenuously urge upon the Government of the United States the propriety of refunding to King Thakombau" this sum, goes on to say that by

"this means tardy justice will be done to King Thakombau, who is now struggling to raise himself and his people from the depths of heathenism to the light of civilisation, and this long vexed and troublesome question be finally and for ever put at rest in a manner creditable alike to the power and generosity of the Government of the United States of America.

* * * * * * * *

" For twenty years these claims have been held over the head of this semi-barbarous and almost helpless king, who has been worried into the belief that we are determined never to be satisfied, while our Government is made to appear vacillating and ungenerous in the eyes of foreign nations. Great care has been taken to arrive at what is believed to be a just decision, and it is to be hoped that nothing in the result of the labours of the present Court may be made the subject of a stringent magazine article by a captain of the British navy, who necessarily views all matters from an English stand-point."

On the manner and result of this tardy inquiry Mr. Calvert makes the following interesting and pertinent observations:—

"It is pleasing to see Captain Truxton styling Thakombau king in Fiji, and sympathising with him in his struggles and helplessness, and in his strong wishes and efforts to set the matter at rest; *but nothing now can repair the injury done to Thakombau,* it is *irreparable*. Indeed the confusion must have been great on this occasion. The Chief was to have a 'calm and patient hearing,' &c., yet I am informed he was not allowed counsel or witnesses before the Court, though he asked for both. And one member of the Court was a claimant for $4500 or $6000. Mr. Williams' claim only was allowed to be reopened, and *and all the rest were to be fully paid,* even their portion of the $15,000 saddled on Fiji, because of the 'interference' of an American naval officer, senior to the man who inflicted the levy. Why not examine these too? Surely the state in which they found the Consul's account was an encouragement to look into the rest. And the claimant-member of the Court—whose long career in Fiji has been honourable, industrious, and influential for good on the whites, half-castes, and natives of his day—could have afforded ample information and evidence to his fellow-jurors. And again, how is it that interest is allowed to the estate of Mr. Williams, and not claimed also on behalf of the others?

"Captain Truxton was evidently one with the upright officers that had preceded him, and it may be fairly concluded that had it not been for the difficulty of the *Polynesian Company,* he would have sifted the whole affair, and settled it. It never can be that reasonable men from such a nation as America can be guilty of injustice and oppression towards such a people as the Fijians."

Meanwhile, in the preceding year, 1868, some gentlemen from Melbourne, taking advantage of the pressure put on Thakombau by the United States Government for a settlement of their claim, and the unsettled state of the Islands, projected an adventure, by which they were to obtain possession of 200,000 acres of the best lands, an unlimited sovereignty over the same, and various other important rights and concessions, the *quid pro quo* proposed for these trifling advantages being an annual allowance to King Thakombau of 200*l*.—which was deemed sufficient for all regal necessities—together with an undertaking to relieve him of the responsibility of the American claim.

Utterly prostrate, by the distracted state of affairs in his country, crushed by the American demand, which he was wholly unable to meet, and yearning for a deliverance by any means, the Chief gladly grasped at this distant gleam of hope, and entered into the proposed agreement, which, along with the various proceedings and certain official correspondence in connection therewith, is fully set out as follows:—

"*British Consulate, Fiji,* 1*st June,* 1868.

"Sir,—I beg to call your attention to the following matters:—

"About the end of July last a Mr. Brewer, of Melbourne, Victoria, visited Fiji; he represented himself as the agent of certain commercial men of that city, whose attention was directed to this group of islands.

"I furnished Mr. Brewer, at his request, with a transcript of the last return (in a tabulated form) of the approximate imports and exports of Fiji. He visited this office once only during his stay in Levuka, and confined himself solely to commercial subjects.

"Mr. Brewer had many interviews with the Chairman of the Wesleyan Mission, Mr. William Moore, the result of which was a scheme to form a banking and maritime insurance company; this much of their intentions I learnt partly from report and partly from Mr. Moore.

"After a short visit Mr. Brewer returned to Victoria, to mature the plan, while Mr. Moore at once built a house in this port suitable for offices, and speculated largely in land.

"My attention was next called to Mr. Brewer, by the reports in Melbourne newspapers, of a meeting held in that city, to consider the propriety of forming a company to trade with Fiji. The Chairman of the Chamber of Commerce presided. The promoters of the scheme were Mr. Karl Vandamme, Mr. Cairns, and Mr. Brewer. Lengthy communications relative to Fiji were read by Mr. Vandamme; they were in disaccordance with fact, and highly calculated to mislead the Colonial public.

"Mr. Cairns spoke with the same prospective effect.

*   *   *   *   *   *   *   *

"Mr. Brewer followed, and announced the principal feature of their scheme, viz., the liquidation of Thakombau's debt to the United States Government, and the acceptance by the Company of lands, &c. in security.

"A resolution to form a company was finally moved, but no one being found to second it, the meeting broke up. I may here remark that, so far from 'approval,' I never heard of Mr. Brewer's designs; had I been apprised of them, I should, for obvious reasons, have expressed my disapproval.

"Conceiving I had heard the last of Mr. Brewer and his adventure, I dismissed the matter from my attention.

"On the 22nd ult., being at Bureta (south side of Ovalau), I received a note from Mr. Moore, to which I at once replied. My reason for prompt action was that Thakombau was in Levuka, and the arrival of a large steamer with Mr. Brewer and a colleague on board, together with their connection with Mr. Moore, induced me to think that the opportunity of the Chief's visit would not be lost by these persons, who seemed determined to press forward a scheme which would undoubtedly entail loss upon many too confiding persons in the neighbouring colonies, and in the future probably be productive of inconvenience to Her Majesty's Government.

"Referring for a moment to the present American securities, certain islands in Bau territory, I beg, Sir, in part explanation of the steps I have taken, to submit to you that, if the United States Government sell these islands, I will place and keep the purchasers in possession. If this Victorian company advance Thakombau 10,000*l.* sterling to liquidate his debt, accepting his securities, it will do so under the impression that Her Majesty's Government will, if requisite, press any future claims likely to arise from Thakombau's habit of ignoring contracts. With this conclusion I cannot, in view of the past history of Fiji, concur. It is simply transferring for a questionable consideration the onus of an unpleasant procedure from American to British authority, amplified also by unprecedented conditions, containing the germs of

S

trouble and dissension, fatal to the future peace and prosperity of this group of islands.

"I now proceed to the transaction which took place on board the steamer *Albion* upon the 23rd, and my subsequent action in relation thereto, which I venture to hope will meet with your approval.

"In accordance with my note to Mr. Moore, I walked into Levuka, and arrived at my office at 10.30 o'clock A.M., expecting to meet Messrs. Brewer, Evans, and Moore, with the Chief Thakombau. My clerk however informed me the Chief, with four missionaries, had gone on board the *Albion* at 10 o'clock. Under the impression that hoisting Her Majesty's colours would acquaint the above-named persons with my presence in this office, or that courtesy would suggest the propriety of awaiting my arrival to an appointment requested by themselves, I remained disengaged until 2 o'clock P.M., and then gave my attention to other subjects. At noon I was informed that Thakombau was being treated with unbounded hospitality, that he had partaken of a champagne breakfast, and during the morning had consented, through the medium of Mr. Moore, to sign the document, the contents of which were known only to the parties thereto.

"This information I found subsequently to be correct.

"About 3 o'clock P.M. Thakombau came to my office, remained seated in silence for five minutes, and then left.

"In my opinion the Chief was unfit for business of any description. In consequence of the strange rumours which reached me, I proceeded, at 7.30 o'clock P.M., on board the *Albion*, and discovered Thakombau had signed a document prepared and drawn up in Melbourne prior to the *Albion's* departure. This instrument vested Messrs. Brewer and Evans, for the Company, with authority to rule and control all persons, native or foreign, within Thakombau's dominions, to levy taxes, dues, and imposts, as the said Company might think fit, expedient, or proper; granted them a banking monopoly without limit of time, and many rights and privileges not in Thakombau's power to grant. In an annexed schedule Thakombau conveyed to them 200,000 acres of land, not an acre of which he has, in my opinion, any title to.

"The original document, signed in blank by the Chief, was handed me for perusal, together with a printed copy thereof, which I beg to inclose for your information.

"In reply to a query, I declined at that time and place to give an opinion as to the worth of the document, but informed the delegates it was their duty to have submitted the document to me, prior to any negotiation with Thakombau, affecting, as it appeared to me, the commercial interests of a great body of British subjects, both in and out of Fiji, whose capital and industry had called the present trade of the group into existence; also that it was utterly impossible for the Chief to form, in two hours, anything more than a faint conception of the tenor and meaning of the document he had signed.

"On the 25th I addressed a protest to Thakombau, and caused a copy to be posted at this office. I also served on Messrs. Brewer and Evans an injunction to stay further action pending your arrival in Fiji. I acquainted the United States Consul of these facts.

"Having drawn, Sir, your notice to the manner in which Thakombau's signature was obtained, I proceed to the document itself.

"Passing a portion of the premises, I notice the clause or obligation on the part of the Company to well and truly aid and assist in upholding and defending Thakombau's kingdom.

"The meaning of this is that the Company, having purchased the prerogative and power Thakombau may really enjoy, minus his responsibilities, is prepared to receive the Chief's own statement as to the boundaries and limits of his kingdom, and, under the shadow of his name, to take it for themselves by any filibustering measures they may be able to command, or permitted to exercise. This design I learnt from the conversation on board the *Albion*, and that the delegates have held out hopes, flattering to the restless ambition of Thakombau, is beyond doubt. I beg to refer you to a letter from the Rev. Mr. Horsley to me. This part of the Company's design is, I conceive, contrary to the Act of George III. relating to the engagement of Her Majesty's subjects to serve in a foreign service, and the fitting-out and equipping in Her Majesty's dominions vessels for warlike purposes without Her Majesty's permission.

"Referring to the authority vested in the Company, *to ordain and make all laws, and to establish courts, and to appoint judges, magistrates, and other officers to administer such laws*, I beg to observe Thakombau has never enjoyed the right of jurisdiction in any degree over British or other subjects of European Powers. He cannot therefore delegate to others powers he never possessed. Consul Pritchard, in 1860, applied for and obtained similar powers, but received from Lord Russell a reprimand for so doing. Her Majesty's Commissioner to Fiji in 1860–61 distinctly states, Thakombau has no power to make other chiefs submit to his authority. In the present day the natives of Viti Levu would not submit to the rule of Messrs. Brewer and Evans, and Thakombau dare not attempt to enforce it.

"The schedule granting 200,000 acres of land is a document fraught with mischief if permitted to continue, or recognised as valid. Thakombau does not own a rood of land within the described limits. It is occupied and owned, with small exception, by independent tribes now in arms against the Chief of Bau.

"Lavua River, north to the Waidina, is occupied by the important tribe of Namosi, saving such parcels of land as they have sold to British and other subjects; and I have no hesitation in stating this land, ere it can be held by any Europeans under title from Thakombau, must become the theatre of war and bloodshed.

"Thakombau's position in this respect is virtually the same as stated to his Grace the Duke of Newcastle by Colonel Smythe in 1861. Colonel Smythe says : 'He (Thakombau) could not convey to Her Majesty 200,000 acres of land, as consideration for the payment of those claims for him, as he does not possess them; nor does he acknowledge to have offered more than his consent that lands to this extent might be acquired by Her Majesty's Government for public purposes in Fiji.'

"In conclusion, I beg to inform you treaties with Thakombau were made some years ago by France and America, copies of which I shall endeavour to lay before you. The British population of Fiji at the present time amounts approximatively to 600 or 650 persons, and is increasing monthly.

"Many British subjects have invested their labour and capital within the dominions of Thakombau in consequence of his promise to support and protect them, and preserve law and order within his territory. The laws of Bau were enacted in May, 1867, and copies thereof forwarded to the British and American Consulates.

"In order that British settlers in the territories of Thakombau may not have their interests prejudiced by his capricious acts, or by the endeavours of occasional adventurers to obtain privileges opposed equally to law and the spirit of the age, I beg to suggest the propriety of making with Thakombau a treaty of peace and commerce, to remain in force for two years, or such other time as may seem to you sufficient to enable me to submit in detail the present condition of Fiji to Her Majesty's Government, and receive definite instructions.

"I have, &c.,
"(Signed)   JOHN B. THURSTON."

"Commodore Lambert, C.B.,
"Commanding the Australian Squadron."

HISTORICAL NOTICE. 261

"Know all men by these presents that I, King Thakombau, of the Fiji group of Islands, in consideration of William Harry O'Halloran Brewer and John Lavington Evans, of Melbourne, in the colony of Victoria, now on a visit to me as delegates and agents appointed for and on behalf of a certain Company about to be formed in the said Colony, under the 'Companies' Statute, 1864;' hereby undertaking for and on behalf of such Company, and, immediately after its formation, to make suitable provision for the settlement of a claim of 10,000*l.*, or thereabouts, preferred against me as such King, by or on behalf of the Government of the United States of America for losses said to have been sustained by certain American subjects who resided in my kingdom, owing to certain alleged depredations and acts of incendiarism committed and caused by my native subjects, and which said claim the said Government of the United States of America are now threatening to enforce, and also in consideration of the said William Henry O'Halloran Brewer and John Lavington Evans, as the delegates and agents of such intended Company further undertaking, after the formation of the said Company, to pay me, the said King, the annuity or yearly sum of 1,000 dollars: also in consideration of such delegates undertaking that the said Company will at all times, after its formation, well and truly aid, assist me in upholding and defending my said kingdom; do by these presents for ever grant, cede, transfer, and set over unto the said William Harry O'Halloran Brewer and John Lavington Evans, and also Andrew Lyell and Frederick Cook, of Melbourne aforesaid, gentlemen (hereinafter respectively called trustees, for and on behalf of the said intended Company, the several islands, parts of islands, and other territory in Fiji, forming part of my kingdom), which are respectively mentioned and set forth in the schedule hereinafter written, together with the soil or bed of all seas, rivers, and waters adjacent to or abutting on the said scheduled territory, or any part or parts thereof, and also harbours, seas, rivers, creeks, and inlets thereunto belonging or appertaining, or which the said trustees or the said intended Company may now or hereafter think necessary to the settlement and enjoyment of the said scheduled territory, or any part or parts thereof, and also all mines and minerals in or upon the same. And I, the said King, do hereby also grant and give unto the said Trustees, for and on behalf of the said intended Company, and the said intended Company, the sole and exclusive right to impose and levy such duties of custom as to them as may seem fit on the exportation from, or importation into any part of my kingdom, of any goods, wares, or merchandise whatever, with full power to impose and levy wharfage and harbour dues, and also the sole and exclusive right to establish in any part or parts of my kingdom banking institutions, and the sole and exclusive right to issue and circulate throughout all or any part of my kingdom, bank notes; and I, the said King, do hereby pledge myself and my successors, not hereafter to sell, alienate, or cede to any person or persons whomsoever any part or parts of my territory without previously offering the same to the said intended Company, and giving such Company the option and preferential privilege of acquiring the same. And I, the said King, do hereby grant and give unto the said intended Company full power and absolute authority from time to time to ordain and make all such laws for the good government and welfare of the natives, inhabitants, settlers, and people for the time being on the said scheduled lands, and any other portion of the land forming part of my kingdom which may hereafter be acquired as aforesaid, as such Company shall consider just, equitable, and right; and also all such laws as the said intended Company may think necessary or proper, to regulate the trade and commerce of my said kingdom, or of such islands or other portion of my territory as now are, or hereafter may be inhabited by white population, or that of a mixed one, and to establish courts, and appoint judges and magistrates, and other officers to administer and execute such laws. And I, the said King, hereby solemnly pledge myself to uphold and defend such laws, and to protect the inhabitants and settlers for the time being of the lands belonging to the said intended Company, and the property and effects of such inhabitants and settlers, from native or other violence, molestation, or interference, attacks, pillage, and robberies, either from within or without.

"In witness whereof, I, the said King, have hereunto set my hand and seal, the 23rd day of May, in the year of our Lord 1868.

"(Signed) EBENEZER THAKOMBAU,
"*Na Vuneralu, King of Fiji*, his + mark.

"Signed, sealed, and delivered by King Thakombau, in the presence of
"(Signed)   JOHN F. HORSLEY, Wesleyan Missionary.
"SAML. W. BROOKS, Wesleyan Missionary.

"And we the undersigned, being the principal Chiefs under King Thakombau, hereby ratify and confirm in all respects the forgoing Charter.
"(Signed)   RATU SABANAKA NAUIIBIN, his + mark.
"RATU ELIJAH KOROWABALO, his + mark.

"Witnesses to signatures:
"(Signed)   JOHN F. HORSLEY, Wesleyan Missionary.
"SAML. W. BROOKS, Wesleyan Missionary.

"*The Schedule hereinbefore referred to.*

"Two hundred thousand acres, as specified below, including Suva Harbour, and including both banks of the Navua River, and running back to the large Rewa River, that is, all lands within the boundary not already sold, the remainder to be mutually arranged.
"(Signed)   EBENEZER THAKOMBAU, his + mark.
" RATU SARANAKA NAULIRIN, his + mark.
" ELIJAH RAROIWARALO, his + mark.
" Witnesses:
"(Signed)   WILLIAM MOORE.
" JNO. F. HORSLEY.

"This is to certify that the within writing was faithfully and truly explained to King Thakombau in the presence of the undersigned by the Rev. Wm. Moore, of Levuka, Ovalau, the 23rd day of May, 1868.
"(Signed)   JNO. F. HORSLEY.
" SAML. W. BROOKS."

"*Marginal Notes.*

" Be it understood that all privileges, grants, concessions, &c., conferred in this Charter, with the exception of the banking monopoly, shall be understood only to refer to the land in the schedule annexed, or hereafter to be acquired by the Company.
" After the words 'bank-notes,' read 'twenty-one years.'
"(Signed)   W. H. O'H. BREWER.
" J. L. EVANS."

"Know all men by these presents that I, King Thakombau, of the Fiji group of Islands, in consideration of William Harry O'Halloran Brewer and John Lavington Evans, of Melbourne, in the Colony of Victoria, now on a visit to me as delegates and agents, appointed for and on behalf of a certain Company about to be formed in the said Colony, under the Company's Statute, 1864, hereby undertake for and on behalf of such Company, and immediately after its formation, to make suitable provision for the settlement of a claim for 9,000*l*. preferred against me the said King for and on behalf of the Government of the United States of America, for losses said to have been sustained by certain American subjects who resided in my kingdom, owing to certain alleged depredations and acts of incendiarism committed and caused by native subjects, and which said claim the said Government of the United States of America are now threatening to enforce, do by these presents for ever grant, cede, transfer, and set over under the said William Harry O'Halloran Brewer and John Lavington Evans, and also Andrew Lyell and Frederick Cook, of Melbourne aforesaid, gentlemen, hereinafter called trustees, for and on behalf of the said intended Company, the several islands, parts of islands, and other territory in Fiji forming part of my kingdom, which are respectively mentioned and set forth in the schedule hereunder written, together with the soil or bed of all seas, rivers, and waters adjacent to, or abutting on the scheduled territory, or any part or parts thereof, and all harbours, seas, rivers, creeks, and inlets thereunto belonging or appertaining, or which the said trustees, or the said intended Company, may now or hereafter think necessary for the settlement or enjoyment of the said scheduled territory, or any part or parts thereof, and also all mines or minerals in or upon the same ; and in consideration of the Company paying to me annually the sum of 1,000 dollars, I, on the part of myself and my successors for ever, grant to the said Company exemption from all taxation or imposts on the importation into or exportation from any of the lands, harbours, rivers, &c., that now or hereafter shall form part of the said scheduled territory.

"And I also grant to the said Company sole and exclusive right for the term of twenty-one years to establish in any part or parts of my kingdom banking institutions, and the sole and exclusive right to issue and circulate throughout all or any part of my kingdom banknotes.

"And I, the said King, do hereby pledge myself and my successors not hereafter to sell, alienate, or cede any person or persons whomsoever any part or parts of my territory within the following islands, viz., Viti Levu, Kovo, Kautaver, Ono Ongau, Laevai, Ambitiki, Vatu Sile, Motoviki, and Inbenga, without previously offering the same to the said Company, and giving such Company the option and preferential privilege of acquiring the same.

"And I, the said King, pledge myself to protect the inhabitants and settlers of the lands of the Company from native or other violence, molestation, interference, attacks, pillage, and robberies, both from within and without.

"In witness whereof, I, the said King, have hereunto set my hand and seal, this   day of   , in the year of our Lord 1868."

"Acting-Consul Thurston to the King of Bau.

"*British Consulate, Fiji, 25th May*, 1868.

"'Sir,—Whereas Mr. J. Lavington Evans and Mr. W. H. O'H. Brewer, of Melbourne, Victoria, agents and delegates to you from a certain Company about to be formed for the liquidation of your debts to the United States Government, having presented to me for perusal a certain Charter, dated 23rd May instant, granted and delivered by you to them in their representative capacity:

"And whereas the said Charter doth grant and confirm unto the said Company rights and privileges of the gravest importance to yourself, your native subjects, and to European settlers generally residing within your dominions:

"And whereas the said Charter, with its contained rights, privileges, monopolies, &c., was signed and delivered hastily, without the careful deliberation such an important matter demanded:

"And whereas 200,000 acres of land upon Viti Levu, having a frontage extending from Suva to the Lavua river, including both banks of the latter, and extending inland to the Waidini River, hath been granted and confirmed by you unto the said Company for ever:

"And whereas the said included country in its entirety doth not now, or hath in times past been, subject to your authority and control, but is in most part the territory of independent tribes now in arms to prevent your invasion of the country:

"And whereas the grant of this land is illegal by your Fijian laws and those of England, and would be certain to occasion serious complications between the agents of the said Company and the resident landowners:

"And whereas the effect of the rights and power conferred by you upon the said Company for ever is to invest it with absolute and despotic control in your kingdom, enjoying the power and authority of your position, and leaving to you its responsibilities, with power to lock up your lands, absorb revenue, and enjoy interminably a perfect monopoly in all things relative to trade, commerce, and government, to the prejudice and ruin of every trader and settler residing in your dominions, and not being a shareholder in this said Company:

"Now therefore I, John B. Thurston, Esq., Her Britannic Majesty's Acting Consul for Fiji and Tonga, in consideration of the premises, and by virtue of the authority in me vested for the protection and encouragement of British trade and commerce in Fiji and Tonga, hereby protest, and by these presents protest, against the said Charter, its grants, rights, privileges, and monopolies, premises, and habendum, and against all and every act or acts, matters, or things done, or about to be done, relating to the said Charter, pending the arrival in Fiji of Commodore Rowley Lambert, senior officer commanding Her Britannic Majesty's Australian squadron, who is expected about the end of June proximo. In witness whereof I have hereunto set my signature and official seal the day and date first before mentioned.

"(Signed)   John B. Thurston."

" *To Ebenezer Thakombau, King of Bau,*
  "*&c.   &c.   &c.*"

"Acting-Consul Thurston to Messrs. Evans and Brewer.

" *British Consulate, Fiji, 25th May, 1868.*

" Gentlemen,—I have carefully perused a copy of the Charter granted upon the 23rd instant by Thakombau, King of Bau, Fiji, to yourselves, as agents, delegates, or representatives of a certain Company about to be formed in the Colony of Victoria for the purpose of settling a claim of 10,000*l.* sterling, or thereabouts, preferred against King Thakombau, of Bau, by the Government of the United States of America.

" The important subject-matter of this said Charter was not submitted to my notice until after the signature of King Thakombau had been obtained, and the matter so far settled.

" The tenor and meaning of said Charter is to invest your Company not only with great privileges and monopolies, but with the entire government and control of the Bau kingdom.

" These concessions, which would demand the most careful deliberation upon the part of Thakombau, were introduced to his notice after 10 o'clock of the forenoon of the 23rd instant, and by him surrendered at noon of same date. I am therefore morally certain King Thakombau has only a vague and imperfect conception of the obligations incurred.

" Further, the rights and monopolies demanded by and granted to you are virtually such as to place a large part of an important group of islands in your possession, and to enable the Company, if so inclined, to prejudice or ruin those settlers now resident within the Bau dominions, who would be your rivals in trade and commerce.

" As the representative of Her Britannic Majesty in Fiji, it was your duty to submit to me, prior to any negotiating with King Thakombau, the draft of Charter you desired to obtain, and which seriously affects the welfare and interests of hundreds of Her Majesty's subjects resident in, and commercially connected with Fiji.

"I have therefore to inform you that I have this day officially protested against the said Charter, grants, and monopolies of the 23rd instant, and against all the acts, matters, or things done, or about to be done, in or about the said Charter, by all and every person or persons thereunto connected.

"And I herewith require you, J. Lavington Evans and W. H. O'H. Brewer, Esqrs., for the present, and pending the arrival in Fiji of Commodore Rowley Lambert, or other superior officer in Her Majesty's service, with whom I can confer touching the premises, to abstain from any further action in, or by virtue of, the said Charter as it now stands, and by me this day protested.

"I have, &c.,
"(Signed)   JOHN B. THURSTON.
"*J. L. Evans and W. H. O'H. Brewer, Esqrs.,*
"*Delegates, &c., to King Thakombau of Bau.*"

"COMMODORE LAMBERT TO MR. EVANS.

"*Her Britannic Majesty's Ship 'Challenger,' at Ovalau,*
"10*th July,* 1868.

"SIR,—In reply to your communication of the 18th instant, together with the enclosures marked Nos. 1 and 2, I have to observe that I consider no British subject has any right to make or propose any agreement, charter, or, in fact, transact any business involving the conditions as laid down in the Charter presented by you to King Thakombau, to or with a ruler of any country or countries to which an accredited agent of Her Majesty's Government may be appointed, without his knowledge or sanction, nor could he sanction such Charter to be proposed with its conditions. I feel so convinced of this, that I have sent to King Thakombau to meet me here, and I shall have to acquaint him that the paper he has affixed his signature to is valueless, and that no treaty for concession of territory or other negotiations, with the conditions as set forth in that Charter, with British subjects can be deemed valid, however tempting the remuneration may seem to him, without the sanction of the accredited agent of Her Britannic Majesty's Government.

"I have to observe also that the Charter brought up by yourself, and which I believe to have been signed and agreed to by King Thakombau, appears so thoroughly an illegal instrument for the purpose of personal interests, added to which, the communications I have received from Her Majesty's Acting Consul on the transaction, that I shall forward the same, and all correspondence connected therewith, to his Excellency the Governor of Victoria, begging him to take such steps as the law may provide to prevent a recurrence of what I imagine to be an irregular proceeding.

"I have, &c.,
"(Signed) ROWLEY LAMBERT.
"J. L. Evans, Esq. &c."

EXTRACT FROM A DESPATCH FROM GOVERNOR SIR J. H. T. MANNERS SUTTON TO THE DUKE OF BUCKINGHAM AND CHANDOS, dated Government Offices, Melbourne, 12th September, 1868.

"(Received 2nd November, 1868.)
"I have the honour to transmit to your Grace, herein inclosed, copies of letters (two) which I have received from Commodore Lambert, and from Her Majesty's Consul at the Fiji Islands, respecting the proceedings in those islands of two gentlemen (Messrs. Brewer and Evans) who recently left Australia on a mission thither as representatives of a proposed commercial company started but not established in Melbourne.

* * * * * * * *

"At all events, those who are or may be connected with Messrs. Brewer and Evans in their enterprise are not only disentitled, as matters now stand, from claiming British support or protection, but they have been warned of this fact; and although they have not as yet acted upon this warning by relinquishing the endeavour to form a company, they have, by their letters to the newspapers, acknowledged the receipt of it, and, unless I am very much mistaken, the public will appreciate its importance."

CORRESPONDENCE BETWEEN THE COLONIAL OFFICE AND THE FOREIGN OFFICE.

E. C. EGERTON, ESQ., M.P., TO THE UNDER-SECRETARY OF STATE FOR THE COLONIES.

"Foreign Office, 12th October, 1868.

"SIR,—I am directed by the Secretary of State for Foreign Affairs to transmit to you, to be laid before the Secretary of State for the Colonies, a Despatch, with its enclosures, from the Acting British

Consul in the Fiji Islands, relative to the proposal of a Victorian Company to assume sovereign jurisdiction over a part of that territory.

"I am to request that the enclosed papers may be returned to this Office when done with.

"I am, &c.,
"(Signed)   E. C. EGERTON.

"*The Under-Secretary of State,*
"*Colonial Office.*

"(*Extract.*)
"ACTING-CONSUL THURSTON *to the Secretary of State for Foreign Affairs.*

"'*British Consulate, Fiji, 27th May,* 1868.

"'MY LORD,—I beg to inform your Lordship this group of islands is attracting great attention in the commercial circles of the neighbouring Colonies of New South Wales, Victoria, and New Zealand.

"'The British population of Fiji has increased during the present year with unprecedented rapidity, and I have every reason to believe it will continue in an accelerated ratio.

"'British subjects are now settling upon their purchased lands in all parts of this group, but principally at this port and at Rewa.

"'I need scarcely inform your Lordship that among this influx of British settlers are many lawless and unscrupulous persons, who are subject to no control or authority, excepting such as may be vested in this Consulate.

"'The preservation of law and order is therefore at times exceedingly difficult, and as the British population increases, so, in the absence of special instructions and authority, will the difficulty augment.

"'The determination on the part of Australian colonists to invest their capital in Fijian enterprise is so evident that I feel it my duty to submit the fact to your Lordship's notice without loss of time.

"'A late instance of colonial speculation Fiji-ward is especially worthy of your Lordship's attention.

*   *   *   *   *   *   *   *

"'I beg to add that Thakombau repudiates his actions on board the steamship *Albion* on the 23rd instant, and that the "delegates" from Melbourne are respecting my injunction to stay any further action until I can confer with Commodore Lambert.'"

*   *   *   *   *   *   *   *

E. C. EGERTON, ESQ., M.P., TO THE UNDER-SECRETARY OF STATE FOR THE COLONIES.

"*Foreign Office,* 14*th October,* 1868.

"SIR,—With reference to the letter from this Office of the 12th instant, I am directed by Lord Stanley to transmit to you copy of a Despatch from Commodore Lambert, R.N., regarding the negotiation commenced by parties at Melbourne for the purchase of lands at the Fiji Islands; and I am to request that, in laying this Paper before the Duke of Buckingham and Chandos, you will state to his Grace that Lord Stanley would be glad to receive any observations which he may have to make as to the communication to Her Majesty's Consul at the Islands, of the view which Her Majesty's Government take of the proposed sale.

"I am, &c.,
"(Signed) E. C. EGERTON.

"*The Under-Secretary of State,*
"*Colonial Office.*

"COMMODORE LAMBERT TO THE SECRETARY TO THE ADMIRALTY.

"'*Challenger,' at Ovalau,* 21*st July,* 1868.

"'SIR,—With reference to my letter of this date, respecting my arrival at Ovalau on the 9th instant, I beg to acquaint you, for the information of the Lords of the Admiralty, that Her Majesty's Consul brought to my notice that two gentlemen, Messrs. Brewer and Evans, recently came to this place from Melbourne as delegates on behalf of a company about to be formed there for the purpose of paying off the debt due by Thakombau, Chief of Bau, to the American Government, receiving in return a grant of lands and various other rights and privileges.

"'2. They arrived here in the steamship *Albion* during the absence of Her Majesty's Consul, received Thakombau on board that ship a little after 10 A.M., and by noon the Chief had affixed his signature to a charter brought ready prepared from Melbourne by these gentlemen, conveying to them, as delegates, 200,000 acres of land, and conferring on them the right of making laws, fixing the import and export duties, and various other rights.

"'3. As soon as Her Majesty's Consul heard of the proceeding he issued a protest to Thakombau against it, and also an injunction to Messrs. Brewer and Evans to stop further proceedings until my arrival.

"'4. As these gentlemen brought a letter from his Excellency the

Governor of Victoria to Her Majesty's Consul at Fiji, and as I considered their proceedings in the matter to be illegal and unwarrantable throughout, I have forwarded a copy of the whole of the correspondence connected therewith to His Excellency.

" ' 5. This correspondence is very lengthy, and as I am desirous of getting the *Brisk* away, I do not detain her for it, but will forward it to be laid before their Lordships by next mail, by which mail also Her Majesty's Consul will forward his copy to the Secretary of State for Foreign Affairs.

" ' I have, &c.
" ' (Signed)   ROWLEY LAMBERT.
" ' *The Secretary to the Admiralty.*' "

"SIR FREDERIC ROGERS, BART., TO THE UNDER-SECRETARY OF STATE FOR FOREIGN AFFAIRS.

" *Downing Street, 29th October,* 1868.

"SIR,—I am directed by the Duke of Buckingham and Chandos to acknowledge the receipt of your letters of the 12th and 14th instant, relative to negotiations commenced by certain persons, apparently acting on behalf of a company at Melbourne, to acquire sovereign jurisdiction over a portion of the Fiji Islands.

"His Grace is of opinion that the schemes of this kind should receive no encouragement or authority from Her Majesty's Government, and he will be ready to give instructions to that effect to the Governors of the Australian Colonies if Lord Stanley should think that this ought to be done.

" I am, &c.
"(Signed)   FREDERIC ROGERS.
" *The Under-Secretary of State,*
" *Foreign Office.*"

"THE RIGHT HONOURABLE E. HAMMOND TO THE UNDER-SECRETARY OF STATE FOR THE COLONIES.

" *Foreign Office, 30th October,* 1868.

"SIR,—With reference to your letter of the 29th instant, I am directed by Lord Stanley to request that you will state to the Duke of Buckingham that his Lordship concurs in the view taken by his Grace as to the instructions which should be addressed to the Governors of the Australian Colonies in regard to the negotiation undertaken by parties at Melbourne to acquire sovereign jurisdiction over a portion of the Fiji Islands.

"I am to add that Lord Stanley would be glad to be enabled to communicate to Her Majesty's Consul the view thus taken of the matter by the Duke of Buckingham.

"I am, &c.,
"(Signed)   E. HAMMOND.
" *The Under-Secretary of State,*
" *Colonial Office.*"

"THE EARL GRANVILLE, K.G., TO GOVERNOR THE HON. SIR J. H. T. MANNERS SUTTON.

" *Downing Street, 3rd December,* 1868.

"SIR,—I have the honour to acknowledge the receipt of your Despatch No. 142, of the 12th of September last, enclosing copies of papers relating to negotiations entered into, by some persons acting, as it appears, on behalf of a Company at Melbourne, to obtain rights of jurisdiction and property over a portion of the Fiji Islands.

"I approve of the course which you have taken in this matter.

"It should be distinctly understood that undertakings like the present receive no encouragement or authority from Her Majesty's Government.

"I have, &c.,
"(Signed)   GRANVILLE.

" *The Hon. Sir J. H. T. Manners Sutton,*
" *&c. &c. &c.*"

Notwithstanding these official warnings and the prompt action taken in the matter by the British Consul, supported by the Colonial and Home Authorities, 'The Polynesian Company (Limited), Melbourne and Fiji, Incorporated 7th December, 1868,' became *un fait accompli*, excepting, indeed, so far as that authority is concerned which was supposed to vest in the Company, *to ordain and make all laws, to establish courts, and to appoint judges, magistrates, and other officers to administer such laws.*

What is still more important, they have paid most, if not all, of the American claim, and taken possession of at least 90,000 acres of land, as detailed in this statement:—

Account of Lands already conveyed by King Cakobau to the Polynesian Land Company (Limited).

District.	Property.	Planters.	Acreage. Cultivated.	Acreage. Uncleared.	Total.
Mbega	Putrie Island, less the Western end.	None.	None.	All.	Acres. 10,000
Suva	Harbour, the islets in the bay and surrounding lands, including frontages to Leucala Bay and the Waimana River, and rivers entering harbours.	Brewer and Joske. Armstrong Brothers. Fiji Planting Company of Ballarat. Dr. McGrath. Mr. Thomas.	About 400 acres.	About 26,600 acres.	27,000
Viti Levu Bay	Block round the bay and Raku Raku River.	T. B. Matthews, and about thirty small holders or settlers. Trespassers only.	About 50 acres, by trespassers.	49,950	50,000
Natawa Bay	Block 4 miles square, on the north side of harbour.	Thomas Reed, for himself and co-partners in Melbourne.	About 100 acres.	9,900	10,000
			550	96,450	97,000
	Deduct 7,000 acres for adverse claimants				7,000
	Equal				90,000

Now Thakombau hoped to reap some of those doubtful benefits foreshadowed in this agreement, and to obtain a peace and quiet, to which he had so long been a tranger.

But happiness, the dusky monarch's end, was not found even here. From the outset he was sadly put about to find the land which was not his to give, and disputes, claims, quarrels, and counter-claims soon arose, which did not fail to cause him sad disquiet. Old purchasers were ousted from estates previously conveyed to them, the whites not excepted, and club-law and disturbances soon prevailed to such an extent, as to make the Chief regret very bitterly his hasty bargain with the gentlemen from Melbourne.

It is to be hoped that this 'Polynesian Company' may not hereafter also prove a source of embarrassment to our own Government.

There can be no doubt that had it not been for its existence in 1869, the American Commission, presided over by Captain Truxton, would have experienced less difficulty in arbitrating on the matters brought before it, to the satisfaction of all parties, and finally putting the question at rest. Be this as it may, an adjudication has been arrived at, and however much we may deplore the manner of the inquiry and the lameness of its result, it is felt that any attempt now made to re-open the question would be fraught with difficulty, and would be both impolitic and injudicious.

In 1854 Thakombau, smarting from constant reverses and defeat in war, at length yielded to the pious exhortations of the missionaries and an earnest letter from King George of Tonga, and determined on renouncing the flesh*

---

* This was literally the case, for up to that time he had been a cannibal.

and the devil. We are told the precise date of this solemn event was the 30th of April, and that it was heralded by the beating of the death-drum, which but a few days previously had summoned the same people to a cannibal feast.

The truth of the Italian proverb, *Passato il pericolo gabbato il santo* (When the danger is past the saint is mocked), proved by the experience of ages, once more received a confirmation at the hands of Tui Viti, who, relieved temporarily from his difficulties, again returned to his heathen ways. This relapse of Paganism did not long endure.

As, fifteen hundred and sixty-one years since, a Cæsar was convinced of the manifold benefits of Christianity, so now has this dusky potentate of Fiji become persuaded of the necessity and authority of a religion, which, founded on the sublime theory of the Gospel, diffuses among the people a pure, benevolent, and universal system of ethics, adapted to every duty and every condition of life.

A fitting sequel to this reward of missionary labour took place three years later in the baptism of Thakombau and his chief queen, to whom he was then also joined in holy matrimony. She is described as being a stout, quiet woman, about five feet two inches in height.

"I have only seen her once *dressed*, and that at the time of our first official interview about the cession. She then wore a neat bonnet, latest Parisian fashion, a coloured silk dress, and a black mantilla, trimmed with lace. I need scarcely add that the use of crinoline was not unknown even in this remote quarter of the globe. The Queen, at the interview alluded to, was rather bashful, owing to a wish expressed by the Consul that she should sit at her husband's side, instead of, as the rules of the country demanded, behind him. However, she comported herself very well indeed, but I daresay was very glad to get her clothes off as soon as the official interview was over." *

* *Vide* 'Mission to Viti,' B. Seemann.

Here is a description by Captain Erskine of Thakombau himself :—

"It was impossible not to admire the appearance of the Chief: of large, almost gigantic size, his limbs were beautifully formed and proportioned; his countenance, with far less of the negro cast than among the lower orders, agreeable and intelligent, while his immense head of hair, covered and concealed with gauze, smoke-dried and slightly tinged with brown, gave him altogether the appearance of an eastern sultan. No garment confined his magnificent chest and neck, or concealed the natural colour of the skin, a clear but decided black; and in spite of his paucity of attire, the evident wealth that surrounded him showing that it was a matter of choice and not necessity, he looked every inch a king."

Though perhaps in some respects slightly overdrawn, this is, in the main, a fairly good representation of His Fijian Majesty. In reality, there is nothing gigantic in his proportions; at the outside he does not measure more than six feet in height, and neither does he appear to be physically developed in any unusual degree. That he is, however, a powerfully-built man one cannot fail to notice, and especially when he is divested of the uniform which he now always dons on holidays and state occasions. His bearing is dignified; and no one being better aware of his good looks than himself, he feels much piqued that his portraits which are published are not flattering, nor do him justice. To this brief retrospect little else remains to be added.

The idols and the temples overthrown, superstition and priestcraft nearly effaced, a period of savage licence and darkness is about to be succeeded by one of enlightenment and civilisation. The wheel of fortune has accomplished a revolution, and the last relics of barbarism and strife will soon lie buried in a common grave.

APPENDIX.

APPENDIX.

Tonga Islands.*

The kingdom of Tonga is situated about 250 miles to the windward of Fiji, and is composed of some sixty islands, forming the three groups of Tonga, Haabai, and Vavau, running in a direction south-east and north-west, and distant from one another about one day's sail; the number of inhabitants is 16,000, and the area of the three groups about 650 square miles.

The trade is confined to Sydney and Samoa, the same vessels are employed as last year, and their aggregate tonnage amounts to:—British, 2,200; foreign (German), 166.

The exports of Tonga consist almost entirely of cocoa-nut oil, of which the following is the return for the past year:—

Estimated Exports of the Friendly Islands, 1866.

	Tons.	Galls.
Exported by the Tongan Government	308	144
„ by the Wesleyan Mission	90	..
„ by Private Traders	306	..
Total Tons	704	144

At 21*l.* per ton, equal	£14,796
Provisions, Coffee, Cotton, &c.	1,230
Total value of Exports	£16,026

The manufacture of the oil is carried on in the rudest manner the nut is scraped and placed, mixed with a little sea water, in hollow logs, to putrefy. The oil disengages

* Extract from Consular Report for the year 1866.

itself, and is collected at the bottom of the trough. In the year 1850 an enterprising Ceylon house set up a steam oil mill in the Haabai group, but through the fault of the agent, and the irregular system adopted, it failed to answer the expectations formed, and caused its projectors to lose 15,000*l.*

King George of Tonga has endeavoured, both by precept and example, to induce his people to pay attention to the cultivating of coffee, which is found to flourish luxuriantly throughout the Friendly Islands. A Tongan law compels every householder to possess twenty coffee-trees, and some good has been effected by this regulation, as thirty tons of coffee were gathered during the past year; much of this, however, lost its value from the careless manner in which it was picked and dried. An order was also given by the King, forcing each adult to plant 200 cotton-trees; but such is the indolence and indifference of the people, that the greater part of the crop was suffered to run to waste on the plant; and it required a second order on the part of the King, to induce the natives to gather it, which was done in so slovenly a manner that it remains unsaleable to the present time.

The King, in endeavouring to force his people along the path of progress, receives little assistance from those in authority under him. Every innovation is regarded with dislike or indifference. The history of Tongan progress hitherto has been the life of the King; whatever has been done for the advancement of the country has been done by him, unaided, except by the advice of the resident Wesleyan missionaries. He is now an old man, upwards of seventy years of age, but he still possesses more sagacity, energy, and liberality than any man in his dominion.

Three years ago a law was passed by the Tongan Government, that the poll-tax of 16*s.* paid hitherto in cash should, for the future, be paid in oil at the current price of one shilling per gallon; by this step, the Tongan Government increased their revenue thirty per cent., but the resident traders were left without any occupation while this measure was in force. The people also found it oppressive, as much time and oil were wasted in carrying the latter to the district collector, waiting until these chose to measure the oil and give a receipt to the bearers. Many of the districts did not contain sufficient cocoa-nuts for the oil required, and the inhabitants were forced to go elsewhere to seek the means of paying their taxes. These circumstances induced King George to repeal the oil-tax and levy it in money as formerly. the traders agreeing to purchase the oil from the natives, at the rate of five shillings for four gallons. They likewise undertake the risk and expense of collecting it from the villagers, and this, together with the cost of casks, 4*l.* the tun of five, materially lessens their profits; the present price of oil delivered on the beach is 21*l.* per tun.

Tonga was formerly governed by a number of chiefs, who owned the land and the people on it. One of the first acts of King George on consolidating his authority was to emancipate the people, and make all lands the property of the state. A poll-tax of four dollars is levied on all males over sixteen years. From this revenue the dispossessed chiefs receive an annual stipend in addition to a small quit-rent from their former vassals. Each Tongan family can obtain at a nominal rent as much land as they choose to cultivate, estimated at twenty-five acres. The present quantity of food produced in Tonga is however much less than before the emancipation, and this may be accounted for—in addition to the love of indolence, common to all emancipated slaves—by the inconvenient and irregular manner in which the lands have been apportioned, the people are forced to remain in their old tribal villages, while their farms are many miles distant. These are neglected altogether, or only attended to once a week, the proprietor contenting himself with raising a bare sufficiency for himself and family, trusting that his neighbours will share with him their superabundance. Very fair roads have been made throughout the Islands, as they are all, with the exception of Vavau, perfectly level, and free from stone, the only labour required is clearing away the forest and brushwood; but as yet no wheeled vehicles are in use, except by the white traders. The toil of carrying such bulky articles as yams, or taro, under a tropical sun for several miles, is sufficiently severe to exhaust the energies of even a stronger frame than the Polynesian.

Until the Friendly Islands can be brought into more immediate contact with civilisation they must continue in their present unprogressive state. The territory being small, land is not allowed to be sold to foreigners, a prudent regulation, although it has given great offence to the whites; the King was willing to lease land at nominal rents, and some Europeans succeeded in securing farms on easy terms. Unfortunately for the' interest of the others, King George found himself so wearied with the constant and unreasonable demands of those to whom he had leased these lands, that he he is now disinclined to extend the privilege to others.

The fertility of Tonga is such that a very small portion of land suffices for the support of each household; large tracts lie neglected and abandonded, which, under the present regulations, must continue unoccupied. Native labour is obtained with difficulty, even at the high rate of 2s. per diem. Here, as in Fiji, it will be necessary to import labour, which, at the present time, is not encouraged by the Tongan Government.

The complete security of life and property in Tonga, the good police regulations, and the existence of fair roads in the Islands, would attract from the Australian colonies many men (of a class superior to the usual run of island settlers) who would hesitate to trust their families or property in the comparatively lawless district of Fiji, and whenever the Tongan Government proves liberal in granting leases to foreigners, and encouraging the importation of labour either from China or the Western Islands, there is reason to hope that the influx of capital and population, will rouse again the dormant energies of the Tonguese, and force them to continue the work of progress, which they entered on thirty years ago.

Port Levuka, Fiji, December 26th, 1866.

QUEENSLAND.
An Act to Regulate and Control the Introduction and Treatment of Polynesian Labourers.

Assented to 4th March, 1868.

WHEREAS many persons have deemed it desirable and necessary, in order to enable them to carry on their operations in tropical and semi-tropical agriculture, to introduce to the colony Polynesian labourers: And whereas it is necessary for the prevention of abuses and for securing to the labourers proper treatment and protection, as well as for securing to the employer the due fulfilment by the immigrant of his agreement, that an Act should be passed for the control of such immigration: Be it therefore enacted by the Queen's Most Excellent Majesty, by and with the advice and consent of the Legislative Council and Legislative Assembly of Queensland in Parliament assembled, and by the authority of the same, as follows:— [Preamble.]

1. It shall not be lawful for any person or persons to introduce any Polynesian labourers into the Colony of Queensland unless and except in accordance with the regulations contained in this Act and the forms thereunto attached. [Not lawful to introduce Polynesian labourers except according to regulations.]

2. Within four months from the passing of this Act all persons who have in their employment any Polynesian labourers shall make a return to the Immigration Agent, or other authorized agent, of all such labourers in their employment, setting forth the number and names of such labourers, the nature and duration of their agreements, together with all such particulars as may be required. [Present employers to make returns within four months from passing of Act.]

3. Any person employing any Polynesian labourers who shall fail to make a return as required by the foregoing clause shall, on conviction of the same before any two justices of the peace, be subject to a penalty not exceeding fifty pounds. [Penalty for failure in making returns.]

FIJI

Act to apply to employers and labourers at time of passing.

4. The provisions of this Act shall so far as practicable be applied to all Polynesian labourers introduced into this Colony before the passing of this Act and to their employers.

Inspectors to be appointed.

5. The Governor, with the advice of the Executive Council, shall appoint from time to time such person or persons as shall be found requisite for the proper inspection of the said Polynesian labourers, and inforcing the provisions of this Act.

Form of application.

6. All persons desirous of importing labourers from the South Sea Islands shall make application to the Colonial Secretary at Brisbane, in the Form A appended hereto, stating the number required, and how they are to be employed, such application to be accompanied by a bond in Form K, signed by applicant and two sureties, to secure the return of the labourers to their native islands at the expiration of three years or thirty-nine moons from date of arrival. A licence in Form C, may then be issued authorizing the applicant to import the number required.

Vessel to be properly found.

7. The owner or charterer of any vessel so licensed shall provide for the use of the passengers a supply of medicines, medical comforts, instruments, and other things proper and necessary for diseases and accidents incident to sea voyage, and for the medical treatment of the passengers during the voyage, including an adequate supply of disinfecting fluid or agent, together with printed or written directions for the use of the same respectively; and such medicines, medical comforts, instruments, and other things, shall, in the judgment of the emigration officer at the port of clearance, be good in quality and sufficient in quantity for the probable exigencies of the intended voyage, and shall be properly packed and placed under the charge of the medical practitioner, when there is one on board, to be used at his discretion. In case of non-compliance with any of the requirements of this section the master of the ship shall

Penalty

for each offence be liable to a penalty not exceeding fifty pounds, nor less than five pounds sterling.

8. The master of any vessel arriving with Polynesian labourers shall be bound to report on arrival at any of the ports of Queensland the number of such labourers and the names of the employers to whom they have been or are to be indented, and shall not be permitted to land any of the immigrants until he has received the certificate (Form L) of the Immigration Agent, or other officer of the Government empowered to grant same, that the following regulations have been complied with :— *Master of vessel to report arrival, &c.*

(1.) The production by the master of the vessel of a certificate in Form I, or certificates signed by a consul, missionary, or other known person, that the labourers have voluntarily engaged themselves and entered into their agreements with a full knowledge and understanding of the nature and conditions of same, and that when they were embarked they were not known to be afflicted with any disease, and were neither maimed, halt, blind, deaf, dumb, idiotic, or insane. *Master of vessel to produce certificate.*

(2.) The production by the employers or parties to whom the labourers are, or are intended to be, indented, of the certificate in Form C authorizing them to recruit. *Employers to produce certificate of Immigration Agent.*

(3.) That proper means have been taken since the arrival of the ship by the Immigration Agent or other officer by explanations, questions, and inquiries amongst the labourers themselves to ascertain whether they have a proper understanding of the conditions of the agreements, and did voluntarily enter into same: That the agreements have been signed in the form prescribed, and the employers bound to observe the rules laid down for the treatment and management of the labourers. *Immigrants to understand the nature of their agreements.*

9. All agreements (Form D) shall be completed on *Agreements to be*

completed on board ship where practicable.

board the ship if possible, and the immigrants taken from same by their employers; and should there arise a necessity for taking any of the labourers to the Immigration Depôt, their maintenance there shall in all cases be borne by the employer.

Immigrants to be registered on arrival.

10. The arrival of the immigrants shall be registered in the Immigration Office, Brisbane, or at the Custom House in any other port, and in the latter case a copy of the register shall be forwarded by the Customs officer to the Immigration Office by following mail.

Scale of rations.

11. The scale of rations and wages shown in Form G, and printed on the form of agreement, shall in no case be deviated from.

Register to be kept by employer.

12. A register of hired Polynesian labourers shall be kept by each employer in Form E, which shall be open for the inspection of any magistrate or other person appointed by Government for the purpose, who shall record his visit therein. No entry except the state of muster at the expiration of each quarter shall be made in the register of the employer unless from a document of hiring, transfer, death, or desertion, countersigned by the Immigration Agent or other authorized officer.

Transfers how made.

13. No transfer of an immigrant shall be made except with the full consent of the transferror, the immigrant, and the Government in Form F, and no immigrant shall be allowed to leave his employment under transfer until the same has been recorded in the books of the Immigration Office or other appointed office. All transfers shall be signed by the transferror and immigrant in presence of a magistrate, who shall before such signing explain to the immigrant the full meaning and effect of such transfer: Provided that every transferree shall enter into a bond similar to that of the transferror prior to any transfer being consented to.

Deaths or desertions to be

14. All deaths or desertions shall be immediately reported to the nearest bench of magistrates and to the

Immigration Agent by the employer, and in case of death a medical certificate of the cause thereof shall be forwarded if possible. *reported immediately.*

15. All masters of vessels about to proceed to the South Sea Islands in order to obtain labourers therefrom shall enter into a bond, in Form B, with two sufficient sureties for the prevention of kidnapping, and for the due observance of these regulations, so far as they are concerned. *Masters of vessels to execute bonds prior to proceeding to hire labourers.*

16. No ship shall carry a greater number of passengers than in the proportion of one statute adult to every twelve clear superficial feet allotted to their use: Provided that the height between decks shall not be less than six feet six inches from deck to deck; when the height of the 'tween decks exceeds six feet six inches an extra number of passengers may be taken, at the rate of one for every one hundred and forty-four cubic feet of space. Each ship must be fitted with open berths or sleeping places in not more than two tiers; the lowest tier shall be raised six inches from the deck, and the interval between the two tiers of berths shall not be less than two feet six inches. All passengers shall be berthed between decks or in deck-houses. *Number of passengers. (Vide Imperial Act, 16 and 17 Vict. c. 84.)*

17. But no ship, whatever her tonnage or superficial space of passenger decks, shall carry a greater number of passengers on the whole than in the proportion of one statute adult to every five superficial feet clear for exercise on the upper deck or poop, or if secured and fitted on the top with a railing or guard to the satisfaction of the emigration officer at the port of clearance on any roundhouse or deckhouse. *Proportion of passengers to deck area.*

18. The length of the voyage to or from the South Sea Islands shall be computed at thirty days for sailing vessels and fifteen days for steamers. *Length of voyage.*

19. Three quarts of water daily during the voyage shall be allowed to each adult exclusive of the quantity used for cooking purposes. *Water on the voyage.*

20. Provisions shall be issued to each statute adult *Provisions on the voyage.*

during the voyage according to the following scale, namely :—

DAILY PROVISIONS FOR STATUTE ADULT.

	lbs.	oz.
Yams	4	0
Or rice	1½	0
Or maize meal	1½	0
Meat (pork or beef)	1	0
Tea	0	0½
Sugar	0	2
Tobacco (during good behaviour), per week,	0	1½

The undermentioned clothing shall be supplied to each labourer, immediately on embarkation, in advance :—

1 Flannel Shirt,
1 Pair Trousers,
1 Blanket.

Nominal return to be sent at expiration of each quarter.

21. Nominal returns of labourers shall be made by employers of South Sea Island labour to the Immigration Agent at the expiration of each quarter in Form II.

Returns to be forward to Colonial Secretary each quarter.

22. At the end of each quarter the police magistrates or bench of magistrates in each district where South Sea Island labourers are employed shall forward to the Colonial Secretary a return of all cases adjudicated upon in relation to Polynesian labourers employed under these regulations, such returns to include the names of employers and labourers, and the nature of the offences.

Penalty for harbouring runaway labourers.

23. All persons harbouring or employing Polynesian labourers otherwise than under these regulations, without reporting the same to the nearest bench of magistrates and to the Immigration Agent in Brisbane, shall be liable on conviction thereof to a penalty not exceeding twenty pounds.

Breaches of regulations punishable by fine.

24. All breaches of these regulations shall be punishable by fine, to be recovered in a summary manner before two justices of the peace; for the first offence a fine not exceeding ten pounds, for second and subsequent offences not exceeding twenty pounds, nor less than five pounds.

25. All engagements made or to be made with Polynesian labourers already in the colony, or to arrive, are hereby expressly declared to be subject to the provisions of the Act twenty-five Victoria, number eleven. *Engagements subject to 25 Vict. No. 11.*

26. A tax of twenty pounds per head for every Polynesian labourer introduced contrary to the provisions of this Act shall be levied on all vessels in which such labourers may be brought to this colony, and in default of payment of such tax such vessel shall be absolutely forfeited to Her Majesty. *Tax on vessels in default of compliance.*

27. All expenses incurred by the Government in affording hospital relief to sick Polynesian labourers, or by their detention in immigration depôts, shall be chargeable to the employers of such men, and may be recovered from them by summary process on the information of Immigration Agent or other authorized officer. *Expenses incurred by Government chargeable to employers in certain cases.*

28. Any person who shall without the consent of the labourer and the written permission of the Government remove or attempt to remove any such labourer out of the Colony of Queensland, except for the purpose of his return to his home, shall be liable to a penalty of twenty pounds for every such labourer so removed or attempted to be removed, and it shall be lawful for the Government in any case to prevent the removal of any such labourer except for the purpose of his return to his home as aforesaid. *Labourers not to be removed out of the colony without permission or consent.*

29. Any person supplying Polynesian labourers with spirits shall be punishable as at present in the case of aboriginals under fifty-first section of "*Licensed Publicans Act*," twenty-seven Victoria, number sixteen. *Polynesian labourers not to be supplied with spirituous liquors.*

30. It shall not be lawful for any employer of Polynesian labourers to charge such labourers with the payment of any moneys on account of stores supplied, or to deduct any sum in respect thereof from any wages due to them. *Store accounts not to be deducted from wages.*

31. This Act shall be styled and may be cited as the '*Polynesian Labourers Act of 1868.*' *Short title.*

FORM A.

Application for permission to introduce South Sea Island agricultural or pastoral Labourers.

I, , request to be allowed, in accordance with the Act now in force, to procure from the South Sea Islands immigrants for agricultural or pastoral purposes to be employed in the district.

A. B.
Applicant's signature.

The above requisition lodged with me this day of 18 .

G. H.
Immigration Agent, Queensland.

FORM B.

Bond to be entered into by Shipmasters.

Know all men by these presents, that of of , and of are held and firmly bound unto our sovereign Lady Victoria, by the grace of God of the United Kingdom of Great Britain and Ireland Queen, Defender of the Faith, in the sum of five hundred pounds of good and lawful money of Great Britain, to be paid to our said Lady the Queen, her heirs and successors; to which payment well and truly to be made we bind ourselves and every of us jointly and severally for and in the whole our heirs, executors, and administrators, and every of them firmly by these presents.

Sealed with our seals
Dated this day of one thousand eight hundred and

Whereas by the *Polynesian Labourers Act* of 1868 it is amongst other things enacted that all masters of vessels proceeding to the South Sea Islands in order to obtain labourers therefrom shall enter into a bond with two sufficient sureties for the prevention of kidnapping, and due observance of the requirements of the said recited Act: Now the condition of this obligation is such that if the above-bounden J. K., master of ship , about to proceed to the South Sea Islands to procure labourers, shall faithfully observe the requirements of the said recited Act, and shall satisfy the Government of Queensland, through its officer duly appointed for the purpose, that

no kidnapping was allowed countenanced or connived at, then this obligation to be void, otherwise to remain in full force and virtue.
Signed, sealed, and delivered by the above-bounden   [L. S.]
and   in the presence of
I hereby certify that the above bond was duly signed, sealed, and delivered by the said   , and in my presence, this day of   18   .
                                        Immigration Agent.

FORM C.

Licence to recruit Labourers from the South Sea Islands.

This is to certify that   [or his agent] is hereby licensed to recruit   immigrant labourers from the South Sea Islands for Queensland, in conformity with the Act passed regarding such recruiting. This licence is to remain in force only until the number mentioned above have been recruited.
  Dated this   day of   18   .
                                        Colonial Secretary of Queensland.
  Immigration Agent, Queensland.
  N.B.—This licence is to be returned to the Immigration Agent when the labourers have been received.

FORM D.

                                                    18   .
MEMORANDUM OF AGREEMENT made this day between   of   of the first part, and   native of   , per ship   ,of the second part. The conditions are that the said party of the second part engages to serve to the said party of the first part as a   , and otherwise to make   generally useful for the term of   calendar months, and also to obey all   or   overseer's or authorized agent's lawful and reasonable commands during that period, in consideration of which services the said party of the first part doth hereby agree to pay the said party of the second part wages at the rate of not less than six pounds (6*l.*) per annum, to provide   with me understated rations daily, to provide suitable clothing and proper lodging accommodation, and to defray the expenses of   conveyance to the place at which   to be employed, to pay wages in the coin of the realm at the end of each year of the agreement, and provide them

U 2

with a return passage to their native island at the expiration of three years. No wages shall be deducted for medical attendance.

DAILY RATION.

	lbs.	ozs.
Beef or mutton (or 2 lbs. of fish)	1	0
Bread or flour	1	0
Molasses (or sugar)	0	5
Vegetables (or rice 4 oz., or maize meal 8 oz.)	2	0
Tobacco (per week)	0	1½
Salt (per week)	0	2
Soap (per week)	0	4

CLOTHING.

	Yearly.
Shirts (one of flannel or serge)	2
Trousers (pairs)	2
Hat	1
Blankets	1 pair.

In witness whereof they have mutually affixed their signatures to this document.

Witness:
  The above contract was explained in my presence to the said immigrants, and signed before me by them with their names or marks, and by   or his authorized agent at   , this   day of 186 .

         G. H.
      Immigration Agent or Custom House Officer.

Registered at the   office, Brisbane, Queensland, this
  day of   18

         G. H.
         Immigration Agent.

APPENDIX. 293

FORM E.

Register of South Sea Island Labourers employed on the Plantation of _____, in the District of _____; Name of Plantation _____; Post Town _____

Number	Name	From	Date of Arrival	Date when due for return to South Sea Islands	Return for Quarter ended 31 Mar., 1868. 1st Quarter.	Return for Quarter ended. 2 Q.	Return for Quarter ended. 3 Q.	Return for Quarter ended. 4 Q.	Return for Quarter ended. 5 Q.	Return for Quarter ended. 6 Q.	Return for Quarter ended. 7 Q.	Return for Quarter ended. 8 Q.	Return for Quarter ended. 9 Q.	Return for Quarter ended. 10 Q.	Return for Quarter ended. 11 Q.	Return for Quarter ended. 12 Q.	REMARKS. Date of Deaths, Transfers, Desertions, Special Reports, visits of Inspector or Magistrate, punishments inflicted by Magistrates, &c.
					No. Transferred.												
					Less Deaths Transferred.												
					Total												

I visited the plantation on _____, and found all in good order.

J. P.

FORM F.

We [*name and designation of employer and names and numbers of immigrants engaged*], being respectively the master and servants under a contract of service made before the Government Emigration Agent at   , on the   day , do hereby agree that the whole rights and obligations of the said first party under the said contract shall be, and the same are hereby transferred, as at the date hereof, to [*name and designation*], who hereby agrees to accept the said transfer and the contract hereby transferred, with all its rights and obligations.

X. I.
A. B. } *Signatures or marks of all the parties.*
I.

The above transfer, signed by all the parties thereto, its nature and effect having been first fully explained to the immigrants above-named, all in my presence. The said transfer also approved and concurred in by me as on behalf of the Government.

At   this   day of   18

G. H.
Immigration Agent [*or* Justice of the Peace].

Registered this , day of   18

G.H.
Immigration Agent.

FORM G.

SCALE OF RATIONS.

Daily.

	lbs.	oz.
Beef or mutton (or 2 lbs. of fish)	1	0
Bread or flour	1	0
Molasses or sugar	0	5
Vegetables (or rice 4 oz., or maize meal 8 oz.)	2	0
Tobacco (per week)	0	1½
Salt (per week)	0	2
Soap (per week)	0	4

Wages—Not less than six pounds (6*l.*) per annum, in the coin of the realm.

FORM II.

QUARTERLY RETURN.

Return of South Sea Islanders employed on the Plantation of   , in
the district of   ; Name of Plantation   ; Post
Town   , for quarter ending   .

No.	Name.	From.	State of Muster on 31st March, 1868.	Transfers.	Desertions.	Deaths.	Remarks.

RECAPITULATION.

Number at date of last return . . . .
Number transferred to plantation during above quarter . . . .

    Deduct:—
Number died during above quarter . . . .
Number transferred from plantation during above quarter .

Number remaining on   . . . .

                                              Proprietor of

Registered at Immigration Office, Brisbane, on   and acknowledged

                                                  Immigration Agent.

FORM I.

Whereas   , duly licensed by the Government of Queensland to recruit South Sea Island labourers according to licence exhibited to us, and   natives of   , appeared before us this   day of   18 : The said agent has hired the said natives to serve various employers in Queensland as labourers for a term of three years, and undertakes that they shall be furnished with the undermentioned rations and clothing, that they shall be paid at the rate of not less than six pounds (6l.) per head per annum in coin of the realm, that they shall be provided with proper lodging accommodation, and that the cost of their passage to and from Queensland, and all other costs and charges, shall be defrayed by their employers, and that they shall be returned free of expense to this place at the expiration of three years, and that the Government of Queensland shall exercise supervision over their employers and otherwise protect them during their term of service, and during their passage to and from Queensland.

Now we certify that this document has been read, and its full meaning and effect explained to the said before-mentioned natives, in the presence of the said agent and of ourselves, and that the said natives have consented to accompany said agent to Queensland. And we further certify that to the best of our belief none of the said natives are suffering from any disease, or are maimed, halt, blind, deaf, dumb, idiotic, or insane.

    In witness whereof we have hereunto attached our signatures, this day of   18   at

           Missionary [*or* European Resident, *or* Chief Interpreter].
           Agent.
           Natives.

CLOTHING PER ANNUM.

Hat	1
Shirts (one flannel or serge)	2
Trousers, pairs	2
Blankets, pair	1

RATIONS PER DIEM.

	lbs.	oz.
Bread	1	0
Beef or mutton (or fish 2 lbs.)	1	0
Molasses, or sugar	0	5
Vegetables (or rice 4 ozs., or maize meal 8 ozs.) . .	2	0
Tobacco, per week	0	1½
Salt	0	2
Soap, per week	0	4

                      Countersigned by Master of Vessel.

    To be furnished to Immigration Agent or Custom's officer, with report of arrival.

FORM K.

Form of Bond to be given by Employer.

    Know all men by these presents, that we, A. B., of C. D., and E. F., of   , are held and firmly bound unto our Sovereign Lady Victoria, by the grace of God of the United Kingdom of Great Britain and Ireland Queen, Defender of the Faith, in the sum of ten pounds of good and lawful money of Great Britain for each Polynesian labourer employed by us, to be paid to our said Lady the Queen, her heirs and successors; to which payment well and truly to be made we bind ourselves and every of us, jointly and severally, for and in the whole, our heirs, executors, and administrators, and every of them, firmly by these presents.

Sealed with our seals

Dated this   day of   18 .

Whereas by the *Polynesian Labourers Act of* 1868 it is amongst other things enacted, that all persons desirous of importing labourers from the South Sea Islands shall enter into a bond, with two sureties, to secure the return of the labourers to their native Islands at the expiration of the three years or thirty-nine moons from date of arrival, at the rate of ten pounds sterling for each labourer introduced : Now the condition of this obligation is such, that if the above-bounden A. B. shall pay to the Immigration Agent at the rate of fifteen shillings per quarter for every Polynesian labourer in his employment, for the purpose of providing a return passage for each and every South Sea Islander introduced by him under his application, and also all the charges or expenses incurred by the Government of Queensland in connection with the same, then this obligation to be void, otherwise to remain in full force and virtue.

Signed, sealed, and delivered by the above-bounden A. B., C. D., and E. F., in the presence of   [L S.]

I hereby certify that the above bond was duly signed, sealed, and delivered by the said A. B., C. D., and E. F., in my presence, this day of   18 .

Immigration Agent [*or* Justice of the Peace].

FORM L.

I hereby certify that the master of the   arrived from   on the   day of

18   has produced to me the necessary certificates (Form I) that the whole of the labourers on board have voluntarily engaged themselves, &c., &c.

2. I further certify that the licence (Form C) has been produced in all cases.

3. I also certify that by careful examination of the labourers I have ascertained that they appear to have a proper understanding of the full meaning and effect of the agreements, and that they voluntarily entered into the same, and that the agreements have been signed in the form prescribed (Form D).

Dated at   this   day of   18 .

Immigration Agent [*or* Officer of Customs].

LIST of TOWNS on the banks of the Wai Ni Ki, proceeding from Kamba to the Wai Levu (Rewa River), and entering it about six miles from its principal mouth.

Left bank (ascending).

Kamba.
Ndaku.
Nai Vakathau.
Na Mbo thirva.
Mhuretu.
Kiuva. ⎫
Kiuva i ra. ⎬ Kiuva.
Mbulia. ⎭
Namoli. ⎫ Nakelo.
Vaturua. ⎭
Tokatoka. ⎫
Ndromuna. ⎪
Vanua Ndina. ⎪
Lomai na sau. ⎬ Tokatoka.
Nuku tolu. ⎪
Na Suekau. ⎪
Vuthe. ⎭

Right bank (ascending).

Thaulata.
Vatoa.
Wai thoka.
Mokani.
Nai songo Vau. ⎫
Ndravo. ⎪
Thakova. ⎬ Ndravo.
Matai. ⎭
Ndravotu.
Wai Kele.
Narna si saisai.
Namuka.
Va Kele.
Nakelo.
Na Kau levu.
Vutu Vou.
Muana.
Ndravuni.
Tumavia.
Na luna.
Nuku na Tonga Ndravu.
Nuku Nasilai.

LIST of TOWNS on the Wai Levu, commencing at the mouth of the Wai Levu and running to the point, where it divides into the Muna Ndouu and the Wai Ndina.

Lauthala, a small town occupied solely by the U.S. Commercial Agent and some foreign residents.

Nambulok.

Mataisuva, Wesleyan Mission Station.
Vutia.
Narothivo.
Na sau.
Muana.
Nandoi.
Rewa.
Natho.
Nakorovau.
Nde ni vula.
Nalasi.
Nambuli.
Nandungutha.
Waivo.
Mburembasanga.

Vuni ivi Ndeke.
Na Koro levu.
Na Vasa.
Koro i Mbithi.

Wai loa.
Navuso.

Nakaudi.

Viti.

Moli-tuva.
Na Ndoru.
Vusuya.
Lewa i ra.
Na ndali.
Nousouri.
Verata i wai levu.
Na linga.
Kasavu—At the westward bend of the river.
Koronggangga.
Naitasiri.
Tovutovu.
Natoa ika.
Matai Mati—Shoals commence.

LIST of Towns on the Wai Ndina, or left branch of the Wai Levu.

Nanggali—Tidal influence ceases here.
Na vei sama sama.
Na tho sui.
Na Mbitu vula.
Na Mbi Kau.
Na Kuluva.
Na Vakandua.
Vuni Mbua.
Na Koro Vulavula.
Nondra yavu na ta tkoka.
Nau.

Na vunga yanga.

Wai ni Mbi.
Nailili.

Ndelavu.
Karavatu.
Na ulu vatu.
Nai Vakaruku.
Mataimbau.
Na Mbulimbulia.
Na Seivou (Hot springs).
Ndelai Lasakau.
Na sinu mata.
Tumbu waivaka.

Namosi.

LIST of Towns on the Muna Ndonu.

Viria.
Wai Mali.
Na Vuthu.
Vuni Tavola.
Na samu.
Na tavea—Tidal influence ceases.

Tausa.
Vuna.
Na mi Ka.
Ndere i valu.

Koro Mbaumbau.

List of Towns on the Wai Manu.

Na ivi Kinda.
Nai vui vui.
Koroi.

Rough estimation of Distances.

	Miles.
From the mouth of the Rewa River to Navuso	12
„ Navuso to Naitasiri	12
„ Naitasiri to the mouth of the Wai Ndina	12
„ the latter to Na Mbai Vatu	12
„ Na Mbai Vatu to Vakandua	7
Here we obtained our nearest position to Mbuggi Levu, which was about two miles off.	
From Vakandua to Vuni Mbua	4
„ Vuni Mbua to Nondra yavu	4
„ Nondra yavu to Na seivau	12
„ Na seivau to Namasi	12
„ Namasi to Motivaitala	4
Total	91

The forest country of both Vanua Levu and Na Viti Levu lies to the southward; but it is that of the latter island alone which demands notice in the present Report.

We were credibly informed that forests of Dammaras occur along the banks of the Navua river, which opens on the southern coast about thirty miles from Matai Suva; so that timber to almost any amount might be felled and rafted down the river, by native labour, at a trifling cost. Kuro Ndua Ndua, who is the independent sovereign of the whole district from Navua on the coast to Namosi in the interior, is the Chief with whom all such matters may be satisfactorily negotiated. Forests of Dammaras and other valuable woods abound between Namuka and Serua, on the southern coast. Although the following list gives a general summary of trees available as timber, it cannot profess to include all.

List of Trees used for the Manufacture of Canoes, and applicable to other purposes requiring large Timber.

1 Ndakua ndina (true) Dammara.
  b „ leka (short) „
  c „ Mbalavu (long) „
2 „ salusalu. ⎫ Small-leaved Taxinere, bearing ex-
3 Kau tambua. ⎬ cellent timber, particularly the
4 Kau solo. ⎭ Ndakua Salusalu.
5 Vaivai (ni Veikau) .
6 Vaivai (ni wai). A leguminous plant, generally used for boat boards.

7 Visi. A durable reddish-brown hard wood, probably the green heart of India.
8 Ndanamu ndina. (Calophyllum) straight, and much used for the masts of canoes.
  b Ndamanu ndongondongo. Not very serviceable.
  c   ,,   thevatheva. A very good wood.
  d   ,,   Ulu ni Kati Kati.
9 Yasi. Hard, heavy, and durable.
10 Ndawa. An excellent wood; the fruit used as food.
  b   ,,   vatu. Fruit hard.
  c   ,,   mali. Fruit large.
  d   ,,   sere. Fruit white outside, red in.
  e   ,,   Kuluidamu. Fruit red-skinned.
  f   ,,   sisithi. Fruit small (like a gasteropod shell).
  g   ,,   Mbuka. Fruit yellow.
  h   ,,   Nduru i yanasmu. Fruit small, like the Karawan.
  i   ,,   nda ni Kalavu.
  k   ,,   sawa. Fruit has flavour of arrowroot.
  l   ,,   yambia.
  m   ,,   lemba. Fruit like the lemba.
11 Ndoi (of Viti Levu). A white wood, large.
  b ,, (of Vanua Levu). A red wood.
12 Uto (bread-fruit). A light close-grained white wood.
13 Tavola. Fruit edible, timber useful.
14 Tarawau. This fruit, having no false or unfruitful blossoms, is chosen as the emblem of the truth-speaking man.

  b Tarawau Kei na Kaka. With strongly-scented flowers.
15 Lekutu.
16 Ndavata.
17 Tivi.
  b ,, tavola. Like the Tavola.
18 Mbau. A beautiful reddish or brown wood.
  b ,, tandra.
  c ,, Vuti.
  d ,, somi. Timber; very useful.
19 Vulavula. White, soft, and perishable.
20 Masi i ratu.
21 Nduvula.
22 Ndilo. (Calophyllum), wood durable and susceptible of polish.

  b ,, mbalavu.
  c ,, Leka. Valuable in ship-building for knees, &c.

22 Ndilo.
    d   ,,   ndilo, or Ndamanu.   The 'Tamanu' of Tahiti according to the Rev. D. Hazlewood.
23 Malamala.
    b   ,,   vuti.   Rough.
    c   ,,   ndamu.   Red.
24 Malili.
25 Sa.
26 Laumba.
27 Kau ndamu.
28 Ngati.
29 Kavika.   (Eugenia.)
30 Maku.   A light, straight, soft grained wood.
31 Kau loa.   (Black tree.)
32 Ndrala.   (Erythrina Indica.)
33 Mokosui.   Straight and tall, but not very good for spars.
34 Sathau.   Bears its fruit octennially.
35 Ra Maia.
36 Laulaungai.
37 Mbausa.
38 Vure.
39 Ndulewa.   A heavy and hard wood.
40 Kautoa.
41 Mbaka.   A very majestic tree.
42 Kau Karo.
43 Vutu ndina.
    b   ,,   votho.
    c   ,,   Kalau.
44 Wathi wathi.
45 Uthu uthu.
46 Mbu me mbeka.
47 Sausaula.
48 Nomosa.
49 Ivi.
50 Ndaago.   A large mangrove.
51 Ulu bu Kura,
52 Ndirini.
53 Lindi.
54 Veiwarn.
55 Nggulia.
56 Noko.
57 Ta ndalo.
58 Makita.   Useful for spears, and leaves used for thatching.
59 Serua.

60 Wi.
61 Mbua Ndromu.
  b „ toko.
62 Mbuambua.   Wood resembling box.
63 Loaloa.

Trees employed in the Manufacture of Clubs.

64 Nokonoko.   (Casuarina), a hard and durable wood.
65 Velau.
66 Saulaggi ndina.
  b „ ndamu.   } Useful woods.
67 Saru Saru.
68 Vunga.
69 Lava rua.
70 To manu.
  b „ wiwi.
71 Vatu ni mboro.
72 Masi.   The leaves are rough, like sand-paper, and applied to the same use.

73 Se lavo.
74 Vau.   (Hibiscus), the bark is used for cordage.

PALMS.

Niu.   Cocoa-nut, several species.
  „ sawa.   Species of Areca.
Viu.   With flabelliform leaves.

ZOOLOGICAL LIST—Drawn up with the Native Names to facilitate further inquiry.

Bats.

Mbeka ndina, or loa.
  „ ndamu.
  „ lulu.   } Tailless.
Mbekambeka.   Tail included in the inter-crural membrane.
Manumanu vaka Mbui.   With a long exserted tail.

Birds of the River.

Nga Viti, or loa.   Wild duck.
  „ ndamu.   Teal.
Mbele.   Bittern.
Visako.   Smaller species.
Visaka.   The smallest species (light fawn colour).

Snakes.

Ngata ndamu Kuro.	Takes its name from the similarity of its colour to that of a Fijian pot.
Ngata ndamu.	Red snake.
„ mbambawavuti.	Reddish, with an ashy or slate-coloured belly.
„ yasi.	The largest of all.
Mbolo loa.	Small, black.
„ ndamu.	Small, dull-red.

Fishes peculiar to the Fresh Water.

Ka loa (black).	Mugil, with the habits of a rock fish.
Ndeke loa.	About ten inches long.
„ ndamu.	
Mbau.	About the size of Ndeke.
Voloa, or Vola.	Small.
Teatia.	
Ngandro.	
Voseu.	
Vovuti.	
Ndandarikai.	Spotted muræna.
Mbandira.	Large eel.
Nggio.	Shark (?)

Fishes found in the Fresh Water, but said also to exist in the Sea.

Sangka.	Large fish (Scowberidæ).
Ika ndamu.	Red fish.
Yawa.	
Mbati Kasivi.	Called Matamba on the coast, and said to be daily taken down with the floods. (Percidæ.)
Vetakau.	A broad fish.
Kanathi.	A mullet (?)
Nggiawa.	(Percidæ.)
Revo, or wruwru.	(Percidæ.)
Vuvula, or singa.	(Large.)
Yawa.	(In ponds); when large it is called Wailangi. One is said to have been caught at Navuso five feet long and three in girth (?).
Ika Ndroka.	(Percidæ.)

List of Macrourous Crustacea.

Motho.
Lua.
Kandikandi.
} Transparent Palæmonidæ, believed by the natives to be different stages of the same species, but such is not the case.

Ura ndamu.
„ mbala.
„ mbati.
„ „ tambua.   At Vuni Mbua.
„ ndina.
„ ivi.
„ vulu.   (Atya).
„ loa.
„ ndu.
„ ngauvithotho.
„ ngasau.

* * * * * * * *

SYSTEMATIC LIST OF ALL THE FIJIAN PLANTS AT PRESENT KNOWN.*

The Vitian Islands were until 1840 a virgin soil, and still offer a tempting field for botanical explorations. Absolutely nothing was known of their flora until Messrs. Hinds and Barclay, who accompanied Sir Edward Belcher in H.M.S. 'Sulphur,' collected a few specimens in the neighbourhood of Rewa, Viti Levu, and Bua Bay in Vanua Levu, afterwards described by Mr. Bentham in the 'London Journal of Botany,' vol. ii., and the Botany of H.M.S. 'Sulphur.' About the same time (1840) Viti was visited by the United States Exploring Expedition, Commander Wilkes, and considerable collections were made by Messrs. Brackenridge, Rich, and Pickering, furnishing the materials for Professor Asa Gray's celebrated 'Botany of the United States Exploring Expedition.' In 1856, H.M.S. 'Herald,' Captain Denham, R.N., explored different parts of the group, and Mr. Milne, his botanical collector, was enabled to add a good number of species to our knowledge. Another visit was paid to the group by that indefatigable

* *Vide* Seemann's 'Mission to Viti.'

botanist, Professor Harvey, of Trinity College, Dublin, productive of many new types. In 1860 I collected about 800 species, and made a great many notes of the country explored. Whilst part of the latter, relating to the resources and vegetable productions, were embodied in an official report, addressed to his Grace the Duke of Newcastle, and presented to Parliament by command of Her Majesty, a preliminary list of the former was published by me in the 'Bonplandia,' vol. ix. p. 253 (1861). Since then I have had time to examine the plants more closely and correct a few errors crept in. Other botanists have also been led to study the materials collected by me and publish the result. Professor A. Gray has carefully collated my plants with those published by him in the 'Botany of the United States Exploring Expedition' and the 'Proceedings of the American Academy,' the result of which has been given in the 'Bonplandia.' x. 34 (1862), and also in the 'Proceedings' of the Academy named. As there are very few original specimens in Europe of the numerous new types described by that eminent *savant*, these papers are invaluable to the working botanist. Mr. Mitten has examined all my Mosses and Hepaticæ ('Bonpl.' ix. 365, and 'Bonpl.' x. 19); amongst the thirty-five species collected there being twenty new ones. For the determination of the Ferns I am indebted to Mr. Smith, at Kew; for that of the Fungi, to the Rev. M. J. Berkeley; for that of the Palms, to Mr. Wendland; the Lichens, to the Rev. Churchill Babington, and the Aroideæ to Mr. Schott, at Vienna, who has also described the new species ('Bonplandia.' ix. 367, seq.). For my own part, I have begun to describe the new genera and species in the 'Bonplandia,' ix. and x., and given coloured illustrations drawn by the skilful pencil of Mr. Fitch. In the following catalogue will be found embodied the result of all these labours, and also all the species enumerated by previous authors. The numbers which follow the different species refer to my distributed collections and those remitted to me by Mr. J. Storck, who was my able assistant, and is now a permanent resident in Fiji.

Ranunculaceæ.
Clematis Pickeringii, A. Gray (1).

Dilleniaceæ.
Capellia biflora, A. Gray; vulgo 'Kulava' vel 'Kukulava' (2).
C. membranifolia, A. Gray.

Anonaceæ.
Anona squamosa, Linn. Cultivated (3).
Richella monosperma, A. Gray.
Uvaria amygdalina, A. Gray.
U. odorata, Lam.; vulgo 'Makosoi' (5).
Polyalthia Vitiensis, Seem. (4).

Myristicaceæ.
Myristica castaneæfolia, A. Gray; vulgo 'Male' (6).
M. macrophylla, A. Gray; vulgo 'Male' (7).
M. sp.; vulgo 'Male' (866).

Cruciferæ.
Cardamine sarmentosa, Forst. (8).
Sinapis nigra, Linn. Cultivated and naturalized (9).

Capparideæ.
Capparis Richii, A. Gray.

Flacourtianeæ.
Xylosma orbiculatum, Forst. (10).

Samydaceæ.
Casearia disticha, A. Gray (11).
C.? acuminatissima, A. Gray.
C. Richii, A. Gray.

Violaceæ.
Agathea violaris, A. Gray, et var (12).
Alsodeia? sp.; vulgo 'Sesiraka-vono' (867).

Molluginæ.
Mollugo striata, Linn. (230).

Portulaceæ.
Portulaca oleracea, Linn.; vulgo 'Taukuka ni vuaka' (13).
P. quadrifida, Linn.; vulgo 'Taukuku ni vuaka' (14).
Talinum patens, Willd. (15).
Sesuvium Portulacastrum, Linn.

Malvaceæ.
Sida linifolia, Cav.
S. rhombifolia, Linn. (16).
S. retusa, Linn.
Urena lobata, Linn. (17).
U. moriifolia, De Cand.
Abelmoschus moschatus, Mœnch; vulgo 'Wakiwaki' (19, 869).
A. canaranus, Miq.? (20).
A. Manihot, Med.; vulgo 'Bele,' vel 'Vauvau ni Viti' (18).
A. esculentus, Wight et Arn. Cultivated, according to A. Gray.
Hibiscus Rosa-Sinensis, Linn.; vulgo 'Kauti,' 'Senitoa,' vel 'Seniciobia' (22).
H. Storckii, Seem.; vulgo 'Seqelu' (23).
H. diversifolius, Jacq.; vulgo 'Kalauaisoni,' vel 'Kalakalauaisoni' (21).
Paritium purpurascens, Seem.; vulgo 'Vau damudamu' (24).
P. tiliaceum, Juss.; vulgo 'Vau dina' (25).
P. tricuspis, Guill.; vulgo 'Vau dra.' (26).
Thespesia populnea, Corr.; vulgo 'Mulomulo' (7).
Gossypium religiosum, Linn.; vulgo 'Vauvau ni papalagi' (28).
G. Peruvianum, Cav.; vulgo 'Vauvau ni papalagi' (29).

G. Barbadense, Linn.; vulgo 'Vauvau ni papalago' (30).
G. arboreum, Linn. et var.; vulgo 'Vauvau ni papalagi' (31, 32).

Sterculiaceæ.

Heritiera littoralis, Dryand.; vulgo 'Kena ivi na alewa Kalou' (33).
Firmiana diversifolia, Gray.

Buettneriaceæ.

Commersonia platyphylla, De Cand. (34).
Büttneriacearum gen. nov. aff. Commersoniæ (83).
Kleinhovia hospita, Linn.; vulgo 'Mamakara' (35).
Waltheria Americana, Linn. (36).
Melochia Vitiensis, A. Gray (37).

Tiliaceæ.

Triumfetta procumbens, Forst. (38).
Grewia persicæfolia, A. Gray (= G. Mallococca, var.?); vulgo 'Siti' (39).
G. prunifolia, A. Gray; vulgo 'Siti' (40).
G. Mallococca, L. fil.
Trichospermum Richii,' Seem. (= Diclidocarpus Richii, A. Gray); vulgo 'Maku' (41, 870).
Elæocarpus laurifolius, A. Gray.
E. cassinoides, A Gray.
E. pyriformis, A. Gray.
E. Storckii, Seem. sp. nov. (E. aff. speciosi, Brongn. et Gris.); vulgo 'Gaigai' (874).

Ternstrœmiaceæ.

Draytonia rubicunda, A. Gray; vulgo 'Kau alewa' (42, 872).
Eurya Vitiensis, A. Gray (43).
E. acuminata, De Cand. (44).
Ternstrœmiacearum gen. nov. (45).

Guttiferæ.

Discostigma Vitiense, A. Gray.

Calysaccion obovale, Miq. (=Garcinia Mangostana, A. Gray in United St. Expl. Exped.); vulgo 'Vetao' vel 'Uvitai' (46).
Calophyllum Inophyllum, Linn.; vulgo 'Dilo' (48, 873).
C. Burmanni, Wight; vulgo 'Damanu' (49).
C. (polyanthum, Wall.? v. lanceolatum, Bl.? = C. spectabile, United St. Expl. Exped.; vulgo 'Damanu dilodilo') (47).
Garcinia sessilis, Seem. (Clusia sessilis, Forst. 51).
G. pedicellata, Seem. (Clusia pedicellata, Forst. 50).

Pittosporeæ.

Pittosporum arborescens, Rich.
P. Richii, A. Gray; vulgo 'Tadiri' (54).
P. Brackenridgei, A. Gray (55).
P. tobiroides, A. Gray (56).
P. Pickeringii, A. Gray (53).
P. rhytidocarpum, A. Gray (52).

Aurantiaceæ.

Micromelum minutum, Seem. (M. glabrescens. Bth.; Limonia minuta, Forst.); vulgo 'Qiqla' teste Williams (57).
Citrus vulgaris, Risso (C. torosa. Picker.); vulgo 'Moli kurikuri' (58).
C. Aurantium, Risso; vulgo 'Moli ni Tahaiti.'—Cult.
C. decumana, Linn.; vulgo 'Moli kana.' Cultivated and naturalized.
C. Limonum, Risso; vulgo 'Moli kara.'

Meliaceæ.

Aglaia edulis, A. Gray (Milnea edulis, Roxb.); vulgo 'Danidani loa.'

A. ? basiphylla, A. Gray.
Didimochyton Richii, A. Gray.
Xylocarpus Granatum, Kœn.; vulgo 'Dabi' (61).
X. obovatus, A. Juss. (var. præcedent. ? (62).
Vavæa amicorum, Benth. (63).
Melia sp. nov. (64).

Sapindaceæ.

Cardiospermum microcarpum, H. B. et K.; vulgo 'Voniu' (65).
Sapindus Vitiensis, A. Gray (66).
Cupania falcata, A. Gray (70).
C. Vitiensis, Seem. (an var. præced. ? 68).
C. rhoifolia, A. Gray; vulgo 'Buka ni vuda' (74, 69).
C. apetala, Labill. (67).
C. Brackenridgei, A. Gray.
C. leptobotrys, A. Gray.
Nephelium pinnatum, Camb.; vulgo 'Dawa,' et var. plur. (71).
Dodonæa triquetra, Andr.; vulgo 'Wase' teste Williams (72).

Malpighiaceæ.

Hiptage Javanica, Bl. ?
H. myrtifolia, A. Gray.

Ampelideæ.

Vitis saponaria, Seem. (= Cissus geniculata, A. Gray, non Bl.); vulgo 'Wa Roturotu' (76).
V. Vitiensis, Seem. (Cissus Vitiensis, A. Gray).
V. acuminata, Seem. (Cissus acuminata, A. Gray) (77).
Leea sambucina, Linn. (78).

Rhamneæ.

Smythea pacifica, Seem. Bonpl. t. 9 (79).
Ventilago? Vitiensis, A. Gray (an Smytheæ spec. ?=cernua, Tul.).
Colubrina Asiatica, Brongn.; vulgo 'Vuso levu' (80).

C. Vitiensis, Seem. sp. nov. (85).
Alphitonia zizyphoides, A. Gray (= A. franguloides, A. Gray); vulgo 'Doi' (81).
Gouania Richii, A. Gray (82).
G. denticulata, A. Gray.
Rhamnea dubia (84).

Chailletiaceæ.

Chailletia Vitiensis, Seem. sp nov. (86).

Celastrineæ.

Catha Vitiensis, A. Gray (86).
Celastrus Richii, A. Gray.

Aquifoliaceæ.

Ilex Vitiensis, A. Gray (87).

Olacineæ.

Ximenia elliptica, Forst.; vulgo 'Somisomi,' 'Tumitomi,' vel 'Tomitomi' (88).
Stemonurus? sp.; vulgo 'Duvu' (877).
Olacinea? (878).

Oxalideæ.

Oxalis corniculata, Linn.; vulgo 'Totowiwi' (89).

Rutaceæ.

Evodia hortensis, Forst.; vulgo 'Uci,' vel 'Salusala' (91).
E. longifolia, A. Rich (92).
E. drupacea, Labill. ? (90).
Acronychia petiolaris, A. Gray.
Zanthoxylon varians, Benth. (= Acronychia heterophylla, A. Gray, (102, 879).
Z. Roxburghianum, Cham. et Schlecht. (103).
Z. sp. (n. 104).

Simarubeæ.

Soulamea amara, Lam.
Amaroria soulameoides, A. Gray (880).
Brucea? sp. (105).

Ochnaceæ.
Brackenridgea nitida, A. Gray (93).

Anacardiaceæ.
Oncocarpus atra, Seem. (O. Vitiensis, A. Gray; Rhus atrum, Forst.); vulgo 'Kau Karo' (94, 881).
Buchanania florida, Schauer (882).
Rhus simarubæfolia, A. Gray (95).
Rh. Taitensis, Guill.? (96).

Burseraceæ.
Canarium Vitiense, A. Gray (97).
Evia dulcis, Comm.; vulgo 'Wi' (98).
Dracontomelon sylvestre, Blume; vulgo 'Tarawau' (99).
Dr. sp.? (100).

Connaraceæ.
Rourea heterophylla, Planch.
Connarus Pickeringii, A. Gray (101).

Leguminosæ.
I. Papilionaceæ:—
Crotalaria quinquefolia, Linn.
Indigofera Anil, Linn. (106).
Tephrosia purpurea, Pers. (T. piscatoria, Pers. 107),
Ormocarpus sennoides, De Cand.
Uraria lagopodioides, De Cand. 108).
Desmodium umbellatum, W. et Arn. (109).
D. australe, Bth. (Hedysarum, Willd.)
D. polycarpum, De Cand. (111).
Abrus precatorius, Linn.; vulgo 'Qiri damu,' 'Lere damu,' vel 'Diri damu' (110).
Canavalia obtusifolia, De Cand. (122).
C. turgida, Grah. (112).
C. sericea, A. Gray.

Glycine Tabacina, Bth. (123).
Mucuna gigantea, De Cand. (119).
M. platyphylla, A. Gray (200).
Erythrina Indica, Linn.; vulgo, 'Drala dina,' (125) et var. fl. albis.
E. ovalifolia, Roxb.; vulgo 'Drala kaka' (124).
Strongylodon ruber, Vogel (113).
Phaseolus rostratus, Wall.
Ph. Mungo, Linn.?
Ph. Truxillensis, H. B. et K. (116).
Vigna lutea, A. Gray (121).
Lablab vulgaris, Savi; vulgo 'Dralawa' (118).
Cajanus Indicus, Spr. Introd. (115),
Pongamia glabra. Vent.; vulgo 'Vesivesi,' v. 'Vesi ni wai' (126, 884).
Derris uliginosa, Benth.; vulgo 'Duwa gaga' (127, 883).
Dalbergia monosperma, Dalz. (128).
D. torta, Grah.
Pterocarpus Indicus, Willd.; vulgo 'Cibicibi' (129).
Sophora tomentosa, Linn.; vulgo 'Kau ni alewa' (130, 886).

II. Cæsalpineæ:—
Guilandina Bonduc, Ait.; vulgo 'Soni' (132).
Poinciana pulcherrima, Linn.—Cult.
Storckiella Vitiensis, Seem. in Bonpl. t. 6; vulgo 'Marasa' (133).
Cassia occidentalis, Linn. vulgo 'Kau moce' (134).
C. obtusifolia, Linn.; vulgo 'Kau moce' (135).
C. lævigata, Willd.; vulgo 'Winivikau' (136).
C. glauca, Lam.
Afzelia bijuga, A. Gray; vulgo 'Vesi' (137).

Cynometra grandiflora, A. Gray (138).
C. falcata, A. Gray.
Inocarpus edulis, Forst.; vulgo 'Ivi' (371).

III. Mimoseæ :—
Entada scandens, Bth.; vulgo 'Wa lai,' v. 'Wa tagiri' (139).
Mimosa pudica, Linn. Naturalized (140).
Leucæna glauca, Bth. (141).
L. Forsteri, Benth. (142).
Acacia laurifolia, Willd.; vulgo 'Tatakia' (143).
A. Richii, A. Gray; vulgo 'Qumu' (144).
Serianthes myriadenia, Planch.
S. Vitiensis, A. Gray; vulgo 'Vaivai' (145, 887).

Chrysobalaneæ.

Parinarium laurinum, A. Gray (= P.? Margarata, A. Gray = P. insularum, A. Gray); vulgo 'Makita' (146).

Rosaceæ.

Rubus tiliaceus, Smith; vulgo 'Wa gadrogadro' (147).

Myrtaceæ.

Barringtonia speciosa, Linn.; vulgo 'Vutu rakaraka' (148).
B. Samoensis, A. Gray; vulgo 'Vutu ni wai' (149).
B. excelsa, Blume; vulgo 'Vutu kana' (150).
B. sp.
Eugenia (Jambosa) Malaccensis, Linn.; vulgo 'Kavika:' var. α, floribus albis, vulgo 'Kavika vulovulo;' var. β, floribus purpureis, vulgo 'Kavika damudamu' (161).
E. (Jambosa) Richii, A. Gray; vulgo 'Bokoi' (164).
E. (Jambosa) sp. (an Richii var.?); vulgo 'Sea' (165).
E. (Jambosa) quadrangulata, A. Gray.
E. (Jambosa) gracilipes, A. Gray; vulgo 'Lutulutu,' vel 'Bogibalewa' (158).
E. (Jambosa) neurocalyx, A. Gray; vulgo 'Leba' (159).
E. rariflora, Benth. (160).
E. Brackenridgei, A. Gray (155).
E. confertiflora, A. Gray.
E. sp. nov. confertiflor. proxima (156).
E. effusa, A. Gray (151).
E. amicorum, Benth. (152).
E. rubescens, A. Gray; vulgo 'Yasi dravu' (151).
E. corynocarpa, A. Gray (153).
E. rivularis, Seem.; vulgo 'Yasi ni wai' (162).
E. Grayi, Seem. sp. nov. fl. purpureis (163).
Nelitris fruticosa (A. Gray).
N. Vitiensis, A. Gray; vulgo 'Nuqanuqa' (166, 888).
Acicalyptus myrtoides, A. Gray.
A. Seemanni, A. Gray (168).
Metrosideros collina, A. Gray; vulgo 'Vuga' (169, 889).
M. sp. fl. luteis (170).
M. sp. fl. coccineis (171).

Melastomaceæ.

Memecylon Vitiense, A. Gray et var. (172).
Astronia Pickeringii, A. Gray.
A. confertiflora, A. Gray (174).
A. Storckii, Seem. sp. nov.; vulgo 'Cavacava' (890).
Astronidium parviflorum, A. Gray (465).
Amplectrum? ovalifolium, A. Gray.
Medinilla heterophylla, A. Gray (175).
M. rhodochlæna, A. Gray; vulgo

'Cararaea ra i resiga' (177, 891).
M. sp. (182.
M. sp. 75).
M. sp. (175).
Melastoma Vitiense, Naud. (180).
M. polyanthum, Bl. ? (179).
Melastomacea (181).

Alangieæ.

Rhytidandra Vitiensis, A. Gray.

Rhizophoreæ.

Haplopetalon Richii, A. Gray.
H. Seemanni, A. Gray (184).
Crossostylis biflora, Forst.
Rhizophora mucronata, Lam.; vulgo 'Dogo' (185).
Bruguiera Rhumphii, Bl. (186).

Combretaceæ.

Lumnitzera coccinea, Willd.; vulgo 'Sagali' (189).
Terminalia Catappa, Linn.; vulgo 'Tavola' (187).
P. Moluccana, Lam.; vulgo 'Tivi' (188).
T. glabrata, Forst. ?

Passifloreæ.

Passiflora, sp. fl. viridibus (190).

Papayaceæ.

Carica Papaya, Linn.; vulgo 'Oleti,' Introd. (190).

Cucurbitaceæ.

Karivia Samoensis, A. Gray (192).
Luffa insularum, A. Gray (193).
Cucumis pubescens, Willd. (194).
Lagenaria vulgaris, Ser. (195).

Saxifrageæ.

Spiræanthemum Vitiense, A. Gray.
Sp. Kataka, Seem. sp. nov.; vulgo 'Katakata' (196).
Weinmannia affinis, A. Gray, (197,) et var. (199 et 200).

W Richii, A. Gray.
W. spiræoides, A. Gray.
W. sp. (198).
Geissois ternata, A. Gray; vulgo 'Vuga' (201).

Umbelliferæ.

Hydrocotyle Asiatica, Linn.; vulgo 'Totono' (202).

Araliaceæ.

Aralia Vitiensis, A. Gray (203).
Panax fruticosum, Linn.; vulgo 'Danidani' (204).
Paratropia? multijuga, A. Gray; vulgo 'Dauidani' (205).
Plerandra Pickeringii, A. Gray.
P. Grayi, Seem. sp. nov. (206 et 209).
P. ? sp. nov. (208).
P. sp. (207).

Loranthaceæ.

Loranthus insularum, A. Gray; vulgo 'Saburo' (211).
L. Vitiensis, Seem. (210).
L. Forsterianus, Schult.
Viscum articulatum, Burm. (212).

Balanophoreæ.

Balanophora fungosa, Forst.

Rubiaceæ.

I. Coffeaceæ:—
Coprosma persicæfolia, A. Gray.
Geophila reniformis, Cham. et Schlecht. (239).
Cha-alia amicorum, A. Gray? (214).
Psychotria Brackenridgei, A. Gray.
P. Forsteriana, A. Gray, var. Vitiensis, A. Gray (236).
P. turbinata, A. Gray.
P. tephrosantha, A Gray.
P. parvula, A Gray.
P. gracilis, A. Gray.
P. calycosa, A. Gray? (216).

P. macrocalyx, A. Gray (243).
P. filipes, A. Gray.
P. hypargyrea, A. Gray.
P. (Piptilema) cordata, A. Gray.
P. (Piptilema) Pickeringii, A. Gray (251).
P. (Piptelama) platycocca, A. Gray (249).
P. insularum, A. Gray? (250).
P. collina, Labill. (244 et 254).
P. sarmentosa, Blume (245).
P. sp.; vulgo 'Wa kau;' ramis scandentibus sarmentosis (895).
P. sp. foliis bullatis (248).
P. sp. nov. aff. filipedis (253).
P. sp. nov. aff. Brackenridgei (255).
P. sp. aff. Brackenridgei (259).
Calycosia petiolata, A. Gray.
C. pubiflora, A. Gray (214).
C. Milnei, A. Gray; vulgo 'Kau wai' (213, 892).
Ixora Vitiensis, A. Gray (247); Pavetta triflora, De Caud.; Coffea triflora, Forst.; Cephaelis? fragrans, Hook. et Arn.
I. sp. nov. (258).
I. sp.; vulgo 'Kau sulu' (893).
Canthium sessilifolium, A. Gray.
C. lucidum, Hook. et Arn.; Coffea odorata, Forst. (220 et 221).
Morinda umbellata, Linn. (222).
M. myrtifolia, A. Gray; foliis majoribus (an v. M. umbellatae?) (223).
M. mollis, A. Gray (224).
M. phillyreoides, Labill. (226).
M. citrifolia, Linn.; vulgo 'Kura,' v. 'Kura kana' (225).
M. lucida, A. Gray.
M. lucidaefolia, A. Gray.
Hydnophytum longiflorum A. Gray (= Myrmecodia Vitiensis, Seem.) (216).
Vangueria? sp. (257).
Guettarda speciosa, Linn.; vulgo 'Buabua' (297).

G. (Guettardella) Vitiensis, A. Gray (= 257?).
Timonius sapotaefolius, A. Gray.
T. affinis, A. Gray.
Coffeacea; vulgo 'Kau lobo' (893).

II. Cinchoneae :—
Hedyotis tenuifolia, Sm. (231).
H. deltoidea, W. et Arn.? (232).
H. paniculata, Roxb. (233).
H. paniculata, Roxb. var. crassifolia, A. Gray (234).
H. bracteogonum, Spr. (235).
Ophiorrhiza laxa, A. Gray (227).
O. peploides, A. Gray (228).
O. leptantha, A. Gray (229).
Lindenia Vitiensis, Seem. Bonpl. t. 8 (217).
Lerchea calycina, A. Gray.
Dolicholobium oblongifolium, A. Gray.
D. latifolium, A. Gray.
D. longissimum, Seem. (215).
Stylocoryne Harveyi, A. Gray.
S. sambucina, A. Gray (S. pipericarpa, Benth.) (242).
Griffithiae sp.? (260).
G.? sp. v. gen. nov. (240).
G. sp. fl. odoratis.
Gardenia Vitiensis, Seem. (218).
G.? (an gen. nov.?) (240).
Mussaenda frondosa, Linn.; vulgo "Bovu."

Compositae.

Monosis insularum, A. Gray.
Lagenophora Pickeringii, A. Gray.
Erigeron albidum, A. Gray; vulgo 'Wavuwavu,' v. 'Co ni papalagi' (261).
Adenostemma viscosum, Forst. (262).
Siegesbeckia orientalis, Linn. (263).
Dichocephala latifolia, De Cand. (264).
Myriogyne minuta, Linn. (265).

Sonchus oleraceus, Linn. (n. 266).
Ageratum conyzoides, Linn. ; vulgo 'Botebotekoro,' vel 'Matamoce moce' (267).
Wollastonia Forsteriana, De Cand. ; vulgo 'Kovekove' (268).
Eclipta erecta, Linn.; vulgo 'Tumadu' (269).
Bidens pilosa, Linn.; vulgo 'Batimadramadra' (270).
Glossogyne tenuifolia, Cass. (271).
Blumea virens, De Cand. (272).
B. Milnei, Seem. (sp. nov. aff. B. aromaticae, De Cand. 273).

Goodeniaceæ.

Scævola floribunda, A. Gray (S. saligna,'Forst. ?); vulgo 'Totoirebibi' (274, 896).
S. Kœnigii, Vahl (275).

Cyrtandreæ.

Cyrtandra acutangula, Seem. (276).
C. Vitiensis, Seem.; vulgo 'Betabiabi' (277).
C. anthropophagorum, Seem. (278).
C. involucrata, Seem. (279).
C. coleoides, Seem. (280).
C. Milnei, Seem. (281).
C. ciliata, Seem. (282).
C. Pritchardii, Seem. (283).

Vaccineæ.

Epigynum? Vitiense, Seem. (284).

Epacrideæ.

Leucopogon Cymbula, Labill. ; vulgo 'Tagatagalesa.'

Myrsineæ.

Mæsa Pickeringii, A. Gray.
M. persicæfolia, A. Gray (287 ?).
M. corylifolia, A. Gray (288).
M. nemoralis, A. Gray (286 ?).
Myrsine myricæfolia, A. Gray (290 ex parte).
M. ? Brackenridgei, A. Gray.

M. capitellata, Wall. ? (289).
Ardisia ? capitata, A. Gray.
A. grandis, Seem. (293).
A. sp. (292, 897).
A. sp. (291).

Styraceæ.

Symplocos spicata, Roxb.; vulgo 'Ravu levu.'

Ebenaceæ.

Maba foliosa, Rich.
M. elliptica, Forst.; vulgo 'Kau loa' (295, 296, 297, 898).

Sapotæ.

Sapota ? pyrulifera, A. Gray.
S. ? Vitiensis, A. Gray.
S. sp. (ex A. Gray).

Jasmineæ.

Jasminum tetraquetrum, A. Gray.
J. gracile, Forst.; vulgo 'Wa Vatu' (298).
J. didymum, Forst.; J. divaricatum, R. Brown (299).

Loganiaceæ.

Geniostoma rupestre, Forst. (301).
var. puberulum, A. Gray (G. crassifolium, Bth.) (300).
G. microphyllum, Seem. (304).
Strychnos colubrina, Linn. (302).
Courthovia corynocarpa, A. Gray (= Gærtnera pyramidalis, Seem.); vulgo 'Boloa' (303).
C. Seemanni, A. Gray (Gærtnera barbata, Seem.) (305, 899).
Fagræa gracilipes, A. Gray (F. viridiflora, Seem. (306).
F. Berteriana, A. Gray; vulgo T. Vitiensis, Seem. (307).
'Bua' (308).

Apocyneæ.

Alyxia bracteolosa, Rich; vulgo 'Vono' (310, 900); var. α macrocarpa, A. Gray (A. macrocarpa,

Rich); var. β angustifolia, A. Gray (A. stellata, Seem.); var. γ parviflora, A. Gray.
A. stellata, Labill.
Cerbera lactaria, Ham.; vulgo 'Rewa' vel 'Vasa' (309).
Melodinus scandens, Forst. (311).
Tabernæmontana Vitiensis, Seem.; T. citrifolia, Forst. non L. = ? T. Cumingiana, A. De Cand.
T. sp.
Rejoua scandens, Seem. sp. nov.; vulgo ' Wa rerega ' (901).
Ochrosia parviflora, Hensl. (O. elliptica, Labill.?) (318).
Alstonia plumosa, Labill. (318).
A.? sp. (317).
Echites scabra, Labill.? (315).
Lyonsia lævis, A. Gray.

Asclepiadeæ.

Tylophora Brackenridgei, A. Gray.
Gymnema subnudum, A. Gray.
G. stenophyllum, A. Gray; vulgo ' Yaupau ' (322).
Hoya bicarinata, A. Gray; Asclepias volubilis, Forst.; vulgo ' Wa bibi ' vel ' Bulibuli sivaro ' (319).
H. diptera, Seem. (320).
H. pilosa, Seem. (321).

Gentianeæ.

Erythræa australis, R. Brown.
Limnanthemum Kleinianum, Griseb.; vulgo 'Bekabekairga' (323).

Convolvulaceæ.

Ipomœa campanulata, Linn.; vulgo ' Wa vula ' (324).
I. peltata, Chois.; vulgo ' Wiliao ' teste Seemann, ' Veliyana ' teste Williams (325).
I. Pes-capræ, Sw.; vulgo ' Lawere ' (326).
I. Turpethum, R. Brown; vulgo ' Wakai ' (327).

I, sepiaria, Koen. (328).
I. cymosa, Rœm. et Schult.; vulgo ' Sovivi ' (334).
Aniseia uniflora, Chois. (329).
Batatas paniculata, Chois.; vulgo ' Wa Uvi ' vel ' Dabici ' teste Storck (330, 902).
B. edulis, Chois.; vulgo ' Kamara ' vel ' Kawai ni papalagi.'—Cult.
Pharbitis insularis, Chois.; vulgo ' Wa Vuti ' (331).
Calonyction speciosum, Chois. (332).
C. comospermum, Boj. (333).

Boragineæ.

Tournefortia argentia, Linn. (335).
Cordia Sprengelii, De Cand.; vulgo ' Tou ' (336).
C. subcordata, Lam.; vulgo ' Nawanawa ' (337).

Solaneæ.

Physalis Peruviana, Linn. (338).
P. angulata, Linn. (339).
Solanum viride, R. Brown? (340).
S. anthropophagorum, Seem. (sp. nov. Bonpl. t. 14); vulgo ' Borodina ' (341).
S. repandum, Forst.; vulgo ' Son,' ' Sousou,' vel ' Boro sou ' (342).
S. inamœnum, Benth. Lond. Journ. ii. p. 228 (343).
S. oleraceum, Dun.; vulgo ' Boro ni yaloka ni gata ' (344).
S. sp. (S. repand. var. ?) (345).
Capsicum frutescens, Linn.; vulgo ' Boro ni papaligi ' (346).
Nicotiana Tabacum, Linn.—Cultivated (347).
Datura Stramonium, Linn.—Introd. (348).

Scrophularineæ.

Vandellia crustacea, Benth. (349).
Limnophilia serrata, Gaud. (350).

Acanthaceæ.

Eranthemum laxiflorum, A. Gray (351, ex parte).
E. insularum, A. Gray (351, ex parte).
Apenosma triflora, Nees ab Esenb.; vulgo 'Tamola' (252).

Verbenaceæ.

Clerodendron inerme, R. Brown; vulgo 'Verevere' (353).
Vitex trifolia, Linn.; vulgo 'Vulokaka' (354).
Premna Tahitensis, Schauer (Scrophulariodes arborea, Forst.); vulgo 'Yaro' (355).
P. Tahitensis, Schauer; var.? (356).
Gmelina Vitiensis, Seem. (sp. nov.).

Labiatæ.

Leucas decemdentata, Sm. (357).
Ocimum gratissimum, Linn. (358).
Plectranthus Forsteri, Benth.; vulgo 'Lata' (359).
Teucrium inflatum, Swartz (360).

Plumbagineæ.

Plumbago Zeylanica, Linn. (361).

Plantagineæ.

Plantago major, Linn.—Introd. (362).

Nyctagineæ.

Pisonia Brunoniana, Endl. (363).
P. viscosa, Seem. (sp. nov.) (364).
Boerhaavia diffusa, Linn., var. pubescens (365).

Amarantaceæ.

Amarantus melancholicus, Moq., var. tricolor; vulgo 'Driti damudamu' (366).
A. paniculatus, Moq., var. cruentus, Moq.; vulgo 'Driti.'—Introd. (367).

Euxolus viridis, Moq.; vulgo 'Driti' vel 'Gasau ni vuaka' (368).
Cyathula prostrata, Blume (369).

Polygoneæ.

Polygonum imberbe, Sol. (370).

Laurineæ.

Hernandia sonora, Linn.; vulgo 'Yevnyevu' vel 'Uviuvi' (372).
Cassytha filiformis, Linn.; vulgo 'Waluku mai lagi' teste Williams (373).
Cinnamomum sp.; vulgo 'Macou' (376).
Laurinea. Arbor 15-20 ped. (374).
Laurinea (375).
Laurinea (377).
Laurinea; vulgo 'Siqa' vel 'Siga' (378).
Laurinea; vulgo 'Lidi' (903).

Thymeleæ.

Drymispermum sp. (379).
D. montanum, Seem. (sp. nov.)
D. subcordatum, Seem. (sp. nov.); vulgo 'Matiavi' (381).
D.? sp. (382).
Leucosmia Burnettiana, Benth. (= Dais disperma, Forst.); vulgo 'Sinu damu' vel 'Sinu dina' (383).
Wikstrœmia Indica, C. A. Mey.; vulgo 'Sinu mataiava' (884).

Santalaceæ.

Santalum Yasi, Seem. (sp. nov.); vulgo 'Yasi' (385).

Ceratophylleæ.

Ceratophyllum demersum, Linn. (386).

Euphorbiaceæ.

Euphorbiacea? (387).
Acalypha? (388).
Acalypha Indica, Linn.? (389).

APPENDIX.

A. sp. (390).
A. rivularis, Seem. (sp. nov.); vulgo 'Kadakada' (391).
A. virgata, Forst. (= A. circinata, A. Gray); vulgo 'Kulabuci damu' (392).
A. grandis, Benth.; vulgo 'Kalabuci' (393).
Claoxylon parviflorum, Juss. (394).
Mappa Molluccana, Spreng.? (395).
M. macrophylla, A. Gray; vulgo 'Mavu' (396).
M. sp. (397).
M. sp. (419).
M. sp. (420).
Excœcaria Agallocha, Linn.; vulgo 'Sinu gaga' (398).
Manihot Aipi, Pohl; vulgo 'Yabia ni papalagi' (399).
Curcas purgans, Juss.; vulgo 'Wiriwiri ni papalagi' (400).
Ricinus communis, Linn.; vulgo 'Bele ni papalagi' (401).
Omalanthus pedicellatus, Benth.; vulgo 'Tadauo' (402).
Aleurites triloba, Forst.; vulgo 'Lauei,' 'Tutui' vel 'Sikeci' (403).
Euphorbia Norfolkica, Bois.; vulgo 'Soto' (404).
E. pilulifera, Linn.; vulgo 'De ni osi' (405).
E. Atoto, Forst. (E. oraria, F. Muell.) (406. 904).
Rottlera acuminata, Vahl (407).
Croton metallicum, Seem. sp. nov. (408).
C. sp.; vulgo 'Sacasaca loa' (409).
C. sp. (an var. n. 409?) (410).
C. Storckii, Seem. sp. nov. aff. C. Hillii, F. Muell.; vulgo 'Danidani' (905).
Codiæum variegatum, A. Juss.; vulgo 'Sacaca' vel 'Vasa damu' (411).
Melanthesa sp. (aff. M. Vitis-ldææ) (412).

M. sp.; vulgo 'Molau.' Arbor (413).
Glochidion sp. (414).
G. ramiflorum, Forst.; vulgo 'Molau' (415).
G. cordatum, Seem. sp. nov.; aff. G. mollis (416).
Bischoflia sp.; vulgo 'Kaka.' Arbor (417).
Phyllanthus fruticosa, Wall. (418).

Urticeæ.

Elatostemma? nemorosa, Seem. sp. nov. (422).
Gironniera celtidifolia, Gaud.; vulgo 'Nunu' (423).
Missiessya corymbulosa, Wedd.; vulgo 'Matadra' (424).
Maotia Tahitensis, Wedd.; vulgo 'Waluwalu' (425).
Laportea Harveyi, Seem. sp. nov.; vulgo 'Salato.' Arbor 30–40 ped. (426).
L. Vitiensis, Seem. sp. nov. (aff. L. photinifol.); 'Salato' (427).
Fleurya spicata, var. interrupta, Wedd.; vulgo 'Salato ni koro' vel 'Salata wutivali' (428).
Pellionia elatostemoides, Gaud. (429).
Procris integrifolia, Don, Hook., Arn. (430).
Bœhmeria Harveyi, Seem. sp. nov.; vulgo 'Rere' (431).
B. platyphylla, Don (432).
B. platyphylla, Don, var. virgata, Wedd. (433).
Malaisia? sp. Arbor (431a).

Moreæ.

Morus Indica, Linn.—Introd.(434b).
Trophis anthropophagorum, Seem. sp. nov.; vulgo 'Malawaci' (435).
Ficus obliqua, Forst.; vulgo 'Baka;' (436).

F. tinctoria, Forst. (437).
F. sp.; vulgo 'Loselose.' Frutex fruct. edul. (438).
F. sp.; vulgo 'Loselose ni wai.' Frutex rivularis (439).
F. sp. (440).
F. sp. Frutex 16 ped., caule subsimpl. (441).
F. sp. (442).
F. sp. (443).
F. sp. (444).
F. scabra, Forst.; vulgo 'Ai Masi' (445).
F. aspera, Forst. (446).
F. sp. (447).
F. sp. (448).

Artocarpeæ.

Autiaris 'Bennettii, Seem. Bonpl. t. 7 (sp. nov.); vulgo 'Mavu ni Toga' (449).
Artocarpus incisa, Linn., var. integrifolia, Seem. (aff. A. Chaplashæ, Roxb.); vulgo 'Uto lolo' v. 'Uto coko coko' (450).
A. incisa, Linn. var. pinnatifida, Seem.; forma vulgo 'Uto dina' dicitur (551).
A. incisa, forma vulgo 'Uto Varaqa' (452).
A. „ „ „ 'Uto Koq' (453).
A. „ „ „ 'Balekana' (454).
A. „ „ „ 'Uto buco' (455).
A. „ „ „ 'Uto assalea' (456).
A. „ „ „ 'Uto waisea' (457).
A. „ „ „ 'Uto Bokasi' (458).
A. „ „ „ 'Uto Votovoto' (459).
A. incisa, Linn. var. bipinnatifida, Seem.; vulgo 'Uto Sawesawe' vel 'Kalasai' (560).

Gyrocarpeæ.

Gyrocarpus Asiaticus, Willd.; vulgo 'Wiriwiri' (561).

Celtideæ.

Sponia orientalis, Linn. (562).
Sp. velutina, Planch. (563).

Chloranthaceæ.

Ascarina lanceolata, Hook. fil. (564).

Piperaceæ.

Peperomia sp. (565).
Macropiper latifolium, Miq. (566).
M. pubernlum, Benth.; vulgo 'Yaqoyaqona' (567).
M. methysticum, Miq.; vulgo 'Yaqona' (568).
Piper Siribon, Forst.; vulgo 'Wa Gawa.' Frutex scandens (569).

Casuarineæ.

Casuarina equisetifolia, Forst.; vulgo 'Nokonoko' (570).
C. nodiflora, Forst.; vulgo 'Velao' (571).

Cycadeæ.

Cycas circinalis, Linn.; vulgo 'Roro' (572).

Coniferæ.

Dacrydium elatum, Wall.; vulgo 'Lewenimini' vel 'Dakua salusalu' (573, 906).
Podocarpus (elatus, R. Br.?); vulgo 'Kuasi' (574).
P. (polystachya, R. Br.?); vulgo 'Gagali' (575).
P. cupressina, R. Brown; vulgo 'Kau tabua.'
P.? v. gen. nov.; vulgo 'Kau solo' (576).
Dammara Vitiensis, Seem.; vulgo 'Dakua' (577).

Orchideæ.

Dendrobium Mohlianum, Reichb. fil. sp. nov. (578).

D. crispatum, Swartz (579).
D. (580).
D. Millingani, F. Muell. (581).
D. biflorum, W. (582).
D. sp. (an var. praeced.?) (583).
D. Tokai, Reichb. fil. sp. nov.;
 vulgo 'Tokai' teste Williams
 (584).
D. sp. (591).
Limodorum unguiculatum, Labill.
 (585).
Bletia Tankervilliæ, R. Brown
 (586).
Oberonia (587).
O. brevifolia, Lindl. (Epidendrum
 equitans, Forst. (588).
O. Myosurus, Lindl. (589).
Microstylis Rheedii, Lindl. (Ptero-
 chilus plantagineus, Hook. et
 Arn.) (590).
Appendicula (592).
Tæniophyllum Fasciola, Seem.
 (Limodorum Fasciola, Swartz);
 vulgo 'De ni caucau' (593, 907).
Saccolabium sp. (594).
S. sp. (595).
Eulophia macrostachya, Lindl.?
 (596).
Eria sp., aff. E. baccatæ, Lindl. ?
 (597).
Cirrhopetalum Thouarsii, Lindl.
 (598).
Rhomboda (599).
Sarcochilus (600).
Dorsinia marmorata, Lindl. (601).
Monochilus sp. (602).
Corymbis disticha, Lindl. (603).
Pogonia biflora, Wight (604).
Calanthe (605).
C. sp. florib. pallide aurantiacis
 (606).
C. veratrifolia, R. Brown (607).
Habenaria (608).
Orchidea (609).
O. (610).
O. (611).

O. (612).
O. (613).
O. (614).
O. (615).
O. (616).
O. (617).
O. (618).

Scitamineæ.

Musa Troglodytarum, Linn.; vulgo
 'Soqo' (619).
Gen. nov.; vulgo 'Boia' (620).
Alpinia sp. (621).
Curcuma longa, Linn.; vulgo
 'Cago' (622).
Zingiber Zerumbet, Linn.; vulgo
 'Beta' (623).
Amomum sp.; vulgo 'Cevuga
 (624).
Canna Indica, Linn.; vulgo 'Gasau
 ni ga' (625).

Dioscoreæ.

Helmia bulbifera, Kth.; vulgo
 'Kaile' (626).
Dioscorea alata, Linn.; vulgo 'Uvi'
 (627).
D. nummularia, Lam.; vulgo
 'Tivoli' (628).
D. aculeata, Linn.; vulgo 'Kawai'
 (629).
D. pentaphylla, Linn.; vulgo
 'Tokulu' (630).

Smilaceæ.

Smilax sp.; vulgo 'Kadragi' vel
 'Wa rusi' (631).

Taccaceæ.

Tacca sativa, Rumph.; vulgo 'Yabia' (632, 909).
T. pinnatifida, Forst.; vulgo 'Yabia dina' (933, 908).

Liliaceæ.

Cordyline (634).
C. sp.; vulgo 'Ti kula.'—Colitur
 (635).
C. sp.; vulgo 'Qai,' v. 'Masawe.'—
 Colitur (636).

Allium Ascalonicum, Linn.; vulgo 'Varasa.'—Colitur (637).
Geitonoplesium cymosum, Cunn.; vulgo 'Wa Dakua' (638).
Dianella ensifolia, Red. (639).

Amaryllideæ.

Crinum Asiaticum, Linn.; vulgo 'Viavia' (640).

Asteliew.

Astelia montana, Seem. (sp. nov. bacca trilocul.); vulgo 'Misi' (641).

Commelyneæ.

Commelyna communis, Linn. (= C. pacifica, Vahl?); vulgo 'ai Rorogi' vel 'Rogomatailevu' (642).
Aneilema Vitiense, Seem. (sp. nov.; florib. pallide cæruleis) (643).
Flagellaria Indica, Linn.; vulgo 'Sili Turuka' vel 'Vico' (644, 910).
Joinvillea elegans, Gaud. (= Flagellaria plicata, Hook. fil. (645).

Typhaceæ.

Typha angustifolia, Linn.; vulgo 'De ni ruve' (646).

Bromeliaceæ.

Ananassa sativa, Lindl.; vulgo 'Balawa ni papalagi.'
A. sativa, var. prolifera.

Pandaneæ.

Freycinetia Vitiensis, Seem. sp. nov. (647).
F. Milnei, Seem. sp. nov. (648).
F. Storckii, Seem. sp. nov. (695).
F. sp. (696).
Pandanus odoratissimus, Linn.; vulgo 'Balawa' vel 'Vadra' (649).
P. caricosus, Rumph.; vulgo 'Kickie' vel 'Voivoi' (650).

Aroideæ.

Alocasia Indica, Schott; vulgo 'Via mila,' Via gaga,' 'Via sori,' v. 'Via dranu' (651).
Amorphophallus? sp. nov.; vulgo 'Daiga' (652).
Cyrtosperma edulis, Schott, sp. nov.; vulgo 'Via kaua' (653).
Raphidophora Vitiensis, Schott, sp. nov.; vulgo 'Wa lu' (654).
Cuscuaria spuria, Schott, sp. nov. (655).
Colocasia antiquorum, Schott, var. esculenta, Schott; vulgo 'Dalo' (655 b).
Aroidea (911).

Lemnaceæ.

Lemna gibba, Linn.; vulgo 'Kala' (656).
L. minor, Linn. vulgo 'Kala' (657).

Palmæ.

Cocos nucifera, Linn.; vulgo 'Niu dina.'
Sagus Vitiensis, Herm. Wendl. (Cœlococcus Vitiensis, Herm. Wendl.); vulgo 'Niu soria' vel 'Sogo' (558).
Pritchardia pacifica, Seem. et Herm Wendl. gen. nov.; vulgo 'Sakiki,' Niu Masei,' vel 'Viu' (659).
Kentia? exorrhiza, Herm. Wendl. sp. nov.; vulgo 'Niu sawa' (660).
Ptychosperma Vitiensis, Herm. Wendl. sp. nov. (662).
P. filiferum, Herm. Wendl. sp. nov.; vulgo 'Cageeake' (661, 663).
P. Seemanni, Herm. Wendl. sp. nov.; vulgo 'Balaka' (664).
P. perbreve, Wendl.
P. pauciflorum, Wendl.

P. Pickeringii, Wendl.

Cyperaceæ.

Baumia sp. (665).
Hypolytrum giganteum, Roxb. (666).
Lepironia mucronata, Rich (667).
Cyperus sp. (668).
C. sp. (912).
Mariscus lævigatus, Rœm. et Schult. (669).
Kyllingia intermedia, R. Brown (670).
K. sp. (671).
Lamprocarya affinis, A. Brongn. (672).
Gahnia Javanica, Zoll. (673).
Fimbristylis marginata, Labill. (674).
F. stricta, Labill. (675).
Scleria sp. (676).
S. sp. (677).
Elæocharis articulata, Nees ab Esenb.; vulgo 'Kuta' (678).

Gramineæ.

Zea Mays, Linn.; vulgo 'Sila ni papalagi.'—Cult.
Oplismenus sp. foliis purpurascentibus; vulgo 'Co damudamu' (679).
O. sp. foliis albo-maculatis.—Cum præcedente colitur (680).
O. compositus, Rœm. et Schult. (681).
Paspalum scorbiculatum, Linn.; vulgo 'Co dina' (682).
Eleusine Indica, Gærtn. (683).
Centotheca lappacea, Desv. (684).
Andropogon refractum, R. Brown (= A. Tahitense, Hook. et Arn.) (685).
A. acicularis, Retz. (686).
A. Schœnanthus, Linn.; vulgo 'Co boi' (687).

Cenchrus anomoplexis, Labill. (688).
Sorghum vulgare, Pers.—Colitur (689).
Digitaria sanguinalis, Linn. (690).
Saccharum floridum, Labill. (691).
Coix Lacryma, Linn.; vulgo 'Sila' (692).
Panicum pilipes, Nees ab Esenb. (693).
Bambusa sp.; vulgo 'Bitu' (694).

Equisetaceæ.

Equisetum sp.; vulgo 'Masi ni tabua' (697).

Lycopodiaceæ.

Psilotum complanatum, Sw. (698).
P. triquetrum, Sw. (699).
Lycopodium cernuum, Linn.; vulgo 'Ya Lewaninini' (700).
L. flagellare, A. Rich (701).
L. Phlegmaria, Linn. (702).
L. varium, R. Br. (703).
L. verticillatum, Linn. (704).
L. sp. (705).
L. sp. (706).
L. sp. (707).
L. sp. (708).

Filices.

Acrostichum aureum, Linn.; vulgo 'Boreti,' vel, teste Williams, 'Caca' (709).
Stenochlæna scandens, J. Smith (710).
Lomariopsis leptocarpa, Fee (711).
L. cuspidata, Fee (712).
Lomogramme polyphylla, Brack. (713, 421).
Goniophlebium subauriculatum Blume (714).
Hemionitis lanceolata, Hook. (716).
H. elongata, Brack. (715).
Antrophyum plantagineum, Kaulf. (717).
Diclidopteris angustissima, Brack.,

Y

vulgo 'Mokomoko ni Ivi' (718, 914).
Vittaria revoluta, Willd. (719).
V. elongata, Sw. (720).
Arthropteris albopunctata, J. Smith (721).
Prosaptia contigua, Presl (722).
Phymatodes stenophylla, J. Smith (723).
Niphobolus adnascens, Sprengel, Sw., J. Sm. (724).
Loxogramme lanceolata, Presl (725).
Hymenolepis spicata, J. Smith(726).
Pleuridium cuspidiflorum, J. Smith (727).
P. vulcanicum, J. Smith (729).
Phymatodes Billardieri, Presl (730).
P. alata, J. Sm. = Drynaria alata, Brack. (731).
P. longipes, J. Smith; vulgo 'Caca,' teste Williams (732).
Drynaria muscæfolia, J. Smith (728).
D. diversifolia, J. Smith; vulgo 'Bevula,' 'Teva,' vel 'Vuvu' (733).
Dipteris Horsfieldii, J. Smith ; vulgo 'Koukou tagano' (734).
Meniscium sp. (735).
Nephrodium simplicifolium, J. Smith (736).
N. sp. (737).
N.; vulgo 'Watuvulo' (738).
N. sp. (739, 740).
Lastrea sp. (741).
Polystichum aristatum, Presl (742).
Nephrolepis ensifolia, Presl (743).
N. hirsutula, Presl (744).
N. repens, Brack. (745).
N. obliterata, J. Smith (831).
Dictyopteris macrodonta, Presl (746).
Aspidium latifolium, J. Smith; vulgo 'Sasaloa' (v. Saloa?) (747).
A decurrens, J. Smith (748).
A. repandum, Willd. (749).

Oleandra neriiformis, Cav. (750).
Didymochlæna truncatula, Desv. (751).
Microlepia polypodioides, Presl (751 b).
M. sp. (752).
M. papillosa, Brack. (753).
M. Luzonica, Hook.(gracilis, Blum.) (754).
M. flagellifora, J. Smith (Wall.) (755).
M. (fructif.) (An var. n. 751 b? B. Seem.) (756.)
Humata heterophylla, Cav. (759).
Davallia elegans, Sw. (757).
D. Fijiensis, Hook. (758).
D. fœniculacea, Hook. (760, 762).
D. gibberosa, Sw. (761).
D. Moorei, Hook. (830).
Schizoloma ensifolia. Gaud. (763).
Synaphlebium davallioides, J. Smith (764).
S. Pickeringii, Brack. (765).
S. repens, J. Smith (766).
Sitolobium stramineum, J. Smith (767).
Cyathe medullaris, Sw. (768).
Trichomanes Javanicum, Blume (769).
T. rigidum, Sw. (780. 829).
T. meifolium, Bory (781).
T. bilingue, Blume (= n. 789 ?) (772).
T. angustatum, Carm. = T. caudatum, Brack. (783).
T. erectum, Brack. (784 ex parte).
Hymenophyllum (784).
H. formosum, Brack. (785).
H. parvulum, Poir. (786).
Todea Wilkesiana, Brack. (787).
Marattia sorbifolia, Sw.; vulgo 'Dibi' (788).
Angiopteris evecta, Hoffm. (789).
Lygodictyon Forsteri, J. Smith; vulgo 'Wa Kalou' (790).
Gleichenia dichotoma, Hook. (791).

Schizæa dichotoma, Sw.; vulgo 'Sagato ni tauwa' (792).
Actinostachys digitata, Wall. (793).
Ophioglossum pendulum, Linn. (794).
Blechnum orientale, Linn. (795).
Lomaria attenuata, Willd. (796).
L. elongata, Blume (797).
Pellæa geraniifolia, Fee (798).
Cheilanthes tenuifolia, Sw. (799, 800).
Adiantum lunulatum, Sw.; vulgo 'Kau ni vi vatu' (801, 915).
A. hispidulum, Sw. (802).
A. aff. A. setulonervi, J. Smith (803).
Pteris quadriaurita, teste Hook. Sp. Fil. (804).
P. sp. (Litobrochia divaricata, Brack.?) (805).
P. tripartita, Sw. (806, 913).
P. esculenta, Forst. (809).
P. crenata, Sw.; vulgo 'Qato,' teste Williams (811).
Litobrochia sinuata, Brack.; vulgo 'Wa Rabo' (807).
L. sinuata var. (808).
L. comans, Presl (810).
Neottopteris australasica, J. Smith (812)
Asplenium vittæforme, J. Smith (813).
A. falcatum, Lam. (814).
A. sp. (815).
A. brevisorum, Wall. (827).
A. obtusilobum, Hook. (828).
A. induratum, Hook. (816).
A. lucidum, Forst. (817).
A. sp. (820).
A. resectum, Sm. (821).
A. laserpitiifolium, Lam. (822).
A. (Darea) sp. (784 ex parte).
Callipteris ferox, Blum. (= C. prolifera, Hook. var.) (818).
C. (sine fructif.) (819).
Cryptosorus Seemanni, J. Smith =

Polypodium contiguum, Brack. non Sw. (823).
Diplazium melanocaulon, Brack. (824).
D. bulbiferum, Brack. (825).
D. polypodioides, Blume. (826).
Tænitis blechnoides, Sw. (? abnormal.) (832).

Musci.

Leptotrichum flaccidulum, Mitt. sp. nov. (841).
L. trichophyllum, Mitt. sp. nov. (inter 862).
Leucobryum laminatum, Mitt. sp. nov. (844).
Leucophanes densifolius, Mitt. sp. nov. (inter 862).
L. smaragdinum, Mitt. sp. nov. (inter 863).
Syrrhopodon tristichus, Nees (inter 846).
S. scolopendrius, Mitt. sp. nov. (843).
Meteorium longissimum, Dozy et Molk (inter 863).
M. (Esenbeckia) setigerum, Mitt. (Pilotrichum, Sullivant) (846).
Trachyloma Junghuhnii, Mitt. (Hypnum, C. Mueller) (842).
T. arborescens, Mitt. (845).
Neckera flaccida, C. Muell. (836).
N. Lepineana, Montagn. (863).
N. dendroides, Hook. (838).
Spiridens Reinwardti, Nees (840).
Trachypus helicophyllus, Mont. (838).
Leskea glaucina, Mitt. (inter 847).
L. ramentosa, Mitt. sp. nov. (inter 863).
Racopilum spectabile, Hsch. (inter 863).
Sphagnum cuspidatum, Ehrh. (839).

Hepaticæ.

Cheiloscyphus argutus, Nees (inter 862).

Plagiochila arbuscula, L. et L. (inter 862).
P. Vitiensis, Mitt. sp. nov. (862).
P. Seemanni, Mitt. sp. nov. (864).
Trichorolea tomentella, Nees (inter 862).
Radula amentulosa, Mitt. sp. nov. (inter 837).
R. scariosa, Mitt. sp. nov. (inter 837).
R. spicata, Mitt. sp. nov. (inter 837).
Lejeunia (Bryopteris) Sinclairii, Mitt. sp. nov. (inter 843).
L. eulopha (Phragmicoma, Tay.) (inter 846).
Frullania deflexa, Mitt. sp. nov. (inter 834).
F. meteoroides, Mitt. sp. nov. (inter 834).
F. cordistipula, Nees (inter 846).
F. trichodes, Mitt. sp. nov. (inter 846).
Sarcomitrium plumosum, Mitt. (847).
Marchantia pileata, Mitt. (838).

Lichenes.

Sticta damæcornis, var. caperata, Nyl. (848).
S. (Stictina) filicinella, Nyl. (849)
Ramalina calicaris, Nyl.; vulgo 'Lumi' (ni Vanua) (851).
Coccocarpia molybdæa, Pers. (852).
Leptogium tremelloides, Fries (853)
Sticta (Stictina) quercizans, Ach. (854).
Sticta Freycinetii, Del. (861).
Verrucaria aurantiaca, Nyl. (865).
Parmelia peltata, Ach. var.

Fungi.

Rhizomorpha sp.; vulgo 'Wa loa' (855).
Lentinus sp. (856).
Polyporus sanguineus, Fries (857).
P. affinis, Fries (858).
P. hirsutus, Fries (859).
Hoomospora transversalis, Brebisson (860).
Agaricus (Pleuropus) pacificus, Berk.
Schizophyllum commune, Fries.
Xylaria Feejeensis, Berk.

Algæ.

Hoomonema fluitans, Berk. (gen. nov.) (860).

INDEX.

ABORTION, Criminal, 46
Adultery, 75
Aged and infirm, barbarous treatment of, 30
Agriculture, for the years 1864 and 1866, p. 195 ; for the year 1867, p. 196
Ambassadors, 69
Ambati, 52
American claim on Thakombau, 239 ; also see Financial Liabilities.
Amusements, 130
Anchorage, 4
Annexation, 121; desirability of, 84; petition for to United States Government, 90; colonists concerned about, 93 ; petition by Dr. Lang for, 98 ; to New South Wales, entertained, 104 ; also see Cession.
Anthropophagism ; see Cannibalism.
Appendix, 277
Arcana imperii, 113
Arms and Ammunition, return of, 120
Arrowroot, 129 ; also see Agriculture.
Atonement or expiation for offences, 76

BANANAS, 132
Barbers, 27
Baskets, materials for, 141
Bays, 4
Bêche-de-mer, 144
Betrothal, 54
Beverage, national, intoxicating, 140 ; see also *Yaqona*.
Bokola, 57
Boutwell, Captain, questionable proceedings of, 239 *et seq.*
Bread-fruit, 131 ; native manner of preparing, 132 ; theory regarding, 209
Burying alive, 30

CALENDAR, Fijian, 20
Canal, see Kele Musu.
Cannibals, famous, 59

Cannibalism, 56; cannibal-vegetables 58; origin of, 60
Canoe-building, 62
Carpentery, 63
Cattle; see Agriculture.
Ceremonies, funeral, 31
Cession of Fiji, an account of the various proposals for the, 79; declined, 85; New Zealand in favour [of, 87; again declined, 100; last proposal for the, 114; conditions attached to, 115; signature of deed of, 123; legal formality of, concluded, 125
Character, of natives, 23
Child-birth, 54
Church and state, 74
Civilisation, 35; quasi, of the aborigines, 66
Classes, division of the people into, 67
Climate, 17; effect on Europeans, 201
Cloth, manufacture of, 66; also 140
Cocoa-nut, varieties of, 136; see Fibre
Coffee, 129; also see Agriculture.
Colonial produce, 138
Colonists, amount of capital necessary for intending, 202
Commerce, see Trade.
Communications, between Fiji and other places, 167; also 194
Connor, Paddy, 183
Consul, influence of, 26; first British resident, 187
Consular trade returns, 145; for the year 1863, 147; for the year 1864, 149; for the years 1865 and 1866, 153; for the year 1867, 154; for the year 1868, 158; for the year 1869, 159; for the year 1870, 162; for the years 1872 and 1873, 164
Cordage, fibres for, 141
Cotton, excellence of Fijian, 129; also 141; first exported from Fiji, 147; see Consular Trade Returns; also see Agriculture.
Council Houses; see Mbures.
Cowry, Orange, 215
Creation, tradition of the, 50
Crime, punishments for, 75
Crustacea, 216
Customs, see Manners and Customs.
Cyclopean Platforms, 207.

Dancing, 30
Debt, the Fijian, 113; also see Financial Liabilities.
Deluge, Fijian tradition of the; see Flood.

Despotic power, 68
Destroyer of Souls, 51
Dialects, 38 ; also see Language.
Disturbance, between Fijians and Tongans ; see Maafu.
Doctors, Native, 46
Dress, manner of, 39;
Drinking, see *Yaqona*.
Drum, death, 57
Duck (wild), 213

EASTER Island, 206
Economy, Fijian domestic, 39
Education, necessity for, 182
Elysium, Fijian, 48
Emigration, 191
Esculent roots, 137
Ethnology, 204
Etiquette, Fijian, 26
Exploring Expedition, the Rewa, 6 *et seq.*
Exports, from Sydney to South Sea Islands, 146; see also Consular Trade Returns.

FASTNESSES, 15
Fauna, 213
Feasts, 27, 33, 53
Fidelity, see Adultery.
Fiji, discovery and history of, 219; first resident Consul at, 220; also see Consul; physical aspect and extent of, 1 ; situation and importance of, 127, etymology of, 38
Fijians, see Natives.
Financial liabilities, disposal of, 123; amount of, 119
Fish, varieties of, 214 ; manner of catching, 41
Flies, a nuisance, 217
Flood, tradition of, 49
Food, staple article of, 41 ; principal articles of, 139
Friendly Islands, see Tonga.
Fruits, indigenous, 132; see also Consular Trade Returns.
Future state, belief in, 48

GEOLOGICAL formation of islands, 2
Gods, numerous, 48 ; classes of, 50; consulting of, 52
Government, Native, 68 ; attempt to form a, by Settlers, 105
Groves, Sacred, 48; also 142
Gum, see Kaurie.

HADES, Fijian, 51
Hairdressing, 27
Half-Castes, 24
Harbours, 4
Harry the Jew, 186
Harvey, Professor, 304
Hazlewood, David, his works on the Fijian language, 38
Historical Notice, 219
Honour, place of, 45·
Horses first introduced, 217; also see Agriculture.
Hotels, 12
Houses, description of, 63; manner of building, 64
Hybridisation and Selection, 210

IMMOLATION, self, 30
Imports to Sydney, from South Sea Islands, 145; see also Consular Trade Returns.
Indigo, 129
Industries, Fijian, 62
Infanticide, 55
Invertebrates, 215
Islands; see Physical Aspect of; situation of; number of; area of; and survey of, 1

JUSTICE, Fijian law and, 75

Kai Colos, 56
Kalous, see Gods.
Kandavu, island of, 1, 4
Kaurie, gum, 138
Kava, see *Yaqona*.
Kele Musu, the canal of, 6

LABOUR, 170; regulations regarding, 174; Mr. Anthony Trollope on, 174; the Marquis of Normandy on, 175; India future mart of, 181.
Lakemba, Island of, 2
Land, tenure of, 71; notable feature of, 72; question, 122; still plentiful, 191; area of, held by settlers, 191; sales and purchases of, 192
Language, 37
Laying out the dead, 32
Levuka the town of, 12
Liku, 39

INDEX.

Lime, inexhaustible supply of, 138
Lying, propensity for, 23

Maafu, subscribes to Cession, 124; ambitious designs of, 225; checked by H. B. M's Consul, 227; Chief of the Windward Islands, 234
Magruder, Captain, U. S., visit of, to Fiji, 241
Manufactures, see Industries.
Manners and customs, 39
Mariner, on preparing *Kava*, 43
Markets, 193
Marriage, 54
Mats, materials for, 141
Mbau, native capital, 13; supremacy of, 67; history of, 223
Mbuggi levu range, 8
Mbures, or temples, 64; *ni-sa*, or sleeping-houses, 26
Medicinal plants, 46; also 140
Messages, mode of sending, 30; also 70
Meteorological tables, 18
Midwifery, 46
Missionaries, 55
Mosquitoes, 217
Moti-vei-tala, 11
Mountains, 2
Mourning observances, 34
Mythology, see Gods.

NAITASIRI, 6
Naithombothombo, 49
Namosi, 11
Natives, the, 23; origin of, 205; characteristics of, 206
Navua, the river and the Hundred Waterfalls, 12
Ndengei, 50
Nduri, town of, 15
Nephew, privilege of, as *Vasu*, 73
Nets, fishing, 42; also see 215
New Hebrides, 171
New Zealand, the, and Polynesian Company, 168
Nursing of children, 54

OFFICIALS, native, 70
Offerings to Gods, 48 and 53
Oil, cocoa-nut, 66; see also Consular Trade Returns.
Origin of the race; see Ethnology.
Ornaments, 25; also 69

Ovalau, Island of, 13; calamity to residents of, 188
Ovens, cannibal, 57

PAGANISM, decline of, 35
Palms, 141
Paper mulberry, 66
Parents, peculiar mode of showing affection for, 31
Paroquets, beautiful species of, 213; source of attraction to Tongans, 214
Patteson, Bishop, murder of, 170
People, see the Natives.
Perfumes, scents and, 140
Philips, Mr., or Thakonauto, 234; death of, 238
Physical, the, aspect of the Islands, 1
Pine, New Zealand, 138
Plants, ornamental, 142
Poisons, vegetable, 140
Politeness, native, 26
Polity, 67
Polygamy, 54
Polynesian Company, Limited, Melbourne and Fiji, 255 *et seq.*; statement of land, conveyed to, 273
Population, native, decrease of, 136; number of, 67; number of white, 189
Pottery, manufacture of, 66
Priests, see Ambati.
Printing, native, 66
Productions, 129
Provisions—fruit, see Consular Trade Returns.
Punishments, native, 75

RAINFALL, see Climate.
Rank, indication of; native, 25
Ratu Nggara, of Rewa, 238
Reefs, 4
Religion, 18; Phallic and Ophidian worship, 208
Reptilia, 217
Respect shown on meeting; see Politeness.
Rewa, the river, 5; town of, 14; history of, 234
Rivers, 5
Roads, 194
Robinson, Sir Hercules, Negotiation of, Cession by; see Annexation.

SACRIFICES, 56
Sailors, native, skilful, 63
Salutation, mode of, 26
Sandalwood, 5
Savage, Charley, 185
Savu-Savu, 3; bay of, 5
Scenery, on the *Wai Manu*, 6; on the *Wai Levu*, 7
Seasons; see Calendar.
Seymour, Commodore, timely visit of, to Fiji, 230
Sharks, 214
Sheep, 218; also see Agriculture.
Shipping and tonnage; see Consular Trade Returns.
Sick, native treatment of the, 46
Sinnet, plaiting of, 65
Sleeping, peculiar custom regarding, 26
Smythe, Colonel W. J., 84
Society, state of Fijian, 77
Soil, 5
Soloira, 8
Somosomo, 45
Spices, 129
Springs, hot, 3; also 10
Strangling, practice of, 30; also 34
Submission, the different kinds of, 71
Succession, law of native, 69
Sugar, important article of trade, 130; see Agriculture; see Consular Trade Returns; also p. 196
Strongholds, Fijian, see Fastnesses.
Swine, see Agriculture.
Sydney, see Exports; also see Imports.

TABERNACLES of nature, 49
Tamboo, 34
Tanoa, 224
Taro, "the staff of life," 137
Tattooing, strange belief regarding, 29
Temperature, see Climate.
Temples, see Mbures.
Thakombau, his claim to the title of *Tui Viti*, 221; description of his queen, 275; renounces "the flesh and the devil," 274; baptism of, 275; his difficulties with the United States, 79; his war club, 125; Maafu a dangerous rival, 225

Timber, valuable kinds of, 141; see also Consular Trade Returns and Appendix.
Tobacco, 129; see also Agriculture; see also Consular Trade Returns.
Toddy, theory regarding, 211
Toilette, native, 27
Tonga, King George of; his interference in Fijian affairs, 239; an account of the islands of, 277; intercourse between the natives of, and Fijians, 225
Tortoise-shell, 144; see also Consular Trade Returns.
Trade, 143; development of, 147; see also Consular Trade Returns.
Trepang, see Bêche-de-mer.
Tribes, number of, 221
Tui Viti; see Thakombau.
Turban, or *sala*, 28
Turtle-fishing, 215

Uluna Ndonu, 9
United States claim, 239; see Financial liabilities; investigation of by the United States Government, 253; payment of, 272
Unnatural affection, see Parents.

Vasu, privileges of; see Nephew.
Vegetables, indigenous, 131; foreign, 130
Vicarious suffering, 75
Victory, celebration of, 57
Vogel, Mr. Julius, 108
Volcanic, formation of the islands, 2; disturbance, 3

Wages for labour, 171
Wai Levu, see Rewa.
Wai Ndina, 8
Whippy, David, 183
White population, 183; number of, 189; character of, 190
Wigs, native, 28
Wilkes, Commodore, 219
Winds, prevailing, see Climate.
Women, morality of, 40; degradation of, 41
Wool; see Consular Trade Returns.

Yams, staple article of food, 136
Yaqona, 30; preparation of, 42; also see Mariner.

THE END.

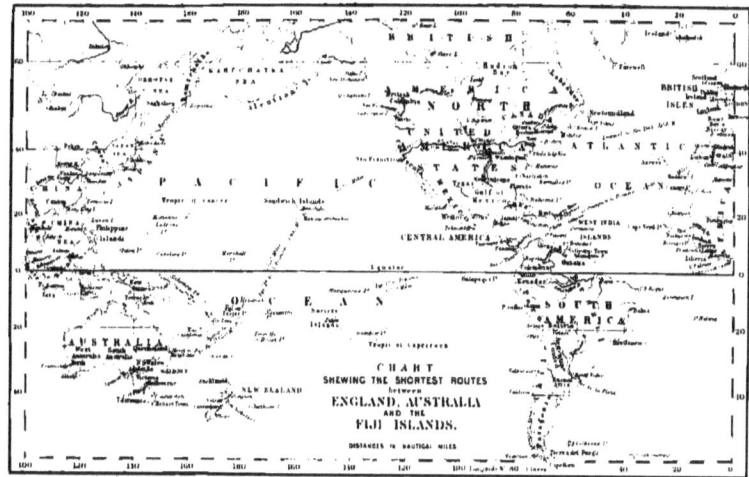

www.ingramcontent.com/pod-product-compliance
Lightning Source LLC
Chambersburg PA
CBHW031858220426
43663CB00006B/672